Dynamics among Nations

The Evolution of Legitimacy and Development in Modern States

Hilton L. Root

The MIT Press
Cambridge, Massachusetts
London, England

MIT Press books may be purchased at special quantity discounts for business or sales promotional use. For information, please email special_sales@mitpress.mit.edu or write to Special Sales Department, The MIT Press, 55 Hayward Street, Cambridge, MA 02142.

This book was set in Sabon by the MIT Press. Printed and bound in the United States of America.

Library of Congress Cataloging-in-Publication Data
Root, Hilton L.
Dynamics among nations : the evolution of legitimacy and development in modern states / Hilton L. Root.
pages cm
Includes bibliographical references and index.
ISBN 978-0-262-01970-5 (hardcover : alk. paper) 1. International economic relations. 2. Globalization. 3. State, The. 4. Economic development. 5. Evolutionary economics. I. Title.
HF1359.R66 2013
337—dc23
2013010260

10 9 8 7 6 5 4 3 2 1

Contents

Preface and Acknowledgments

Nature's evolutionary processes have generated a burgeoning area of inquiry, the study of complexity, which examines how environments and their constituent parts continuously adapt to and transform one another. Complex systems, found everywhere from rain forests to ant colonies to birds in flight, can help us understand how complexity also arises in socioeconomic systems, which is the subject of this book.

Descriptions of international relations routinely concede complexity, but not in the scientific sense. Employed here, complexity is a property of systems comprising many interdependent parts, arising when the behavior of the whole emerges from the interactions of its components. A change in one part of the system affects other parts until the system acquires new properties that its individual components did not possess. Thus, to understand the collective behavior of a social system, and how it arises from the relationships of its constituent parts, one must think about systems in ways that differ significantly from conventional approaches to solving large-scale social problems.

Shifts in trade and in geopolitical influence have created new networks and brought about an interconnectedness of the world's many social and economic systems that exist at different stages of development. These networks are not only interconnected, they are constantly reacting to the behaviors, or anticipated behaviors, of other networks that are also repositioning themselves as the landscape they share is altered. Together they shape the larger system, creating rules and identities at the macro level that differ from those at the micro levels.

Interdependence among connected but diverse parts is a characteristic that distinguishes complex from merely complicated systems. In a complex system, the removal of a single part will change the behaviors of the remaining components; in a merely complicated system, such as a clock or a nuclear reactor, the removal of one part will not cause a change in the remaining parts, although the system itself may cease to function. Complex systems may be organized hierarchically, but they can also self-organize without design, making it impossible to predict the behaviors of numerous components in constantly shifting environments and organization formations. What happens in one component may affect seemingly unrelated components, so distinguishing cause and effect is not easy

My own search for the rules of social complexity began without any idea or language to describe what I was trying to unravel. First, there was a dissertation on the social origins of different land-use patterns in premodern Europe, completed at the University of Michigan in 1983. Interest in economic history took me to the California Institute of Technology later that year. Upon my arrival, Professor Murray Gell-Mann, the Nobel laureate in physics and part-time specialist in economic history, greeted me with harsh words, warning that I should expect little progress toward understanding economic development or how to accelerate its progress around the world. The tools of contemporary economics, he maintained, were insufficient for the understanding of a complex world. Instead of trying to comprehend the implications of complexity for policy, economists were using tools that dealt only with systems in equilibrium or that treated one part of a system as a microcosm of the whole. It made just as little sense, he warned, to look to the sister social sciences, which were similarly reductionist and just as likely to envision economic development as a universal change agent that would advance all societies along the same institutional and social trajectory.

In 1984, Gell-Mann embarked upon the establishment of the Santa Fe Institute, the pivotal center for the study of complex adaptive systems. SFI's work also began to call into question many of the key assumptions of contemporary economics. But at the same time, mainstream academic political economy circles were framing a new theory, in "all you need to know" packaging, about the causes of economic growth. New institutional economics became the blueprint of enlightened social engineering, with prescriptions for boosting the level of a society's positive incentives for economic growth when they did not occur naturally.

I too was swept up with the NIE and institutional development. I owe much of my intellectual development that followed to constructive engagement with economic historians Lance E. Davis, Philip T. Hoffman, Douglass North, and Roger. S. Schofield; comparative politics specialist Robert Bates; political theorist Norman Schofield; and philosopher Brian Barry. All were essential architects of the new consensus on the primacy of institutions. I left Caltech in 1985 for the University of Pennsylvania, where my career took an unexpected turn toward global development policy, thanks to economists and global rainmakers Mancur Olson and Larry Summers. Both were seeking a holistic approach to economic development, one that included social institutions. Olson invited me to participate in field studies for his USAID-funded program, "Institutional Reform and the Informal Sector" (IRIS), applying perspectives on the economics of organization developed by regulatory economists (Armen Alchian, Harold Demsetz, and Michael Jensen) to the study of institutional capacity in francophone Africa. A schema of good governance began to take shape. An invitation by Summers, then chief economist at the World Bank, to research the institutional foundations of East Asia's high-performing economies strengthened that framework of good governance. For the next decade, with many international organizations standing behind my efforts, I explored the functional and structural attributes of the institutions required for emerging regions to yield capitalist economies.

Real-time opportunities to implant good governance through donor assistance kept coming my way. In 2001, John Taylor, then undersecretary at the Treasury Department, provided an opportunity to work on a concept that eventually became a major US foreign aid program, the Millennium Challenge Corporation. Several years later, I was tapped by USAID to lead a multi-country program, "Enhancing Government Effectiveness," in Islamic-majority countries that were heavily dependent on US donor assistance. Over a five-year span, we examined government institutions in justice, finance, and planning, along with the social programs in education and health, and later, the management of investments in physical infrastructure, water, sewerage, and transportation. The demand for expertise on building institutions in targeted third world environments became a major specialization within the development community. But setting functional goals and delegating instructions for filling gaps of social capacity has rarely proved successful.

All of these opportunities ultimately helped clarify why institutional reform is not sufficient to define a functioning social system. Explanations of economic growth that focus on institutions do not define how relationships among the institutional components give rise to the collective behavior of the system of international relations. They reveal too little about how collections of parts form functioning wholes, which details are critical, or even what rules of interaction transform the collections of parts into wholes. Even when well-intentioned institutional reforms result in seemingly successful projects and programs, donor assistance is rarely found to be the source of the rise of a functioning society equipped to undertake complex collective tasks.

To decrease the gaps between good intentions and failed outcomes, we must improve our understanding of how collective and networked properties of a system arise. And to understand how these properties arise, we must understand why. For this, two key ideas of complexity science—emergence and interdependence—are needed. *Emergence* is what occurs in a system when the behaviors between and among agents contribute to a more complex behavior of the whole. The system acquires new structures and properties that its individual components did not possess. *Interdependence* describes how the parts of a system affect other parts.

Conventional approaches to international relations and to other complex human environments presume the necessity of a hierarchical command, but when an activity requires the coordination of many different levels of knowledge, experience, and organization, then the problem-solving capacity of any single individual or institution, and their efforts to centralize control, will fail. Solving problems of complexity requires specialization in distributing action and authority. For this reason increasing competition among firms and nations for obtaining resources needed to produce and distribute goods and services is creating a networked global civilization.

Moreover many different network systems arise in global political economy; some can strengthen system-level adaptability while others can weaken it. Already the global environment faces an important change as various control structures arising locally compete as standards of global governance. At the end of the cold war, modernization theory described a globalization that would propel all aspirants to higher income-generating economies along the developmental trajectory already traveled by the West. Instead, many emerging democracies are becoming full-fledged threats to the stability of international system. This should caution us that no particular developmental pathway of either failure or success attains universal rank. Social systems evolve in the local contexts in which they find themselves. The iconoclastic seeds that Murray Gell-Mann planted are growing into a large and fertile forest.

The economist and social psychologist Herbert Simon has demonstrated the extent of human cognitive limitations. We can never fit into our minds the entire system of which we are a part, so we work from maps, metaphors, or other systems of symbolic representation. We are part of whatever prediction or strategy we devise, and this impedes our objectivity. Acknowledging these constraints, let us consider the implications of the scientific study of complex systems for social policy. My hope is that this effort will demonstrate how policy makers can better manage change as the world we inhabit becomes increasingly interdependent.

Discovering complexity in social systems has been a journey, but the path has not been a lonely one. I have encountered many fellow travelers, and much of the knowledge that I have gained and hope to impart in writing this book is from scholars and policy practitioners who share little in common with my own background. Here are some of the landmarks.

In 2010, Sven Steinmo commented on one of the chapters at an annual meeting of the American Political Science Association. Robert Axtell invited me on two occasions to share views with colleagues and students in the Department of Computational Social Science at George Mason University's Krasnow Institute for Advanced Study.

In March 2011, Mercatus Center program director Claire Morgan organized a book conference at the Center in which Paul Dragos Aligica, Aaron Frank, Armando Geller, Alexander Hamilton, Garrett Jones, Siona Listokin-Smith, John Nye, Itir Ozer, Jessica Heineman-Pieper, Ian Vasquez, and Chunjuan "Nancy" Wei, offered many different perspectives to consider. What emerged from Jack Goldstone's adept moderating was the wisdom of the crowd, and from it, ideas that will germinate in the works of all the participants.

Later in 2011, Robert Lempert convoked a meeting on the manuscript at Rand's Frederick S. Pardee Center for Longer Range Global Policy and the Future Human Condition. Michael D. McGinnis and Elinor Ostrom organized a talk on "Dynamics in Social Systems: The Study of Complexity and Institutional Change" at The Workshop in Political Theory and Policy Analysis Fall 2011 Colloquia at Indiana University. On Michael

Woolcock's invitation I presented chapter 7, "Accelerators of 'Stateness,'" at the World Bank's Development Economics Research Group (DECRG) Social Science and Policy Seminar Series.

In June 2011, a National Endowment for the Humanities fellowship allowed me to participate in the Institute for Advanced Topics in the Digital Humanities at the University of North Carolina, Charlotte, and gave me access to the expertise of Jason McKenzie Alexander, Aaron Bramson, and Patrick Grim. The research on Chinese influence in Sri Lanka was collected under a Fulbright Specialist Grant, Project 3945, Grantee ID No. 8841810. In-country interviews were conducted between June 23, 2011, and July 2, 2011, under strict assurances by the author of complete anonymity.

In December 2011 at Peking University, a multi-departmental, two-week workshop/course on this book manuscript was organized by Jun Fu, dean of the university's School of Government; Shiding Liu, a professor of the university's Center for Research on Development of China Society; Zeqi Qiu, dean of the Center; and Tianbiao Zhu, vice dean of the School of Government. Two brilliant students, Wanshun Liu and Hu Peng, made all the local arrangements. Noel D. Johnson chaired a meeting of the Economic History Workshop at George Mason University's Department of Economics in 2012.

Alice Amsden, Philip Auerswald, Ray Bowen, Yi Feng, William Ferguson, Lloyd Fernando, Jacek Kugler, Peter Lewis, Yan Li, Shoji Nishimoto, Paul Ormerod, Nancy Overholt, Ben Ramalingam, and Qing Tian shared insights on the manuscript at various stages.

The graduate students who have taken my PhD seminar on global public policy deserve mention. I thank them all for their interest and their time. Special thanks go to PhD students at the George Mason School of Public Policy who acted as research assistants, Kanishka Balasuriya, Ammar Malik, and Ha Vu.

Dinah McNichols's editing has been indispensible. Victor Teicher provided generous financial support.

The voice of each one of my mentors, some now gone, grows more audible every day of my life. I would like to thank Kenneth Arrow, Gary S. Becker, Marvin Becker, David D. Bien, James Coleman, Milton Friedman, François Furet, Robert Hartwell, Robert P. Inman, Alan Charles Kors, Emmanuel Le Roy Ladurie, Bruce Bueno de Mesquita, Douglass North,

Mancur Olson, Elinor and Vincent Ostrom, George Schultz, John Taylor, Charles Tilly, and James Allen Vann. The record reveals I have been a taker for far too long. I hope it is not too late to reform myself.

Washington, DC
January 2013

1

Post-Globalization: Complexity in the Governance of a Networked Global Society

All development and security policies presume a theory of change. This book considers the partnership of *modernization theory*, the dominant theory of social change since World War II, and *liberal internationalism*, the foreign policy agenda the West has promoted in political and economic development since the cold war.[1] It will contrast the analytical framework of modernization theory with that of the evolutionary theory of complexity to explain unforeseen development failures, governance trends, and alliance shifts.

International liberalism presumes that if developing societies adopt trade, and monetary and fiscal reforms that integrate them into the global economy, the intensified speed of economic change will lead to changes in other societal structures and expedite a sociopolitical convergence toward global cooperation—a truly international society. It did not anticipate that social and political change move at a much slower pace than economic and technological change, and that considerable divergence can occur between the pace of economic and technological transition and the more glacial pace of cultural and societal transitions. Instead of the anticipated convergence toward a common framework of values, the growing economic interconnectedness is establishing new norms of optimal governance based on growing diversity and disparity between the West and newly rising powers.

As it transitions from regional applications to global repercussions, liberalism must face many challenges it did not anticipate, and for which it is ill prepared. The world's population growth and the flow of interregional trade are concentrating among regimes that operate far from liberal conceptions of optimality. Both of these trends, trade shifts and demographic pressures, have implications for the evolution of global cooperation and for the kinds of policies that can be sustained through international co-operation. Liberal internationalism's linkages with modernization theory fail to provide convincing explanations for the unanticipated variations in governance that can arise from the local pursuit of wealth and power.[2]

The liberal West, which has existed at the summit of liberal internationalism's hierarchical ladder since the end of the cold war, anticipated a period of stable and consistent evolution toward the best practices in governance that its economic success had made legitimate. But the predictions of modernization theory, which presumes that as societies urbanize and prosper, they will converge to adopt the values of liberal internationalism, have not materialized. Since the collective behavior of the global system depends on the behavior of its parts, variations in the latter can cause systemwide effects that make the maintenance of system's stability more complex.

Although liberal internationalism is premised on the classical idea of cooperation among equals, which obviates the need for a "central enforcer," to make it a global standard of development requires top-down guidance from the West.[3] A central administrator, the United States, provides the system's organization and management. In the future, however, there may be no place at the top for a central power that can organize and manage the system. There may not be a "top" at all. Conventional thinking in geopolitics holds that a world in which no single nation can maintain an undisputed place at the top cannot be stable: it is a world adrift, in search of a leader. Every facet of global interaction is being affected by this transition from hierarchies to networked systems, requiring a new language for comprehending change processes.[4]

The system of international relations, like most complex ecosystems, such as the nervous system or a rain forest, is yielding to its rules of complexity. In complex systems, a central administrator rarely guides the collective behaviors that characterize developmental processes. The system itself has a collective behavior that depends on all its parts. Rather than convergence toward a dominant model, or "global optimum," the interactive dynamics are coevolutionary; their interactions result in reciprocal and evolving change. In the global social system, interdependence is causing a transition with qualitatively different impacts for each of its affected regions. Illiberal and liberal regimes alike engage in a pattern of cocreation, each shaping the other. This coevolutionary process is dispelling expectations of convergence, and it can cause shifts to the larger system.

As environments become more interdependent, strategies for survival depend increasingly on the "cost functions" agents must face under local circumstances. Instead of the mimicry of higher order adaptations that conventional social theorists predict, functional segregation intensifies as new tiers of organization emerge. Unfilled niches in ecosystems are rare. As nations jostle for wealth and power, competition and aggression co-exist within webs of symbiosis and cooperation, creating an unforeseen range of governance variations (Smil 2008, 163–65). An analogy is the physics of aviation, although they are the same for all aircraft, wartime requirements cause cascades of innovation to fill special functions, re-sulting in the rapid divergence of military and civilian aircraft. Combat structures with well-separated traits arise.

Similarly adversaries have become more diverse since the end of the cold war, when the targets were other states. Today's adversaries are de-centralized transnational networks that appear in many sizes and shapes; they are not geographically fixed, hierarchically governed, or bureaucrati-cally managed, and they can come from a number of sources, confront-ing all corners of the globe with the potential for disaster. Islamic fun-damentalism is but one of many forms of stateless adversaries without fixed boundaries that can turn asymmetries of power to their advantage (Treverton and Wilhelm 2009).[5]

Competition in highly interdependent global environments produces far greater local variation and diversity of structures and strategies than modernization theory ever anticipated. Rather than a one-to-one map-ping of the traits of successful incumbents by their emerging challengers, heightened competition drives social agents to alter their environments by creating niches that offer new opportunities for interaction, and that competition in turn reveals new niches that other actors can exploit.[6] Even strategies that are suboptimal or second best, from an economy's production possibility curve, may contribute to overall system durability (Arthur, Durlauf, and Lane 1997).

Collective Security and Collective Values

In the post–cold war period, the long-term security strategy of the West has been based on the belief that as countries embrace liberalism, they become more reliable allies.[7] Thus heavy investments in promoting the values of liberal internationalism have been guided by the hope that establishing a universal norm will ensure global security.

Victories in the Second World War and the cold war placed the liberal market democracies of the West in a position to be administrators of the global system, possessing the authority to determine the rules of legitimate economic and political order by which others might play (Amsden 2007). Economic success bestowed another system-defining role on the West—it could now designate the characteristics of the effective state. But while liberal internationalism enjoys voluntary compliance among like-minded liberal regimes of European descent, its reach is parochial.

A consensus among the Western powers on domestic policy goals, such as social protection against unemployment, disability, poverty, ill health, and the frailties of old age, made it easy to agree on the rules needed to operate within the world economy.[8] Shared values and ideas facilitated agreement about what public goods would enhance collective security and well-being. Enforcement capabilities were thin and the specifics of cooperation never fully articulated, but cooperative security had a mutually reinforcing logic—rather than balancing each other as potential rivals, the Western states built institutions that matched their common outlook. States that shared fundamental principles could act cooperatively without a central enforcer.

The West presumed that aspirants would accept the same values, and that participating in an open system of international trade would signal acceptance of a common framework of the norms that constitute political advancement. By the late 1980s the West's macroeconomic beliefs had also converged toward global optima: the axiomatic Washington Consensus of standard economic policy reform (Williamson 1990). Thus both the future course of political legitimacy and the course of economic effectiveness were framed in terms predicated by the historical experience of the West.

Confidence in the universal appeal and ultimate triumph of liberal internationalism rests on the belief that both markets (the desire to truck and barter) and democracy (the quest for social recognition) arise out of human nature, and that harnessing these two human drives is the most efficient means to resolve complex universal dilemmas of collective action. Democracy is inherent to the nature of politics and can be suppressed, but only for so long (Fukuyama 1992). Its ascendency gains further support from its strong relationship to capitalist market economics and from the forceful example of prosperous democratic states (Mandelbaum 2007a, b).

Liberal internationalists presume that a growing middle-class roster of countries will bolster system stability, and that the rising middle classes will champion liberal values, further stabilizing the global system by changing countries from within. As international relations theorist John Ikenberry writes (2011, 190):

The American Vision of postwar order also had progressive aspirations. . . . One was that the liberal international order, although first established within the West, would spread outward to non-Western and the developing societies. Democracy and integration into the open capitalist system would, in time, envelope the emerging regions of the world . . . and . . . would drive social and political advancement within the societies that became part of it.

Yet the connection between economic growth and the construction of liberal democracy is rarely exemplified in the trajectories of emerging states. Instead of a liberal system based on universal values, the newcomers protest the "invitation" to join a Western system. Brazil, Russia, India, and China enjoy the advantages of international law and organization, but they contest the legitimacy of liberal internationalism's core values—democracy, labor and human rights, an open domestic economy—to be the systemwide ethos. They rebuff limits on state sovereignty, such as the idea of interventionism to protect populations from abuses committed by their own governments. The universal legitimacy of the rule of law, they maintain, need not be bound to Western norms.

The system built upon liberal internationalism is vulnerable to alteration when its values are no longer shared among the dominant powers. If enough actors act myopically, the liberal consensus may collapse or be severely undermined. It only takes enough of these countries, or the right mixes of these countries, and the international ecology will change, calling into question the dominance of liberalism. What will happen to system stability when the core group of liberal democracies no longer constitutes the dominant power but is joined or supplanted by the rising non-Western powers formerly on the periphery of global trade or production?

Policy Diffusion and Unfolding Global Megatrends

The system of global trade has long been characterized by vertical flows overseen by the liberal West, which has assumed that adoption of its values would follow a similar top-town learning process. But emerging economic and demographic trends are changing the global ecosystem in ways that are unfavorable to the continued dominance of liberalism. Changes in the pattern of world trade are transforming its economic geography by reshaping economic borders. In the new geography, the South is moving from the periphery of global trade to the center (Amsden 2001, 2007; Khanna 2008). Emerging economies, which provide 40 percent of global output measured by market exchange rates, are expected to continue growing at rates of 6 percent, while advanced economies stagnate. Economists Uri Dadush and William Shaw (2011) predict that developing countries will increase their share of global exports from 30 to 70 percent of the total by 2050. If they maintain current rates of growth by that time, six of the seven largest economies will be those of developing nations. Economic development scholar Alice Amsden has reported that growth spreads first within regions before it spreads among regions. Being in a fast-growing region makes a difference. In East Asia the growth of interregional trade is motivating the idea of an Asia bloc (2007, 154–59).

The distribution of interregional trade once predominantly North–South is also changing, diminishing the West's centrality to global interregional trade and production. Trade flows are moving along new paths, and the percentage of global trade that is South–South has increased as a percentage of total trade. Between 2001 and 2011 China's trade with Latin American, for example, grew 1,200 percent, from $10 billion to $130 billion. This means that Latin American countries like Bolivia, and Venezuela that have adversarial relations with the West will have new outlets for trade and investment. If those trends continue, at some point along the horizon, horizontal South–South flows will overtake vertical North–South flows. And as trade flows are altered, what began as commercial networks based narrowly on national interests may evolve into cultural, political, and intellectual affinities.

Many countries that have become dependent on China for trade have also become dependent on China for access to military and other vital technologies. South American militaries were once dependent on the West for military supplies, but China is already the primary source of weapons for both Bolivia and Venezuela. At least twenty regimes in Africa similarly depend on Chinese civil and military technology. Dependence on China's technological expertise opens up many venues for reshaping the political rule, along with the economic arrangements, of its partners. Once dependence on Chinese technologies (and integration into technopolitical systems that originate in Beijing) becomes essential to the stability of a regime, the dependency will influence the regime's interactions with the world. This is illustrated by the example of China's relationship with Sri Lanka, addressed in chapter 10. Although the new geopolitical trends are not irreversible, the new patterns of global commercial and technological change will shape how political power will be exercised in the twenty-first century.

Global megatrends raise new questions about the direction of global political economy. As the South increases its share of interregional trade, what will the implications be for the evolution of networks of belief, ideas, and policy? Will it be a source of new alliances and new patterns of international cooperation? Can the global trading system maintain the identity it has acquired through the cold war and post–cold war periods if the new hubs of global trade are also hubs of ideas about global order? Will the rise of new centers of cultural and geographic affinity require new rules for global cooperation?[9]

Can Liberalism Survive Global Complexity in Transition?
From the middle of the nineteenth century, the international system had a geographical center, Europe and North America, with a large influence on the transmission of values and norms to peripheral regions. The West believed that after obtaining independence, countries would seek to emulate their larger trading partners in order to attain peak fitness. But since the end of the cold war, the likelihood of such bottom-up emulation has been reduced as connections among emerging nations, the North–South connections, proliferate faster than those with Europe and North America. As coevolving nations form new coalitions, they unlock new governance frontiers.

The end of cold war bipolarity affords local actors greater freedom to exercise local preferences and parochial identities. Global governance diversity arises from the internal discourse between elites who seek to preserve and increase their power and wealth, and the international system, particularly the international economy in which national elites try to integrate their national economies. In a global economy with no captain at the helm, diverse national and global elites can increasingly eschew the counsels for liberal democratic growth in favor of alternatives that serve their own sectarian interests (Kagan 2009).

The socioeconomic development sequence anticipated by liberal internationalism has failed to materialize for a number of reasons. Chief among them are the economic and social processes at work within the international system that can affect development within a national regime and result in the rise of elite internal factions that form alliances with external powers. Such alliances may speed global economic integration but deepen internal divisions within regimes. National elites enjoying first world incomes and lifestyles not accessible to the majority of their populations may incite resentment that threatens regime stability, producing populist backlashes.[10]

These apprehensions about the survival of liberalism as the ethos of the global trading system raise questions far beyond the scope of modernization theory. Global change processes are being shaped by the properties of networks of interdependent but diverse actors who respond to cues both from their local and their global situations.

Overview

The chapters that follow employ systems analysis, in which institutional change and economic development are understood as self-organizing complexities. An alternative, albeit rational, picture of institutional change and persistence will be constructed that challenges the paradigms of contemporary social theory.

The study of complexity contains a wealth of models and ideas through which global social change processes can be interpreted and understood, thanks to the pioneering efforts of Brian Arthur (1994, 2009); Robert Axelrod (1984, 1997, 2001); Robert Axtell and Joshua Epstein (1996); Albert-László Barabasi (2002); Eric Beinhocker (2006); Samuel Bowles (2004, 2011, 2012); Lars Cederman (1997); Richard Dawkins (1997, 2006); Herbert Gintis (2000a, b); Stephan J. Gould (1982); Mark Granovetter (1973, 1978); Geoffrey Hodgson (1993, 1996, 2006); John Holland (1975, 1992, 1995, 1998); Stuart Kauffman (1993); Susanne Lohmann (1993, 1994); Ian Lustick (2011); Joel Mokyr (1990a, b, 1991); Richard Nelson and Sidney Winter (1982); Paul Ormerod (1994,

1998, 2006); Elinor Ostrom (2005); Scott Page (2007, 2010); Anatol Rapoport (1986); Thomas Schelling (1978); Herbert Simon (1969); John Maynard Smith (Smith and Szathmáry 1995); and Sven Steinmo (2010). Their efforts have brought us to the threshold of what may be a major scientific revolution. This book seeks to carry their efforts further toward an understanding of global political economy by examining large sweeps of history in several important but not very well understood nations.

The topics chosen are among the most salient in scholarly debates about global development and institutional change: the great divergence of East and West; emergence of the European state, its contrast with the rise of China, and the network properties of their respective innovation systems; the trajectory of democracy in developing regions; Turkey's emergence as a bridge between the Islamic countries of the Middle East; and the systemic impact of China on the liberal world order.

Chapter 2 explores how the interactive dynamics of system stability in an increasingly interdependent and networked global society are largely similar to the change processes studied by the sciences of complexity. Scientists from fields as diverse as neurology, ecology, and physics have developed a new understanding of networks as complex integrated systems, with useful applications for the study of social organization.

Chapter 3 asks that we reconsider the autonomy that markets enjoy in conventional theories of social change. It reviews the conventional narratives of modernization in which markets are the *replicators* (vehicles) that transfer liberal values to the rest of the polity. However, cultural and social norms, such as freedom of expression and the role of the individual in society, transfer sluggishly when compared to the rapid transfer of tools for financial management. Thus there is considerable latitude for residual sociopolitical factors to determine the form that a particular set of market institutions will take. Markets arise from and rely on networks of exchange among various buyers and sellers, producers and suppliers, who in turn coevolve in a network of interdependency with other components of the social system.

Chapter 4 traces liberal internationalism's roots in modernization theory, which presumes economic growth and democracy to be mutually reinforcing. But warnings to authoritarian regimes that they will suffer eventual economic stagnation if they refuse to democratize are proving to be unconvincing. Modernization theory became the dominant logic of the liberal West's post–World War II global development agenda, when it was common to argue that the wealthiest succeed because they possess the most virtuous social, economic, and political institutions. But as the global resources controlled by the industrial West shrink, modernization theory will come to be seen as just a triumphalist narrative, a mismatch for the trajectories of developing nations. Newly emerging powers will form their own narratives of modernization based on their own histories.

Chapter 5 examines efforts to unravel the mystery of economic growth by scholars who presume that its "final" building blocks are the institutions of capitalist societies and the rules that govern those institutions. But the comprehensive inventories of individual components of successful capitalist economies do little to solve the mystery of why some countries succeed and others fail at economic growth. Determining the final building blocks of modern capitalism is not sufficient to explaining how it arose or how it can be replicated.

Chapters 6 and 7 elaborate analytical perspectives on the *macroevolutionary* change processes. Chapter 6 examines how interactive agents create a shared ecology of the larger system through *self-organization*.[11] It posits a world in which there is no real distinction between a component (an *agent*) and its environment. To discover the laws that govern the interaction of agents, we construct *fitness landscapes* in which peaks are solutions, the highest being the optimal solution.

In fitness landscapes, the largest determinant of agent behavior comes from the fitness challenges (or time horizon) that a particular agent faces within a given landscape. Whereas global development policy presumes that globalization will produce convergence to a dominant model, here the choices an agent faces reflect its different locations or starting points that frame its position within the global system. The starting point determines the end point.[12] The shapes (or ruggedness) of a given fitness landscape will determine what its population chooses to optimize in order to survive. Many problems of international development require adaptations to a local peak, because paths to the global or highest peak (e.g., liberal democracy) are not visible from the population's starting point. Institutional selection is generally a myopic choice from among local alternatives; the more rugged the landscape, the less likely a globally optimal solution will be found.

Local options are defined by the interactive effects of other agents operating on the same or on the adjacent landscape. As the intensity of interactions deforms the landscape, the optimization problem a particular agent faces becomes more complex, and as its time horizon shrinks, its behavior will become more opportunistic or shortsighted.

Complex, or rugged, environments are not easily controlled through interventions. This gives large developing economies an advantage over their smaller counterparts; they have more control over the key variables within their environments. Their local landscapes are not so easily deformed by the moves of other economies (Amsden 2007, 127–37, 149–64).

Complexity is obviously not a condition unique to contemporary social relations. Diversity and interconnectivity are as old as human civilization and appear in the writings of the ancient Greek and Roman historians Herodotus and Tacitus. Complexity theory, we will see, offers new knowledge of social relations that can be applied to earlier times, the rise and fall of dynasties in old regime Europe or imperial China, just as it can be used to characterize key developments in contemporary governance.

Chapter 7 refocuses the perennial question of why innovations like the use of gunpowder or cannon, which put the class basis of social order at risk, were diffused in Europe. And why were these innovations resisted in other world regions, most notably in China, where they originated, and Japan? Network analysis allows us to postulate that the European state system effectively adjusted to changes and extreme events, such as system-altering technological innovation and warfare that punctuated its evolution, without experiencing the setbacks of prolonged disintegration and collapse that frequently occurred in China during dynastic transitions. The more distributed, multi-nodal, or modular, character of intra-European networks of authority had implications for system-level resilience. Although distribution among a variety of nodes made internally generated extreme events likely, at the system level, Europe was more resilient than China when such events occurred. The European networks of distributed power could adapt to changes even after a critical node had been removed. This drove the intensity of technological innovation and rendered military revolutions recurrent but enabled the continuation of aristocratic domination, even after particular lineages were defeated.

If innovations resulted from frequent military revolution in a system without a central controller, China did not want them. It regulated the diffusion of military technology, as well as a state monopoly over coal, and iron and metal foundries, providing a cost-efficient method to prevent the diffusion of military technologies dangerous to central authority. But China's centralized system thwarted waves of innovations like those that dramatically transformed social relations in the West.

Chapters 8, 9, and 10 ask what we can learn about systemwide changes from the interaction among various states and their impacts on the development trajectory of other states. The focus is on microevolutionary change processes, assessing the impact of national institutions on the local social networks from which they arose.

Since the ending of the cold war, the spread of consumer conveniences, global financial markets, and global mass communication has created a flat world effect; nevertheless, the speed of economic change rarely overlaps with the more glacial speed of change in political and social processes. By contrast, during and after the Second World War, political and social changes among both developed and developing societies were more rapid than economic change processes. Colonialism ended in the global South. In the North, the effects of war on the structure of society and the expectations of the population crystallized in major regime changes at the ballot box, where populations demanded higher standards of social responsibility from the state. Can the rapid pace of economic change incite similar waves of demands for responsible political structures in the developing world?[13] The larger question is how the intensification of economic change will alter the international system and still produce a stable system of international relations.

Chapter 8 asks whether the world is becoming less diverse as more countries practice some variant of democracy. The outcomes of democratic reforms have remarkable capacity to vary, as members of the same society respond differently to pressures and opportunities in the environment. Democratic transitions share many properties identified with complex systems: they exhibit nonlinearity, they are highly sensitive to initial conditions, and they are frequently associated with cascades, or extreme events, like revolution or war.

Chapter 9 compares the emergence of bureaucratic systems from different historical antecedents in China and Europe. The result is parallel political modernization in which trajectories follow divergent paths.

Chapter 10 explores the impact of China's ascendancy on the norms, rules, and institutions that define the liberal international system. It asks what happens if the key actors no longer share beliefs about how the game of international relations should be played. Will the rise of China mean the end of liberal ascendency or simply a change in liberalism's specifications? China's impact on the internal and external dynamics of regime change in Sri Lanka illustrates the nuanced interplay of China's global influence and exemplifies how complex patterns of global interconnectedness are creating networks and incentives that are changing the global policy environment.

Chapter 11 addresses larger questions concerning the connections among globalization, social change, and modernization. For example, what will the difference in network structures—China's centralized hub-and-spoke network versus the denser, more decentralized network structure of Western states—mean as China becomes more important to global trade networks? It offers clear alternatives to the conceptions of globalization that have captured the imagination of the educated public and that have been most influential on the formation of global development policy.

Networks of communication, finance, trade, migration, fashion, and lifestyle trends are transforming our world. And their existence compels us to take an interest in complexity; all networks large or small are complex systems. That complexity has produced remarkable novelty and powerful self-organizing behavior, such as information cascades that impelled the 2011 Arab Spring or the collapse of the Soviet Union after the Berlin Wall was torn down in 1989. The sciences of complexity have already influenced empirical work on power outages, the spread of contagious diseases, market crashes, and traffic jams. In all of these arenas, small events that fall outside the range of normal distributions produce large disruptions. The Industrial Revolution can be thought of as an example of the catalytic properties of informational cascades.

Once the reader makes an initial investment in the terminology of complexity, understanding the concepts and the flow of the ideas is relatively easy. I have tried to balance the need for precise understanding against the necessity of technical concepts, hoping to avoid jargon. But this does not mean that such technically precise terms as *scale-free* or *punctuated equilibrium* can be avoided. For readers who find learning new terminology to be engaging, thinking of social systems as complex adaptive systems is full of rewards and what seems like scientific jargon today will be colloquial tomorrow.

Readers will be correct to suggest the need for quantitative indicators to back up the assumptions. This need can be fulfilled only after the qualitative changes leading economic activity into completely new activities are understood. Complexity alters relationships among the measurable inputs and outputs, changing outcomes by changing the relationships among the components.[14] A new generation of computational social sciences is just beginning to learn how to address key questions of global political economy. Measures of complexity will improve as scholars learn to devise and implement methodologies, such as spatial econometrics, agent-based modeling, and network and cluster analysis.

It is far too early to talk about general principles that link all complex systems the way Newton's invention of calculus unified the science of dynamics. There may never be a coherent and rigorous mathematical theory that unifies the many dynamical properties of complex systems and satisfies the standards of scientific rigor. The calculus of social complexity may be beyond human comprehension. This absence of mathematical simplicity is a challenge to the scientific legitimacy of complexity sciences. Yet biology, evolution, neurology, ecology, and other life sciences have gained major insights from complex systems theory. Similarly, in the study of social change processes, it is well understood that many forms of complexity coexist. Complexity science is not guaranteed to yield algorithmic explanations of complex historical change processes, but it may offer explanations that match the messy richness of those processes.

2

Opening the Doors of Complexity

Complexity thinking means thinking in terms of systems. It will help us to identify the importance of interconnections so that we do not assign value only to what is quantifiable. It will direct us to make policy in terms of feedback loops, and to design social learning into management processes. It will instruct us to optimize what is appropriate for the whole: to uncover the wisdom already in the system and to locate responsibility for action triggered by behaviors within the system. It will help us to better understand why there is a gap between our perception of a problem and the successful implementation of reforms. And it will lead us to see the value in diversity and to challenge the tyranny of disciplines.

Conventional approaches to global political economy excel at counting and classifying the changing properties of particular social constructs, regimes, institutions, political parties, or households. But the behavior of these social institutions is rarely reducible to the sum of the behaviors of their components. Social institutions constantly change in relation to their environments, and the interactive behaviors create "rules" from which emerge larger complex systems with their own emergent properties. Understanding how the dynamics of various change processes differ and give rise to the system being observed is the goal of this book.

Dynamics in Social Systems

The interactive dynamics of system stability in an increasingly interdependent and networked global society are largely similar to the change processes studied by scientists from fields as diverse as neurology, ecology, and physics. They use different terms to explain these systems: dynamical systems theory, the theory of complexity, nonlinear dynamics, networkdynamics, fractals, dissipation, and *complex adaptive systems*, which is the term in use in this book.

Markets and social institutions, such as political parties or the state, are complex adaptive systems in which the interactions of components (*agents*) give rise to networks of linked behaviors that are also complex adaptive components, or levels of organization, within yet larger complex adaptive systems. There is no real distinction between the component and its environment (system). *Networks* are not only the aggregates of components but are also themselves interactive agents that create a shared ecology of the larger system through self-organization. The environment and networks of which it is comprised together form its ecology.

A network is comprised of agents. The agents interact according to shared and evolving rules of behavior that in turn define the larger environment or system. That behavior generates continuous feedback loops that enable agents to learn and to adjust their behaviors to others' actions, thereby re-creating the system in which they operate. Complex adaptive systems are created by interactions and communications of self-adjusting agents. Continuous "feedback" motivates agents to re-evaluate their positions. Because agents are constantly reacting to other agents' behaviors, nothing in the environment is ever fixed or finite. In order to fully understand the impacts of these agents, their behaviors must be understood as they interact with the broader system.

This is very different from traditional social science, where the agents are atomized, independent actors that respond to incentives defined by formal rules and institutions. In conventional theory, change is additive, proportional to what goes in. Thus a society's well-being is computed by calculating the sum of characteristics of individual parts of the system; growth statistics, for example, are obtained by adding the output of all the firms in a nation's economy.[1] But the aggregates of quantities such as employment, output, or inflation disregard the critical data on variation needed to distinguish system complexity.[2] They hide the micro-variation that gives rise to complex outcomes. In complex systems, small variations matter and the interactions of a system's components cannot be reduced to the knowledge of the individual components. It is because of these concerns that institution-centric approaches to social development will be incomplete. It is also for this reason that a universal measure of political performance of nations is elusive.

In complex systems, agents adapt but are not optimizers. The "knowledge" of the actors in a social system, or in systems in general, consists of a limited view of the universe; they cannot predict the future path of the environment, being part of the prediction that is made.[3] They base their actions on the perception of what other agents will do. The agents are heterogeneous and employ both deductive and inductive decision processes to select from a range of options they conceptualize.

Complex adaptive systems show sensitivity to initial conditions. Economists Brian Arthur, Douglass North, and Paul David have each referred to the irreversible quality of institutional design with the term "path dependency" (Arthur 1994; David 1985; North 1981). "Sensitivity to initial conditions," a term coined by meteorologist Edward Lorenz, is an essential property of path dependency. A key implication of sensitivity to initial conditions is that small system perturbations can cause large differences in outcomes. In 1961, Lorenz produced compelling evidence (the length of the string of numbers behind a decimal point) of the huge impact of small perturbations on the outcome of interactions in weather systems. That logic was popularized as the "butterfly effect" and formed the basis of chaos theory. Before Lorenz's demonstration, scientists generally assumed irregular behavior to be uninteresting; but his proof that a tiny perturbation could affect an enormous system, such as the weather, has proved to be equally applicable to systems of human design. Moving the decimal point in measuring movements on the NASDAQ (a mere difference in the third decimal place) had a large, destabilizing effect on the system of financial valuations and price movements (Darley and Outkin 2007).

A given process of institutional development involves multitudes of interactions, and each might cause the results to vary. This insight raises issue with the habit among economists to seek the representative case. In economics, models that consist of a single representative agent carry powerful intellectual authority. But such models fail to identify how agent interactions are affected by connections and change, which can lead to complexity. For example, before the 2008 global financial crisis, the tyranny of thinking in terms of representative agents made it difficult to detect systemic default. When a loss of confidence spread across networks of bankers, traders, and speculators, the models ceased to have any relevance to the prevailing conditions in the real world (Root 2012).

When does a component recognize that it is a contributing agent? Do the parts know they are a wave? The study of complexity helps us recognize the significance of an individual change, in terms of the larger pattern or system of which it is a part. These are elements of collective behavior that must be understood in order to grasp events like the spread of revolutionary violence throughout Europe after demonstrations broke out in Paris in February 1848, the tearing down of the Berlin Wall and the collapse of the Soviet Union, or the global financial crisis of 2008.

Social networks, like living organisms, progress through a series of *bifurcations*, like the branching of an ancestral tree. A minor variation can produce large variations in the branching; the random element it introduces becomes a reference for the next bifurcation, causing lineages with a common ancestor to diverge. A bifurcation can initiate a recursive pattern, the sequential and irreversible construction of one action upon a previous action. The development of the human spine represents a pattern of recursive development that is traceable to nonhuman ancestors. Social examples of irreversible recursive processes are the property rights regime or, more generally, a legal system. Determining the point of divergence, the bifurcation point, is critical since escape from a given pattern is difficult. There is deeply humanistic meaning to irreversibility; it is the mechanism that allows us "to move from the universal to the unique, toward richness and variety" (Prigogine and Stengers 1984, 145).[4]

As we move toward diversity, we move away from equilibrium. A system can only be in equilibrium if it has no spatial structure generating its own internal dynamics. Complex systems have substantial internal structure, and this generates internal dynamics, including the possibility of extreme events.

The development model embraced by economics is a linear sequence that shows convergence toward equilibrium, the way cold and hot water converge to a uniform temperature. Its quantitative characteristics are additive, i.e., the sum of all its inputs. Introducing a variable, such as technological change, is like the effect of adding several drops of water, with the outcome proportional to the number of drops. There is no internal spatial structure to contend with. However, the temperature equalization of mixing cold and warm water droplets—the accumulation of inputs toward a linear goal—does a very poor job at depicting the dynamics of social systems. In complex systems, the agents combine and create something different, the way baking soda and vinegar combine to create an emergent quality, effervescence.

Emergence is any behavior that occurs between agents that contributes to a more complex behavior of the whole. Emergence describes the process through which a system acquires new structures and behaviors that its individual components did not possess. In nature, emergence is the wetness that occurs when atoms of hydrogen and oxygen combine to form water molecules. A complexity approach treats development as an emergent property, rather than the sum of the components that make up citizen well-being. The emergent properties of social organization can be illustrated by an ant colony's capacity to process more information than an individual ant, or by the mass synchrony of fireflies.

Complex adaptive systems comprise levels of organization; agents at one level are the building blocks of the next. A family is a complex system in that it comprises sets of individuals who share relationships with other individuals; there are different types of families: nuclear, blended, and extended. Within families, members base their actions on the behaviors of other members, and the family as an aggregate acts as a unit in response to the behaviors of other families.

At each level of complexity, adaptive agents respond to different *rules* that change the properties of the constituent parts. As complexity increases, the number of rules the system shares with behavior at "lower," or "less complex," levels will decrease. What happens to the shared rules when component entities are part of *more than one system* is a particularly acute conundrum since the behavior of a complex system cannot be predicted or deduced from observing individual behaviors of the "lower level" entities (reductionism).

In complex systems, the "rules" that generate a mass phenomenon can be absurdly simple, such as a conditional *if/then* interaction. For example, flocks of birds can mobilize by following a simple sequence of rules: "Be near, but not too far. Follow at least one other bird. The more birds you are near, the better. Follow the average direction of the birds ahead of you" (Holland 1995). Such strings of simple rules can generate complex social outcomes and behavior, such as the demonstrations in the streets of Warsaw, Prague, and Budapest that precipitated the fall of the Soviet Union, or the Arab uprisings of 2011, which began without a sophisticated political agenda. People did not text their friends, "Let's topple the regime of Hosni Mubarak." Something as simple as a message to "meet me at Tahir Square at 11 a.m.," with no political agenda or leader, is a movement as powerful as the flocks of birds that head south every winter and then back north again in the spring. Because adaptive agents respond to the reactions of other agents, even simple rules can produce complex outcomes.

As the number of interactions between agents in a complex system (either social or biological) increases exponentially with the addition of new or different agents, any number of novel behaviors can emerge. Furthermore, due to the richness of the interactions and communications among its agents, the complex system itself will inevitably undergo spontaneous self-organization to form new tiers of organization. However, levels of organization are never permanent; they evolve, adapt, and acquire new motivations.

Because the rules are conditional and evolve at each level of complexity, change in a complex system becomes nonlinear. Change is the interaction of different parts of the system with each other, and is not the sum total of the inputs. What goes in may not be what comes out. Development is an emergent quality that results from the way different parts of the economic and social system interact with each other. Macroevolutionary changes that create new adaptive zones occur at the level of the system.

Merely complicated mechanisms, such as a pendulum or a watch, a sewing machine, or a nuclear reactor, are not adaptive, making optimal solutions possible. However, if one part is removed or damaged, the other parts will not respond, and the system will most likely shutdown. Complex systems are more resilient; a change to one of the parts will not result in the collapse of the system but will change the behavior of the remaining components. In complex systems, no single attribute, strategy, or type can solve all optimization problems. But adaptive systems need not result in optimal structures, and fit organisms need not be the most complex.

Evolution or Complexity?

Questions about variation and networks are central to both the study of evolution and complexity. Both share complementary perspectives on such questions as what drives systems toward greater complexity, what drives the evolution of system components toward greater diversity, what makes some changes more likely than others, and how the speed of change alters the variation and the complexity of adaptation. So what justifies the choice of complex adaptive systems to explain social change processes, such as the rise of the modern state? Why not just stop with evolution?

Evolutionary systems move slowly. The environment in which an organism must survive determines the viability of its structure. Each change to one cell or a network of cells requires adaptive variations among other cells. Evolution is tenacious and unrelenting. It never gives up. It will always exhaust every option in the attempt to find a fit order. But constrained as it is by path dependency, evolution cannot go back and retrieve a design that has been lost. Social systems are not as severely constrained, so they evolve much more quickly, and this is why we do not study them through the lens of evolutionary adaptation.

Moreover diversity within a given gene pool thwarts evolution; highly diverse gene pools cannot interact. Evolutionary change thrives in a world of variation, but great diversity is an obstacle—even slight genetic differences in members of a population will prevent interbreeding. By contrast, since social systems are not gene-based, path dependency is not as binding, and there is no limit to mixing and matching across or among different cultural lineages.

Both evolution and complexity do emphasize the possibility of order from randomness. In both, fit designs arise through continuous adaptation to novelty in a process of trial and error. However, mutability in biology is limited to the mutation or recombination of genetic material, which ensures gradual patterns of transition, and most mutations are actually harmful. According to Charles Darwin (1876, 156), "natural selection acts only by taking advantage of slight successive variations; she can never take a great and sudden leap, but must advance by short and sure, through slow steps." The underlying dynamics of Darwinian *gradualism* are modeled on the domestication of plants and animals by breeding characterized by a slow, smooth rate of change consistent with certain biological limits. In Darwin's theory of natural selection organisms adapt to their environments until they attain a fit that is good enough to ensure survival and reproduction; later variations build up as time goes by.

Societies, by contrast, evolve through the purposeful actions of the agents; they are subjects of conscious design, although purposeful action is not always rational or efficient. The genes in which biological change occurs cannot consciously decide to reorder their structure. This makes evolution an inadequate framework to study the variation among societies, states, and governance regimes. Whereas evolution takes place primarily in genes and their lineages, evolutionary theory offers insufficient explanations for how the interactions of the parts result in collective behavior at the system level.

Social learning involves reinforcement effects: mimicry, copying, emulation, or the threat of ostracism. The influence of social networks can lead to cascades caused by group think, leading to the rise and fall of fashions and fads, or sudden shifts in business sentiment. As a consequence a sudden change in a system's macro-properties, *phase transitions,* rare in biology, occur more frequently in social systems.[5] Information cascades that produce events like the Arab Spring can make up for lost time and promise to end the eclipse of social progress with a great burst of social innovation. Hence the analogy with biological systems breaks down in the analysis of social systems.

Evolution and complexity offer complementary but different perspectives on global change. Evolution helps us discover the capabilities of an individual society, its institutions, or the state itself. Complexity, however, offers a more complete understanding of social systems because they have a wider range of change mechanisms. Simulations have established that evolution through natural selection leads to fewer types, reducing the quantity of fit organisms over time.[6] Blinded by a dominant logic or ideology, human societies can long resist change, and then change suddenly. They are not necessarily constrained by a previous adaptation and can redeploy ideas from the past. They can regress or fail, and incur coups, revolutions, civil wars, conquest, and occupation.

The system of international relations exemplifies the volatility of manmade regimes rarely evolving to a state of permanence. Challenges to the legitimacy of an incumbent order are a constant feature of international relations. Political historian Philip Bobbitt traces the system-altering transitions that have changed the definition of regime legitimacy and effectiveness to the effects of interstate warfare (2002). The end of the Thirty Years' War (1618 to 1648), memorialized by the Treaty of Westphalia, altered the power structure of Europe and created the dynastic state. It recognized the triumph of sovereignty over empire.

But the legitimacy and efficacy of the Westphalian order were ultimately challenged by a series of wars, impelled onto the European stage by the French Revolution, initiated to eliminate dynastic rule in favor of the nation state. The ideology of the nation state was itself contested in a series of conflicts that Bobbitt calls the Long War, which began in August 1914 and finally ended with the end of the cold war (2002). The Long War was fought over three contrasting visions of national welfare: fascism, communism, and liberal democracy. The victory of liberal democracy has only opened a new contest for the rules of the successor regime, one that engages the state to be an engine of economic development that can secure market access for its population.

In sum, core Darwinian principles do not explain the full range of dynamic processes that produce the state, the economy, the trajectory of technology, and other social systems. All exhibit volatility, tipping points, and phase transitions that are rare in evolution. The purposeful outcomes of human actions, such as the French Revolution or the Spanish Conquest of Mexico, can change the course of history. The difference between evolutionary systems and human-made systems resides in the fact that humans erect networks that transmit ideas, spark revolutions, and raze empires.

Analytical Conventions in Political Economy and Their Applications to Global Development

To demonstrate how the fundamental claims of this book differ from analytical conventions widely applied in political economy, this section will consider two of the most far-ranging approaches by contemporary political economists to construct comprehensive theories of international development.[7]

Economists Daron Acemoğlu and Douglass North, two recognized leaders in the field of political economy, both seek to explain why some countries prosper while others stagnate, and both use history and economics to link development and social change into a single line of argument. Both rely on the analytical conventions of contemporary political economy to demonstrate that an "iron law" of democratic and economic convergence exists. Both of their research programs are founded on the conviction that the convergence of political and economic values is required for effective modernization of societies, and both employ widely accredited conventions of social science to offer empirical demonstrations to prove the necessity of this convergence. First we will review those conventions, and then we will show that a wide range of historical and contemporary experience does not fit their assertion of convergence.

In *Why Nations Fail* (2012), a celebrated study of historical political economy, Acemoğlu and political scientist James Robinson claim that "extractive regimes," political institutions that give elites monopoly access to unearned income, can be found with persistent regularity in every part of the world where growth is blocked and end in predictable political failure and economic decline.[8] Inclusive political institutions, by contrast, produce inclusive economies (2012, 429–30). Without the inclusive political institution of democracy, higher incomes for the population will be forfeit to collusive behavior by predatory elites.

Acemoğlu's and Robinson's predictions about why some economies stagnate while others progress share with the earlier work of Noble laureate Douglass North a narrative about the impacts of *institutions* on economic progress. In many books and articles, North argues that institutional structure is the most universal and empirically grounded causal variable that explains economic failure or success, and is the primary driver of large-scale processes of social change. The link from institutions to prosperity runs from property rights to invention, and from entrepreneurship and investment to growth. "Institutions are the rules of the game, the patterns of interactions that govern and constrain the relationships of individuals. Institutions include formal rules, written laws, formal social conventions, and informal norms of behavior. Institutions must also include the means by which rules and norms are enforced" (North, Wallis, and Weingast 2009, 259).

Technological discovery occurs when the investors and inventors are confident that they will reap the economic benefits of their efforts. Institutions that reduce transaction costs to productive exchange will create incentives that motivate individuals to trade and engage in productive behavior. Higher incomes and improved social welfare will result, something that all rational people should hope for. But most social orders in history deliberately erect barriers to efficient exchange to benefit regime insiders.

According to our framework, throughout all of history humans have devised just three social orders: ways of organizing societies that are self-sustaining and internally consistent. The *primitive order* consists of hunter-gatherer societies, and will concern us only in passing.

The *limited access order* creates limits on access to valuable political and economic functions as a way to generate rents. Rents are created both by limits on access to resources and functions—like worship, trade, education, and warfare—and by limiting access to forms of social organization that the larger society will support. Powerful individuals possess privileges and rents, and since violence threatens or reduces those rents, the risk of losing the rents can make it in the interests of powerful individuals and groups to cooperate with the coalition in power rather than to fight. Privileged individuals have privileged access to social tools enabling them, and only them, to form powerful organizations. In limited access orders the political system manipulates the economy to create rents as a means of solving the problem of violence. Acknowledging this direct link between the creation of rents and maintenance of order enables us to integrate economic and political theory in a new way.

The third order, the *open access order*, relies on competition, open access to organizations, and the rule of law to hold the society together. These societies use competition and institutions to make it in the interests of political officials to observe constitutional rules, including consolidated political control over all organizations with the potential for major violence. (North et al. 2007, 4)

North's collaboration with economic historian John Wallis and political scientist Barry Weingast on *Violence and Social Orders* (2009) expanded on this essay presented at the World Bank by defining "the doorstep conditions" through which all countries must pass in order to attain economic modernization. The study traces a developmental sequence in which "limited access orders" (Acemoğlu refers to these as extractive regimes) are replaced with polities of open access. They distinguish their work from previous efforts of quantitative social scientists by claiming that they have discovered the influence of an omitted factor: "the pattern of social relationships in the open access order" (p. 13) where everyone enjoys economic opportunities and political voice, and where competition flourishes (Acemoğlu refers to these as "inclusive regimes").

The Race to Discover the Omitted Variable

The methods of both Acemoğlu and North are representative of what constitutes proof and evidence in normal social science. Both programs draw on a large body of historical research that establishes the relationship between dependent and independent variables, using statistical tools like regression to the mean. Both draw on a wealth of studies that describe development by calculating the sum of characteristics of individual parts to establish standardized aggregates like gross national product, which is measured by adding the output of all firms in a nation's economy.

Traditional economics focuses on incomes as the main measure of development. Believing that development must be less about growth and real income per capita and more about a population's well-being, in 1975 the United Nation's Development Programme (UNDP) introduced sophisticated statistical measurements, called Human Development Indicators.[9] These define the well-being of the population by calculating the sum of all human capital, and by computing the sum of all its components (e.g., health, education, leisure, and gender entitlement) to determine a country's relative level of development. The Human Development Indicators measure social development the same way gross domestic product measures economic growth; both establish linear correlations between inputs and outcomes, and define development by the weighted sum of all the parts.

North's team also rejects income as the main measure of development; but instead of health, education, and living standards, they substitute institutional variables. They call these the "doorstep conditions" that enable impersonal exchange. The doorsteps are the long-sought-after standardized aggregates that correlate democracy and high income. These include the control of violence by the state, consolidated control over the military, a rule of law that allows elites to protect property rights, and the formation of "perpetually lived organizations," in which organizational identity is separate from the identity of its members (North, Wallis, and Weingast 2009, 26, 260).[10] But are these doorsteps the Holy Grail that explains the connection between democracy and high-income levels? The irony of North's "doorsteps" to his open access orders is that they exclude the most successful and open economies in the emerging world. The doorstep is not wide enough to accommodate the newly industrialized East Asian nations, the most impressive contemporary examples of high-speed economic growth since 1960. Contemporary India, which easily fits through the door to enhanced exchange, has not performed as well as its neighbors to the East that are kept out.

The Omitted One-Third of the Human Population

Douglass North's efforts to find the omitted variable omit one-third of the world's population. Asia's development trajectory since 1949 refutes the proposition of democratic and economic convergence. This means that North's definitive causal link of good governance and growth excludes East Asia, and China, and fails to explain India's laggard performance. The East Asian Tigers have a long history of authoritarianism; only Japan held elections during its growth surge, and it has nevertheless reelected the same party for the entire four decades of high growth. China achieved twenty years of continuous high-speed growth as a one-party state without elections. Moreover East Asia's economy grew by deliberately copying the technology of others, not through innovation. India, by far Asia's most democratic regime, is a country of prejudicial regulations and higher barriers to entry than many of its more authoritarian neighbors. For most of its history as an independent state, democratic India's growth rates have been mediocre. This suited India's founders who descended from a priestly caste, Brahmin, which held business to be socially disruptive.

China's growth has not depended on the formal enforcement of property rights either. For North, this is just an anomaly. Although North, Wallis, and Weingast affirm that representative government is a precondition for the security of property rights, they also maintain that a successful capitalist economy is not possible without representative institutions that protect private property (2009). So where do the underlying economic incentives that drive China's growth originate? Within North's framework, the degree of formality versus informality can provide an answer. In China, informal institutions must have mattered more than formal ones. Informal, reputation-based, contract enforcement must have substituted for formal property rights.

History is not kind to either North or Acemoğlu. Unlike European history, the history of the Chinese Empire offers few examples of confiscation, and few regulations that distort markets to create extractive opportunities for the elite. The governing elite in China was the imperial bureaucracy, and it sought legitimacy by provisioning public goods, avoiding the extractive behavior that the theories of North and Acemoğlu would have predicted. Nor does either Acemoğlu or North explain the spectacular rise of imperial Germany after 1850, when it became Europe's major industrial economy without electing its head of state. Its productive capabilities were enlarged by more extensive and wider allocation of social assets, such as health and education, than was practiced among its more democratic or autocratic neighbors. Autocratic Germany, not democratic France or England, fielded the most highly educated European army during the two world wars.

Acemoğlu and Robinson (2012) are more dismissive and less willing to accept the inevitability of China's continued growth. If China refuses to adopt inclusive institutions, they maintain, its current economic success will expire and it will implode, as did the former Soviet Union (p. 441). If the Chinese elite do not give up their tight grip on power, "Chinese growth is likely to end. . . . In this case, history and our theory suggest that growth with creative destruction and true innovation will not arrive, and the spectacular growth rates in China will slowly evaporate" (p. 442).

Even the once-authoritarian East Asians appear to be bending to Acemoğlu's iron law; he asserts that they too have already begun to adopt democracy. But as we will see in chapter 8, the democracy they are adapting has little in common with liberal conceptions of democratic pluralism. Also in the case of East Asia, the pressure to democratize comes from outside—it is not a manifestation of Acemoğlu's iron law of economic and democratic convergence. The East Asian Tigers all depended on access to a principal trading partner, the United States, which emphasized the transition to democracy as a precondition to normal trading relations. Its security umbrella could be withdrawn from governments considered illegitimate due to the absence of electoral democracy.

The same external impetus has enabled Mexico to transition away from the rest of Latin America. However, an external impetus will have little import in China's case. Will Japan eventually converge to the beliefs of its larger neighbor in order to gain greater access to the global investment opportunities through linkage with China's economy? In sum, the institution-centric approach works so long as the interstate component of global political economy can be removed. It leaves us ill prepared to answer questions about systems that are dynamic, interactive and interdependent, and in which global patterns emerge from micro-behavior.

China and Global Spillovers

Acemoğlu and Robinson (2012) predict that China's growth will be interrupted, and North arrives at a more optimistic prediction by emphasizing the possibility that China can succeed by relying on contract enforcement through informal practices. But international policymakers have a different concern from that of both sets of institutionalists: any interruption in China's growth will have a dramatic impact on its partners.

Sustainable long-term global development can no longer be imagined without considering that China's established trade and financial linkages already have dramatic spillover effects on advanced and emerging economies alike. The logic of China's state-centered economy has begun to challenge two centuries of economic rule-making, thus releasing powerful *coevolutionary* forces that are changing the landscape for both small and large nations, for both developing and developed countries. This makes macroeconomic stabilization of the international economy more difficult.

Both Acemoğlu's predictions of China's inevitable drift into political instability and North's prediction of inevitable convergence give little solace to policy makers trying to cope with the global economic transformation under way. They focus on another set of questions. Does the rise of China represent a transition point in the evolution of the international system? Will it lead to dissolution of the global order into regional units and subunits, or even multiple international systems, similar to the ancient world in which city-states, empires, and barbarians all interacted, but where there was no global system? What system-level objectives will be sufficiently inclusive to embrace China, and will these values be sufficient basis for system stability?

Concern for global collaboration necessary to stabilize the international economy has led the International Monetary Fund (IMF) to seek a new policy tool that tracks the spillover effects from the domestic policies of "systemic economies," those like China's, whose domestic policies can have external impacts significant enough to propagate global shocks. Thus the policy conundrum concerning the rise of China is the need to develop new methods to assess and balance systemic risk and reduce the stress of local distortions that can reverberate globally.

Raghuram Rajan, former chief economist of the IMF, likewise confirms that China adds risks to international financial stability. "Because different financial systems work on different principles and involve different forms of government interactions," he warns, "they tend to distort each other's functioning whenever they come into close contact" (2010, 7). When two systems clash (e.g., the state-based economies of East Asia and the privately invested economies of the West), mechanisms to reconcile differences and restore balances are more difficult. Instead, the insecurities of financing by less transparent (informal) methods can now be transferred to the other, more accountable and open system. This magnifies global risk. In other words, the countries that long ago passed the "doorstep of open access" can be affected by spillovers from those still left behind in limited-access orders ("natural states," North et al. 2009).[11]

The IMF has only just begun to identify the information that is needed to describe the macro-state of the global financial system. Considering the size of this system, describing how the behavior of the whole depends on the behavior of its constituent parts represents the single greatest challenge for the organization to steer the global economy toward prosperity.

The IMF recognizes that global interdependency heightens global risk for developed and developing countries alike, and that those once-peripheral economies can force change in the global system. During the nineteenth century, supply-chain disruptions from peripheral regions in the global economy were transitory. When cotton could not be produced from one source, another source could be substituted. Substitutes were easily found for low-quality goods or raw materials. Today, because of China's integration into global manufacturing chains, and because it is both a producer and a market for global technology, a disruption in China's growth has broad consequences for intertwined networks of production.

Complexity science allows us to reframe the most pressing issues in the global policy debate on the emerging international order in order to understand the implications of this message—that the world's economies are not merely interconnected, they are interdependent.

States Grow, They Are Not Built

Complexity suggests a very different formulation of the dynamics of social change and economic development than that of either Acemoğlu or North. Development is emergent, instead of being an aggregate or additive outcome. This difference is especially significant in considering global development policy and the role of the modern state, which is the primary representative of human collectives within the international system and the central implementer of that policy.[12]

States consist of government institutions and rules, as Acemoğlu and North both claim. But if devising those institutions and rules were the whole story, we would not be asking why long and costly efforts at building state institutions—those that enable citizens to perform complex collective tasks—often fail in developing regions.

The greater part of the story concerns the transitions of behavior, expectations, and culture that occur when new institutions are introduced. The interactions that take place as the landscape shifts can trigger new behaviors and characteristics that emerge unintentionally and even in direct contrast to the goals of those who contribute the resources and labor.

States do not result solely from the accumulation of events in a local population. They are parts of the international system and acquire structure by being embedded into a larger systemic whole. They interact with that system, even as their constituent parts interact with each other and the broader system. When a state's interactions shift from being locally based to being regionally or nationally based, its behaviors change across the network and the greater system. *Thus a general theory of the system cannot be deduced from the properties of its constituent parts, just as the universe cannot be reconstructed from the fundamental laws of physics.*

A state is a nested hierarchy of interactive components. Lower (or inner) levels of organization combine into higher (or outer) levels, just as groups of individuals form families, groups of families form neighborhoods, groups of neighborhoods form cities, and groups of cities form metropolitan regions, which connect to provinces. The agents at one level contribute to the behavior of the next, but at each level of aggregation, the behavior of the whole also shifts. None of these levels exhibit the identical behavioral characteristics of their individual components.

The formation of a state changes the rules governing the behavior of the groups it comprises in ways not easily foreseen. The emergence of unanticipated behaviors is a characteristic that states share with other complex systems. A change at one level alters the options for change at another. The agents adapt; they acquire new identities and adjust their behaviors to new sets of rules and to the expected reactions of others, making it difficult to predict the behavior of individuals in constantly shifting environments and organizational formations. At each level, the constituents are likely to exhibit new behaviors, and how they adapt and act together to create the behavior of the whole is not easily reducible to the sum of the parts.

Emergence, the process through which new structures and behaviors arise to create a more complex whole, is critical to the examination of the most fundamental questions of the origin and behavior of modern states. For example, states are catalysts for giant change processes like nationalism, democracy, and industrialization (Gellner 1983). These socioeconomic megatrends are examples of emergence that arise in the context of a state, yet at same time, states are outcomes of those trends. Economic development, democracy, globalization, and liberal internationalism contribute to the environment of one another, but they are also products of one another. The differences between process and structure are rarely as neat as conventional theories presume.

Likewise a state's behavior is not reducible even to the most exhaustive catalog of institutions. In complex, highly connected systems, the rules of interaction matter as much as the specifications of the structures and their component parts; successful adaptation or reform is contingent on other factors in the same environment. The way its component parts, its social networks, are interconnected determines a state's behavior over time. The same institutions in a different network will produce different outcomes; different institutions in different networks may produce similar outcomes (parallel evolution, to be discussed in chapter 9), and reforms that succeed in one environment may fail in another. Even institutions that share a common design will produce qualitatively different outcomes due to the linkages within social networks.

The Intrastate Omission

States do not exist in isolation from larger systems. And changes to the rules of governance are not solely the results of local interactions among domestic elites; states that win wars are positioned to decide the legitimate order for other states. The winners then become the system administrators, deciding the rules by which others will play.

An analogy of the international system that can be drawn from nature would be the evolution of species, a higher-level phenomenon meaningless at the cellular level.[13] Macroevolutionary change, such as the transition from asexual to sexual reproduction or from cold- to warm-blooded organisms, occurs only at the system level.

In today's global political economy, the effects of the last game change, the last big war are slowly being eroded by global trends, including shifts in global demographics. Will these slow-moving but persistent trends altering the relationships between the Western incumbents and the emerging powers be the source of the next global power transition? Will they destabilize regime compacts that constitute the current order and cause unpredictable and potentially catastrophic outcomes? Or will global institutions successfully mediate the necessary adjustments with tolerable but reasonable sacrifices to avoid the possibility of widespread violent conflicts?

If North or Acemoğlu is correct, then open trade and economic growth should lead developing nations into convergence with Western values of individual rights and democratic institutions. Yet current studies of newly developing powers, such as China, Brazil, India, and Turkey, reveal deviations and departures from the "norms" of modernization theory. These departures from Western democratic and market-based norms pose important questions about the need for an alternative framework to understand the development and trajectory of newly emerging powers. North's and Acemoğlu's assertions that they have discovered the causal variables for economic growth that can reinterpret recorded human history need toning down. The exalted golden thread with which they would weave together institutions and development does not glisten the way they claim. Interdependencies in the new global environment reduce its shimmer to that of an ordinary cotton string.

Chapters 3, 4, and 5 will focus on reasons for rejecting current intellectual conventions concerning institutional selection and system stability. Then chapters 6 through 10 will demonstrate the use of complexity models to explore alternate paths to economic and political modernity. Each chapter starts with a comprehensive description and evaluation of previous theoretical approaches. The goal is to reveal properties of systems that might not otherwise be apparent in conventional analysis. Chapter 11 concludes by assessing the policy implications of a world in which there is no guarantee of economic and political convergence, and no captain at the helm to steer the outcome.

It is far too early to assert that the structures and networks in human society are governed by the same underlying regularities as those found in nature. Even if they do not provide a comprehensive explanatory theory for all social behavior, complexity approaches take us far beyond the scope and capacity of frameworks that now make up the lexicon of contemporary political economy and international relations. In the language of self-organization, sensitivity to initial conditions, path-dependency, lock-in, coevolution, adaptation, and bifurcation, a vocabulary does exist for disentangling the processes that generate system-level changes from the structure and evolution of networks that produced those processes. It teaches us to see the changing dynamics of both state-building and development by taking into account how individual states are organized into systems, how state systems arise and disappear, and what rules contribute to system change.

3

Economic Incentives and the Replication of Social Complexity

The Fallacies of Modernization Theory

Modernization theory has had a deterministic influence on contemporary understanding of global development, both within the academy and among the policy community. Its influence is so widespread that it is even difficult to refer to modernization as a theory; its visceral intensity in the framing of US development policy has been a matter of faith under democratic and republican administrations. Under Bill Clinton, modernization theory led US policy makers to believe that open trade and rising incomes would bring democracy to China and Russia. Under George W. Bush, it led to the belief that a democratic transition would spontaneously follow the eradication of dictatorship in Iraq and helped gain bipartisan support for the invasion. Bush's secretary of state, Condoleezza Rice, espoused confidence that a rising middle class in China would assume its "universal" role and demand democratic rights of representation and a free media. The grip of modernization theory on policies of international relations did not change when the Democrats won the 2008 election. President Barack Obama links open economies, open societies, and open governments, just as his predecessors did. All administrations since Jimmy Carter's have asserted that human progress has a single trajectory: it may start with the economy, but it must ultimately end with democracy.

Ronald Ingelhart and Christian Welzel, two celebrated academic exponents of modernization theory, claim that it "integrates socioeconomic development, cultural change, and democratization under the overarching theme of human development" (2005, 1). According to these scholars, modernization is a process that produces objective capabilities, enabling people to base their lives on autonomous choices. Prosperity makes possible the pursuit of freedom of expression and self-realization to lead societies through a series of social changes that will make democracy inevitable. Authoritarian development is not an alternative path, but a transitional stage. Human rights and civil liberties will follow increases in the educational attainment of workers. If a McDonald's is spotted on one corner, writer Thomas Friedman opins, then expect a transition to postmodern values to be just around the next corner.

The strong grip of modernization theory on both development theory and practice is based on its bold claim that to narrow the West's lead in modern science and industry, the rest of the world must replicate its trajectory (McNeill 1992, 806–807). The speed with which Western financial and trade protocols travel around the globe creates the illusion that other Western structures are transported along the same trajectory. Indeed economic change has spread around the world by leaps and bounds, at a rate that surpasses all other change processes, bringing with it physical technology that has homogenized the urban landscapes of many emerging regions. The same fast-food chains do seem to pop up everywhere.

However, the adaptive capacity of local institutions resides in other scales of social order, such as religion, conflict, or identity; and change in these societal processes occurs at a different pace than does change in the economy. Many societies, including China, Russia, and Saudi Arabia, attained near first world levels of economic growth and education without attaining modernization's other virtues, such as democracy, civil liberties, or secure property rights. For this reason, "It is now a commonplace to observe the extraordinary dynamism of the global economy, and the relative underdevelopment of the global polity and global society," observe Barry Buzan and Richard Little, two theorists of international relations (2000, 381). Modernization theory offers only weak account for this gap between the accelerated pace of economic change and the sluggish rate of other social change processes.

This limitation was not apparent in the triumphalist period after the fall of the Berlin Wall, when liberal idealism coalesced with modernization theory to produce a theory of transition from socialism in which economic and political liberalism are examples of a similar process of natural selection. According to this theory, wealth creation leads to openness, which generates more wealth, which in turn increases the demand for openness. So frequently were they found working together that democracy and free markets were assumed to be integrated parts of a single system. The presumed linkage with democracy seemed so certain, and its proliferation so universal, that market liberalism and its theory of transition became a doctrine rather than a process. Democracy and capitalism were no longer the ends, but the prescribed *means* for development as well, to be imitated, replicated, and transplanted.

According to liberal theory, the economy is the replicator of liberal values.[1] It fashions adaptive improvements in social institutions, promotes specialization and the division of labor into useful functional roles, and replicates better-adapted structures of social organization, regardless of the preexisting variation in the environment.[2] This assumption is flawed, and the efforts at transplanting institutions have produced meager results. Neither elections nor the introduction of price-determined markets, the two most powerful change mechanisms in the arsenal of liberal theory, have had the expected transformative effect in developing countries.

The problem with which development policy must increasingly cope is that many of the key institutions of a modern economy arise from different sources and initial conditions.[3] A market economy itself comprises multiple systems of order that function simultaneously, and change moves at different rates among these scales of social action, reducing the capacity for market-based rationality to transform other domains of social order. A lesson drawn by evolutionary ecologists dealing with a parallel analytical problem, that of cross-scale effects, is that optimization models are likely to fail when what happens at one scale is affected by events at other scales. These cross-scale effects make the task of transplanting institutions around the world especially problematic.

The Transplanter's Fallacy

In 2006, I became chief of a project called Enhancing Government Efficiency (EGE) for USAID, the US Agency for International Development, assigned to explore how US technical assistance could help build effective governments in developing regions. The democracy and economic affairs units of USAID designed the project. The collaboration of these two bureaus within the agency led to a focus on fixing broken systems of public administration in predominately Muslim countries with fundamentalist tendencies. I was dispatched to areas where fundamentalist movements were already mobilized, to design diagnostic tools to determine the social impediments to public administration reform. Over the course of five years, we examined more than twenty government agencies concerned with human resource management, recruitment, finance and budget, planning, interagency coordination, and evaluation, in West Bank/Gaza, Yemen, Morocco, Indonesia, and Pakistan.[4]

The ending of the cold war made it possible for the Organization for Economic Co-operation and Development (OECD) to announce in 1992 that good governance was essential to development effectiveness. A recipient country's eligibility for international assistance was no longer based on its opposition to global communism. A World Bank document in 1993 adapted politically neutered language, "transparency, predictability, and accountability," to signal that the governance of a borrowing country had impact on the performance of Bank projects and therefore was a legitimate cause of concern. In 1994 the Bank's "Asian Miracle" report stressed the role of good governance in the rise of East Asia's high-performing economies.

The governance genie was out of the bottle and by the second half of the 1990s, governance reform was a stated policy goal of the development community. The academic community responded by developing frameworks, indicators, and models. One such model, a result of my collaboration with Bruce Bueno de Mesquita while we were both fellows at Stanford University's Hoover Institution, became the analytical basis of the EGE project.[5] According to our model, the leadership of a certain polity is assumed to depend on a particular subset of the population—the winning coalition—for its ability to remain in power (Bueno de Mesquita and Root 2000; Bueno de Mesquita et al. 2003). The leadership in turn rewards this winning coalition, which does not necessarily consist of the exclusive elites but may also include members of various social strata who wield sufficient influence in their operating spheres. The rewards consist of a mix of public and private goods, the distribution of which depends both on the size of the *winning coalition* necessary to maintain the self-interested leader in power and on the larger *selectorate*, the portion of the population with a voice in selecting the leadership.[6]

Since the leadership also has the power to influence the manner in which government revenue is distributed, it might reward its winning coalition by directly providing private goods. This is only sustainable, however, if the winning coalition is relatively small compared to the government's revenue base. If the coalition is large, the value of private goods received by individual coalition members will decrease as the limited revenue is split among many. In such a situation, the leadership runs the risk of losing the support of coalition members who find the amount inadequate. Therefore, it is usually more strategic for the government to redistribute its revenue as public rather than private goods when the coalition is large.

The selectorate model opens up the "black box" of the state and specifically focuses on the preservation of elite power and winning coalitions. Specifically, leaders engage in local, myopic searches for solutions—of which liberalism may be only one. This means that based on their initial starting point (their sensitivity to initial conditions), not all leaders will see the same set of alternatives. Their early choices may be irreversible and will affect future opportunities (creating path dependence). Likewise, the choices of each actor will affect the relative opportunities (interdependencies) and subsequent fitness of others at multiple levels of society (strategic interaction and coevolution).

The transplanter's dilemma is that no part of a complex social system can be isolated from the whole with the expectation that its function will remain the same. Transplanting an institution from a developed society to a developing society will not enable the latter to progress along the same path. For a transplanted institution to replicate identical behavior, the entire developmental process must be replicated, beginning from its primitive condition.[7]

In addition, like most "rational actor" models, our concept assumed that suboptimal policies, institutions, and technologies could be eliminated through the power of market incentives. Much of that work was based on the notion that "in a world of competitive markets, only those who make decisions *as if* they were maximizing will survive" (Simon 1969, 46). Underlying this belief in the remedial power of market discipline was the notion that the optimal decision exists in the menu of options from which a society can actually choose. Even if the optimal decision is among the menu of options, it may be ignored because it conflicts with the economic incentives of key elites (Acemoğlu and Robinson 2012, 69). This puts the focus on class conflict, who has the power and how they exercise it.

However, the elite actors we tried to situate in our model did not possess unlimited foresight to identify the best strategies. Their rationality was bounded, meaning they lacked complete information concerning the social and economic processes that made up their environment. Recognizing this made apparent two misconceptions about the sources of economic incentives: The first stemmed from the presumption that institutions exist because of how they serve the rational interests of winning coalition members. In effect, however, changing the institutions involves levels of coordination with a number of domestic and occasionally external actors. The barriers to the efficiency of public administration are woven into the fabric of society through complex interdependencies and are *not* the result of a conscious design by the elites to conserve power. Coalitions arise as adaptive responses to the institutional ecology; they are shaped by that ecology just as they may attempt to shape it.

The selectorate model is fundamentally a model of elite preservation and the tensions of local and global politics, and does not sufficiently address how sector-level institutions are influenced by macro-variables at the level of systemwide political economy. In the chapters that follow, the complexity lens differentiates the model of adaptive behavior from that of the older selectorate model. It is far more attuned to local conditions and diversity, and the constraints on actors and the way they perceive and evaluate their options. By focusing on the *interdependence* of properties in *public administration* subsystems, the selectorate model did not apprehend the dependency of one component on other affected components of the system. Interdependencies among the components made changing administrative behavior much more difficult than we anticipated.[8] A government official or a business is rarely able to make a decision that reflects an optimal concept of utility. The interrelationships among the components will shape the outcome because of what political economist Stan Metcalfe calls a "combinatorial explosion" (1995, 395).

The complex interdependencies that constrain the adaptive potential of the system arise interactively through coevolution, as a result of the myopic efforts of agents reacting to and anticipating the behaviors of other agents. Each actor adapts to an environment of other agents that evolve simultaneously.[9] And this adjustment occurs in the context of *bounded rationality.*

In fact, the window for reform in all five countries, all poorly governed by international standards, was narrower than we suspected. As in other complex systems, an alteration within one component affected the other components with which it interacted, and what worked well within a single component had unintended and unforeseen effects on the others. General systemwide improvements are obtained only if the benefits from an intervention are greater than the negative side effects on all the other components.

The dilemmas our team encountered applying our rational actor model to the administration of different governmental ministries are familiar to what scientists find in other, often unrelated fields of scientific inquiry, such as epidemiologists studying contagion, geologists working to predict earthquakes, or ecologists assessing the erosion of biodiversity. After the discovery of DNA, for example, biological scientists learned that they had a long way to go before being able to improve life by selecting for mutant genes with positive effects; any mutation in the genes affects a unique sequence of interdependent life processes. Similarly, the likelihood of administrative reform to produce a beneficial outcome depends on complex interdependencies among institutions. A mutation that improves efficiency in one sector may have deleterious consequences for the system as a whole. A single reform will have various effects that can be either negative or positive on the range of institutions with which it interacts. To understand why policies succeed differentially, social planners must address the effects of interdependency, or *epistasis*, that shape development.

Institutional selection is generally a search to attain local optima, discovering a niche that works, rather than what performs optimally by a universal standard. The cost incurred in climbing the particular fitness landscape a population faces is likely to determine the outcome. Thus the pressures that cause an individual regime to select a particular niche in the international system vary considerably from the assumptions of contemporary transition models. Policy planners must confront the dilemma that the systems they seek to reform are locked into local optima and are the best outcomes obtained through narrowly focused strategies of trial and error.

Only great leaps, not small changes, will alter the rules of the game and enable these societies to overcome the causes of uncertainty, corruption, and inequality. However, long jumps, such as the Shah of Iran's White

Revolution, risk grave miscalculation. An exhaustive search of reform possibilities is required that few regimes can realistically undertake. A regime puts its own survival at risk if it allocates all of its resources to such exhaustive searches.

In sum, institutional reform requires that we understand the laws of interaction in the systems from which complexity arises. Although the parts can respond independently to demands placed on them by the environment, those demands are connected to, indeed are responses to, other parts of the same environment. Instead of reducing a problem to one of its parts, our awareness of a problem's origin must be expanded to include the processes that create the system.

The Fallacy of Stages in the Economic Theory of Transition

Karl Marx may have been the first to propose an economic theory of transition in which progress on the institutional tree is additive and linear, driven by technological change. A counter model, Walter Rostow's stages of economic growth, became the guide for international development during the cold war (1960). Dividing history into stages of growth, Rostow mimicked Marx. Instead of a sequence running from feudalism, capitalism, socialism, and finally communism, Rostow's variants placed all nonindustrial order together in one category, traditional; then came preconditions to takeoff, and—instead of communism—high mass consumption is the goal. His anti-Marxist theory shared Marx's belief that technology would drive the efficiency of the system. Rostow's theory was well tailored to the geopolitical objectives of the system's administrator. It allowed the United States to believe that by fostering consumerism, it was contributing to an eventual transition to democracy. US policy makers could reconcile their antipathy toward authoritarian rule with their support of authoritarian leaders, who as vehicles of modernization would drive their countries toward eventual democratization.

During the 1970s, when the pursuit of these ends led to tyrannies maintained by excessive state control and excessive borrowing, a new goal was announced; market liberalism. Government expenditures were reduced, budgets balanced, state-owned enterprises privatized, and domestic economies were opened to international trade. When these objectives (known as structural adjustment and stabilization) failed during the

1980s, institutional economics stepped up with the answer: good governance—defined as credible property protection; transparent and predictable, law-based rule enforcement; and accountable albeit technical governance—that could be copied, imported, and transferred around the world. The good governance consensus targets another malady of transition: poor governance that fosters elite corruption rather than inclusive economic growth. But it failed to account for the most successful developing economies in East Asia and China.

The Fallacy of Evolutionary Institutional Selection

Sophisticated applications of game theory have helped economic historians Douglass North and Avner Greif analyze how norms and markets evolve sequentially from pure-spot market transactions, such as barter in a bazaar, to giant risk pools in contemporary stock markets. The evolutionary steps toward efficient markets involve changes in institutions that change the incentives, and therefore the behaviors, of market participants.

Their sequence begins with a natural, or pre-state pattern, when contract enforcement depends on community sanctions, such as ostracism, and moves along a pathway from face-to-face barter to the large risk pools of modern financial systems—in other words, toward complexity and abstraction. A fully developed market system is one in which contracting is decentralized, or "arm's length," and individual liability is guaranteed by third-party contract enforcement available to all members of society without reference to an individual's family, religious, or ethnic affiliations. At each stage of contract enforcement, society gains greater capacity to manage and mitigate risk, relieving individual economic agents of the necessity to invest their surplus revenue in self-insurance.

To encourage self-organizing networks to form according to economic interest, market societies require sophisticated mechanisms that reduce opportunism. Contract compliance among anonymous market participants depends on institutions that make information available about the probability of noncompliance in a possible exchange. Contract enforcement first appears as a private good, provided by a particular human community to its members on the basis of family or tribal ties. In a community-based exchange system, the members of the collective whole—a family or clan, or business consortium, such as a guild, or corporations—are

responsible for the deeds of individual members. The community moni-
tors and takes responsibility for the actions of individuals and can impose
moral and social sanctions on noncompliant members.

But in this natural setting, few tools exist to deal with malfeasance
or opportunism by nonmembers of the community. The weakness of enforcement keeps the volume of trade low. Nevertheless, as Avner Greif
observes, social enforcement via reputation may facilitate trade on a global scale—the tenth-century Maghribis, Jewish traders in the Maghreb,
conducted trade all over the Mediterranean, but their trading networks
were exclusionary, bounded by marriage ties. Thus, when alternative institutions for building trust are absent, social capital forms through collusion within small homogeneous groups, and contracting is limited to the
extent of lineage (Greif 1993).[10]

Greif's research highlights a critical transition point in economic history crystallized by Genoa's ability to surpass the Maghribi clans and
dominate Mediterranean trade in the eleventh century. That domination
was a consequence of the emergence of public authority and contract
enforcement vested in the institutions of the state. The economic trade
fairs set up by the Duke of Champagne in medieval France and among the
newly consolidating secular powers in Northern Europe arose in a similar
fashion. The trade fairs started in the eleventh century but peaked toward
the end of the twelfth and into the thirteenth centuries. Early state-building added significantly to the scope and scale of economic activities by
providing contract enforcement as a public good to citizens, regardless of
their ethnic or religious affiliations. By increasing the diversity in the pool
of partners, rule-based, third-party enforcement expanded trade, and the
result was a diversity of products and services.

Complexity thinking suggests that change in the structure of economic
institutions is driven by the needs of a given and generally temporary
environment. One form of contractual organization does not subsume an
earlier form, and the simplest forms of social organization do not necessarily disappear. In the same market, both lineage-based and state-based
forms of enforcement may coexist. Among the high-performing economies of East Asia, such as the powerhouse economy of South Korea or
the fast-growing economy of Thailand, large enterprises trade on behalf
of their founding families. Modernization of the state did not eliminate
kinship-based reciprocity, although it added bureaucratic oversight. But

the law-based contract enforcement by an independent judiciary, characteristic of markets in Western Europe, arrived slowly, if at all. China does not provide any meaningful separation of powers or predictable law enforcement—the Communist Party in China stands above the constitution and can reverse it any time (Fukuyama 2011, 248). This requires economic agents to constantly second-guess the possible actions of political managers and, in turn, increases the value of proximity to the party.

Modernization and liberal internationalism view markets as evolutionary mechanisms that cause more complex organisms to evolve over time, and that can spread these changes with the power to transform history or geopolitics. The complexity approach suggests that no global compass exists to lead institutional change toward more complex outcomes, and that there is no mechanism even to ensure that complex institutions will emerge from those that are less complex. So why do we observe greater complexity? Why do the differences between the most complex and the simplest forms of economic organization increase over time?

Variation among economic institutions cannot be entirely explained in terms of increasing levels of complexity. A developed society transacts at many levels simultaneously, employing the norms of widely divergent systems of responsibility and control. Enforcement of community-based norms, firms that are hierarchically managed and centrally planned, and market-based norms all reinforce and support each other through interaction. The direction of institutional selection is determined by the success that economic agents have in finding solutions to current problems. What look like more complex institutions replacing simple, earlier forms may be an illusion caused by an increasing degree of variation between simple and complex structures. Highly developed societies blend private, community, and state-based enforcement. For example, from the time of Charlemagne until after the Second World War Europe was dominated by a network of interrelated families with small world characteristics. Progress and economic success are best understood as the tendencies of social groups "to improve cumulatively their adaptive fit to their particular way of life, by increasing the number of features which combine together in adaptive complexes" (Dawkins 1997, 1016).

Even among advanced industrial economies, third-party contract enforcement does not entirely eliminate networks of relatives and their dependents. Advanced economies are replete with examples of vestigial forms of coordination. Fukuyama observes that even after tribal societies disappear, the practices with which they are associated never completely vanish. "If political development implied movement beyond patrimonial relationships and parasitic politics, one also had to explain why these practices survived in many places and why seemingly modern systems often reverted to them" (Fukuyama 2011, xiii). Chains of dependency and patronage are common even in the den of liberal democracy, the US Congress. Local bosses, typically called "big men," still dominate elections in urban and rural districts, where large numbers of poor people cluster. Checks on the executive power and regular elections have not entirely erased patrimonial distribution anywhere in the world. We will discuss the fallacy of institution-centric explanations of economic growth in chapter 5.

The Fallacy of the Efficient Market

The mystery of the market as a self-organizing institution, in which millions of transactions conducted by billions of buyers and sellers unknown to each other are integrated into a single system, is, according to Friedrich Hayek (1988, 77):

[t]he only known method of providing information enabling individuals to judge comparative advantages of different uses of resources of which they have no immediate knowledge and through whose use, whether they so intend or not, they serve the needs of distant unknown individuals. This dispersed knowledge cannot possibly be gathered together and conveyed to an authority charged with deliberately creating order.

The magic of the efficient market is that regularities defined in terms of deterministic laws, such as supply and demand, exist despite the absence of top-down planning and control. But there are many intervening stages before the arrival of this magic of self-organization, and these do not arise spontaneously but are purposefully constructed, regulated, and maintained. Markets, it turns out, have transaction costs and, like any human-made network, distribute the costs and benefits among members unevenly (Root 1994, 2006). Acemoğlu and Robinson are correct to insist that markets can be created and maintained so that the managers will be recipients of rents that exceed the social value of their contributions. But they ignore the reality that markets do not arise without purpose and are not cost-free to maintain.

The mechanisms of contract enforcement, such as courts and updated legal codes, as well as trained judges who are essential to the governance of markets, do not arise spontaneously. Historically, the costs and benefits have been divided according to the purposeful collaboration of local landowners and town dwellers in a context that is culturally specific and heavily influenced by other sources or levels of order (Casson 2011). Collusion in the extraction of surplus through political or social mechanisms is not exceptional or stationary; the instruments of extraction evolve, but the rate of change, or time lag, may depend on the speed of social processes that are independent of the market.

"When uncertainty exists about the reliability of partners and contracts, collusive relationships supplant missing market institutions" (Root 2006, 246). Collusive practices can mitigate two of the most adverse forms of uncertainty: the opportunism of individual traders and expropriation by the state. The structure of rent-seeking and other forms of collusion varies widely among societies. Intermediary organizations that emerge at different sequences, such as guilds, professional associations, or oligopolies, considered by liberal economic theory to restrain competition and produce collusion, may enhance efficiency and coordination. But they exist in many cases because they are efficient at reducing the transaction costs that arise in a particular setting. A society lacking reliable organization beyond the family may benefit when control of large enterprises is concentrated among a few family groups. Collusion made possible by concentrated family ownership is an adaptive response to the poor quality of public-sector governance.

Another assumption critical to efficient market theory is that prices fully reflect all available information (Grossman 1976, 1981; Grossman and Stiglitz 1980). If this were true, no place would exist for informed traders; they would not find people willing to pay for their expertise. They could not earn a return on their activity if the information they had to offer was costless for others to obtain. Sanford Grossman and Joseph Stiglitz (1980, 405) conclude that "prices cannot perfectly reflect the information which is available, since if it did, those who spent resources to obtain it would receive no compensation. There is a fundamental conflict between the efficiency with which markets spread information and the incentives to acquire information." The information-processing ability of economic systems to set efficient prices depends on the capacity for learning between the agents (the buyers and sellers) of each other's needs. Grossman (1981, 541) observes that "in a world subject to random shocks . . . [a]gents are faced with the problem of forecasting future states of nature and more importantly of forecasting the impact of these states on the actions of other agents."

This learning takes place in a context of preexisting social networks. In conventional risk models, it takes only a minimal number of rational players to drive the market toward efficiency; in real markets, however, when traders with vastly different expectations and goals fail to anticipate each other's actions, the outcomes are volatile. The agents come together with different time horizons; some may react with more immediacy than others. Information may not be immediately absorbed. In the physical world, information about properties of a phenomenon, such as the speed of light or the width of a door, are not altered by being measured and made public. By contrast, the determination of value in trading models collected and disseminated by traders is itself a determinant of current prices. It creates real-time feedback from market participants who short and distort, thereby altering the expectations and behaviors of other players.

The classical risk models of economics work best when they assume that decision-makers are independent. But the same models of risk distribution used in New York and London are available to everyone in the world. Turn on your computer, and you have access to the same information as someone in Tokyo. With a click of the mouse, one dealer can move assets as fast as another, but when everyone uses the same risk assessments, the money just as quickly moves in the same direction. The models change the statistical probabilities in the financial system as participants respond by placing their bets in gigantic symphony—and moving from safety to crisis.

These patterns of volatility reflect limits of the underlying assumptions about the markets' adaptiveness and efficiency. The behaviors of markets are not consistent and timeless; rather, markets themselves are agents within the larger environments, even as they are made up of buyers and sellers who can self-organize.

The discovery of patterns of global behavior that serve a purpose without a central commander is a strength of economics as a discipline, but as a discipline, it poorly describes the rules of interaction among the traders that give rise to the system. As a result, there has been a failure to describe or anticipate the sources of volatility in markets. This is because conventional economics specifies the utility of the individual actor on one hand and the larger view of the market with its iron laws, on the other. But it is in the missing middle, comprised of multiple feedback loops among actors that calibrate their own interest on what they expect others to do, where economic systems acquire their own internal dynamics. As we will see in chapter 6, however, they can self-organize only as far as their fitness landscapes, their information-gathering capabilities, allow.

Knowledge Transmission in Social Networks

Many of the fallacies described in this chapter arise because the models of value formation ignore network effects. Economics is built upon the notion that people respond to incentives, and that they understand economic incentives best. This is not wrong, but it is only a partial representation of reality.

Social learning also occurs in networks and in organizations. Cognitive processes are interactive at many levels; agents base their actions on what they believe other agents will do. One individual's behavior can be directly influenced by another's (Arthur 1994; Arthur, Durlauf, and Lane 1997; Ormerod 2012). Peer pressure is why cognitive physiologists find that people are likely to be fat if their friends are fat or likely to engage in binge drinking if their peers do. Women are most likely to marry and have children once their cohort does. Investors who understand nothing about technology are likely to hold shares in technology stocks if the people they know do the same. Such behavior is adaptive as the members of groups or organizations individuals, despite their cognitive limitations, can find solutions to the risks they face.

A magnificent account of the primacy of peer pressure appears in Patrick French's analysis of why India, and not Pakistan, won possession of a number of the northernmost and largest independent princely states (2011). A third of the British Raj included numerous princely states. Each had its own treaty with London, and the status of the subcontinent's independent kingdoms was unresolved at independence. French recounts how Prince Hanwant Singh of Jodhpur, in what is now the state of Rajasthan, chose to join India. Muhammad Ali Jinnah, the founder of Pakistan, offered extraordinary private incentives for the prince to join Pakistan and maintain his feudal status, including free access to the port at Karachi, acquisition of any weapons system he desired, control over the railway line into Pakistan, and free grain to alleviate local famines. But the prince waited to see what his fellow princely rulers would do. And when they decided to join India, he too gave up the kingdom his ancestors had ruled for generations (2011, 7–11). Rather than join Pakistan, where feudal elites still rule sixty years after independence, the princes of the independent states of India gave up much more of their independence to join India. Peer pressure prevailed over powerful private incentives.

But are professional investors more responsive to market incentives than Indian princes? Does their expertise help them to steer the public and the market away from bubbles and crashes? The research of Nobel Laureate Vernon Smith reveals that they are not more protected from peer pressure than the general public. In a paper published in 1988, Smith et al. tested the assumption that if only experienced traders participated in the market, bubbles would be smaller and less frequent (Smith, Suchanek, and Williams 1988). They concluded that professionals are no better at steering the market toward normalcy than are uninformed novices. Professional traders are not as economically rational as efficient price theories presume. They are not quicker to learn, and they are no less likely than amateur traders to have irrational expectations. Such behavior causes price bubbles to be an empirical regularity of markets.

Bubbles and crashes are the consequences of economic actors reacting to each other and not to the market directly. When market participants across the globe have the same data on risk and returns, and employ the same optimization models, largely similar portfolios result. Undervalued assets are quickly inflated and cause informational shifts, prompting participants to rush to newly designated safe areas and create new risks that condemn the market to cycles of instability (Persaud 2000). The misperceptions shared by market participants clustered in certain urban financial centers are amplified. The possibility increases that the outliers—the fat tails far from the normal distribution—can wreak havoc with the system when everyone puts their bets in the same place. The mix of computers with the human herd instinct produces ever-larger bubbles that are now global in scale. For example, after the publication of the "East Asian Miracle" report by the World Bank in 1993 and the mainstreaming of that phrase by the business media, a glut of investment capital poured into East Asia. But the timing was off. The safe investments had already been placed. Yet investors kept pouring funds in until the region's economies collapsed in 1997.

It seems that even the experts in judging the market behave according to the observation of Keynes—like the judges at a beauty pageant who fix their gaze on each other rather than on the models parading on the stage. They seem to anticipate that the mood of their colleagues will alter the dynamics on the trading floor.

Complexity and the Economy

The fascination of economists with evolution began with giants in the field like Alfred Marshall (1923) and later Friederich Hayek (1973, 1988) who tried to discover analogies between the adaptive agents (genes, parents, offspring, populations) found in biological systems and comparable agents in economic systems. Both were frustrated in their efforts to find appropriate analogies in social change processes to the agents of physics or biology.[11] Such concepts as justice, democracy, and pricing do not exist in biological systems; and genotypes or phenotypes do not exist in social systems. The changing principles of social identity at one level of social organization are not reducible to those of another.

Still, at a higher level of generalization we can observe properties that the economy shares with evolution when we look at both as complex systems. This is what happened in the late 1960s, when researchers began to eschew the search for direct analogies and to think of both economic systems and evolutionary systems as complex adaptive systems, and to ask what general properties such systems share. Bumping up the level of generalization has yielded promising results since it was first suggested by Herbert Simon (1969).[12]

The complexity lens reveals that economics shares many universal principles and simple laws with other complex systems. Where modern economics has attained many of its most notable accomplishments by removing components in order to simplify analysis, complexity theory puts the focus back on the behavior of the components that together constitute the behavior of the whole. Seeing economic systems also as adaptive agents that share properties found among other complex systems allows researchers to visualize a wide range of interactions not observable in the conventional economic models, where interactions between and among agents are presumed to converge in linear fashion toward steady-state equilibria.[13]

Efficient market theory presumes that market components, such as the buyers and sellers of securities, have direct relationships with the market—they are the "price-takers" who react to the market directly. Prices tell them all they need to know about the relative values of various commodities or services. The traders are all independent of each other. But in complex adaptive systems the diverse interacting and adaptive parts cannot be separated in an effort to understand the whole. The interaction of the agents with the environment is part of the system. The environment is also an interactive agent; there are no externalities. A component (or agent) together with its environment constitutes the system, just like the cloud and the cloudbank, or the ripple in the whitewater. No single component may be removed in an attempt to simplify one's understanding of the system. The components are nonetheless heterogeneous. They interpret and communicate their separate realities. Their actions are irreversible and frequently part of more than one higher or lower level activity. Agents strategize in anticipation of the actions of a limited number of other agents. The order of economic systems emerges from agent-based self-organization and continual adaptation. No linear focal point exists toward which all actors aspire or converge, the search for the fittest design never ends.

Peer groups and group learning matter because the behavior of the economic system is a consequence of the behavior of the parts. The parts are not representative agents, such as the "median voter"; the constituents are networks where peer pressure and group learning are critical determinants of collective behavior. Markets arise from and rely on networks of exchange among various buyers and sellers, producers and suppliers. These buyers and sellers *are* the market. Prices reflect how they react to each other. System-level behavior emerges from the countless interactions at the micro level, and the result becomes the market's internal dynamics. The beliefs of market participants are reflected in market-determined prices, and prices themselves are subjected to constant strategic manipulation through collective action in which politics and morality are concurrent influences.

An economy is both a part of a complex system and a complex system in its own right, producing outcomes at other levels. As such, the economy is both the outcome and a trigger of evolutionary change. Like any complex adaptive system, the economic system experiences "reciprocal causation ... between different levels of organization—while action processes at a given level of organization may sometimes be viewed as autonomous, they are nonetheless constrained by action patterns and entities at both higher and lower levels" (Arthur 1994, 6).

The interdependency of economic systems parallels the interactive relationships found between the nervous and immune systems. Robert Ader and Nicholas Cohen demonstrated the connection between the state of mind and body that renders the immune system susceptible to Pavlovian interventions (1975). Their initial insight, that psychological states also affect health, has been confirmed in many studies, and today the immune system is no longer viewed as the beginning and end of protection against infection, malignancy, and the repair of damaged cells. Acquired immunity is related to the central nervous system; depressive disorder, immune response, mental disorders in general, and psychological stress are all linked.

Similarly, understanding markets is insufficient for understanding an economic system. References to the market as a metaphor for the entire economic system ignore the fundamental informational structures that link the market to the larger social system in which it functions. Markets take place in a broader setting and are constructed often to the benefit of their constructors, who might be political leaders who care about consolidating power or religious leaders who care about saving souls (Root 1994).

Francis Fukuyama's *Origins of Political Order* is a source of numerous examples of how an economic system is not only a product of market forces; it depends on sources of trust extraneous to the marketplace. Fukuyama describes how many accidental and contingent relationships exist between political and economic development. The rule of law arose in the West from efforts by religious authorities to preserve their sphere of authority from that of secular leadership (2011).[14] Common law, frequently associated with modern forms of corporate ownership and individual property rights, is linked to Britain's economic advancements in the nineteenth century, had a political purpose, it arose by imposition to consolidate the Norman Conquest of Britain in (1066). "Its existence as a framework for legal decision-making required central political power to bring it into being." And "[w]hile it drew on earlier precedents, it would never have become the law of the land without the Norman Conquest, which displaced the older Danish and Anglo-Saxon nobility and established a single, increasingly powerful source of centralized authority" (2011, 258). If anything, it was neither common nor spontaneous, but imposed by one set of rulers to ensure their domination over a previous set.

Does it matter if institutions are imposed or if they just grow? As systems become more complex and are modified with greater frequency, the difference between design and self-organization vanish. But the variations caused by differences in ascent rarely cease to exist.

Mapping the Path from Complexity to Prosperity

The study of complex systems offers a counterpoint to modernization's elevation of an economy's status to that of the great replicator that determines social order. As complex systems, economic systems are composed of networks of production processes; and these components also participate in the production or transformation of other components in the network. An economy is a network of production processes that can self-organize into patterns of great complexity and play an essential role in the aggregated outcomes. The agents may be autonomous, but as in most complex networks, although the different functions of markets are segmented, certain categories of transactions are linked. In this way the network self-organizes, continually re-creating itself. Similarly "in a living system, the product of its operation is its own organization" (Capra 1996, 98).

The outcome is the spontaneous emergence of new structures. Ilya Prigogne, who originated the idea that dissipation and structure can coexist in his description of living organisms, has speculated that human economies are open systems in which seemingly contradictory tendencies coexist (Nicolis and Prigogne 1989). Yet the points of instability are also the places where the emergence of new structures and new forms of order are likely to arise. An entirely orderly and closed system is prone instead to collapse as internal pressures build up, whereas living systems can achieve stability even in far-from-equilibrium conditions.

By accepting classical notions of nature, in which "stable" means "fixed," conventional economics poorly apprehends these characteristics of economic transition and change. "Our everyday experience teaches us that adaptability and plasticity of behavior, two basic features of nonlinear dynamical systems in far-from-equilibrium conditions, rank among the most conspicuous characteristics of human societies. It is therefore natural to expect that dynamical models allowing for evolution and change should be the most adequate ones for social systems" (Nicolis and Prigogine 1989, 289).

Socioecological systems must be understood by studying more than one scale. Linkages across scales will determine how the system as a whole operates.[15] As systems move away from equilibrium, they also diverge from universal laws and repetition, moving toward the unique and toward diversity and eventual speciation.[16] The strategies, actions, and behaviors of the actors intersect at many levels of aggregation, and what occurs at one level forms the building blocks for the next. For example, critical institutions for the enforcement of contracts and the protection of property rights evolved within a matrix of social forces operating at numerous levels. The economy coevolves with other constituent components of the social environment.

Thus a key policy issue is how to think about systems governed simultaneously by two or more sources of order, and to respond to the interactive risks that result. Historically, for instance, mobilization for warfare has had a large impact on the pace of social reforms and can have a more immediate impact than economic forces on political structures. Economic and political change cycles move along different tracks and travel at different speeds. Mass mobilization during the wars among European states significantly influenced the strengthening of inclusive political institutions. Global wars, more so than integration into global markets, have been the greater stimulant to political change, accelerating institutional developments more than changes in relative prices ever could.

In all economic systems, increasing returns are obtained through the construction of networks of trust and capability. So why do rulers adhere to coercive systems of extraction and experience diminishing returns? Acemoğlu and Robinson (2012), with the support of a wide spectrum of economists, believe they have discovered why some nations transition to inclusive governance. It's the institutions, they insist. But there is a problem with the logic when the problem and the solution are the same. Institutional economics is not suited to play the integrating role of defining the macro change processes. The conjuncture of scales and the divergent speed of change in different sectors are problems of complexity. To fully appreciate the optimization challenges that a society faces requires mapping the linkages of the economy with other facets of a complex social environment.

The next chapter explores the intellectual sociology of ideas that have elevated institutional change to the top of the global change agenda. A surprisingly broad range of social theories shares common roots in debates concerning the rise of the West.

4

Coevolution versus Liberal Internationalism

During the second half of the twentieth century, the liberal democratic nations of the industrialized West generally assumed that their theory of development would serve as the model of modernization for others to follow. But the developed countries are rapidly losing demographic weight and will likely see declines in their future share of world economic growth (Goldstone 2010, 31–43). This has implications for the validity of liberal internationalism as a basis for foreign policy and for modernization theory as a foundation of international development policy.

Evolution was once understood to mediate a series of tournaments for a fixed number of environmental niches, with each contest refereed so that the fittest would survive. In studies of natural ecosystems, coevolution and with it the pull of interdependent behaviors has replaced the idea of convergence to a global optimum, depriving evolution of the role of mediator and referee. When a change in one of the interdependent organisms causes a change in the other, unforeseen consequences will result, both to the organism and to their environments.

The bad news? Without a single administrator, responses to the adaptive moves of others may lower the fitness levels of the coupled environments and thus the overall system. Since there is no march toward a global optimization, the agents are doing their own optimizing, and it is no longer "evolution" that stands as a referee to determine the global optima. In fact there may no longer be global optima; there are multiple adaptive moves and perhaps several optima toward which each agent aspires.

The principles of global order in a coevolving world will also be very different from the conventional theories of sociopolitical development. No longer will the components all evolve toward a single designated point that represents either a local or global optimum (Kauffman 1993, 183).

Coevolution switches the focus of the system's evolutionary dynamics to an emphasis on self-organization. Organisms adapt to an environment that is itself adapting to the actions of other organisms; each provides a niche for the survival of the other. The result is variety without directionality and without an assurance of victory for the fittest. Interdependent states sharing a landscape will still act independently, according to their own self-interests, even as they coevolve in adaption to one another's behaviors. They will not replicate behaviors. When predators and prey, parasites, and hosts coevolve; their evolution does not produce mimicry.

Power Transition

After the cold war ended, it was reasonable to believe that liberal democracy and market economics could produce stability, and that through the joining of these two great attractors, a new world order would emerge. Autocracies and central planning were both retreating by the early 1990s, with electoral democracy and market economies taking hold. National Socialism (Nazism), defeated in World War II, was long buried. Soviet-style central planning too was defeated. The former Soviet bloc seemed to be transitioning toward something that resembled the triumphant liberal democratic consensus of the West.

With China turning toward a market economy, Russia embracing elections, India turning away from inward-looking dirigisme, and Brazil, one of the world's largest economies, bridging its populist and elitist divides, it was reasonable to assume that these countries too would be marching forward, facing the same direction, toward liberalism.[1] Free markets and liberal democracy seemed to have eliminated ideological competition.

No one expressed this certainty about the direction of history more cohesively than Francis Fukuyama, who crystallized post–cold war certainties about the legitimacy of liberal democracy in the seminal *End of History and the Last Man* (1992). "No serious ideological competitors are left," he concluded, asserting that liberal democracy was the "end point of man's ideological evolution." Liberal democracy was the great attractor, "the end point" of the evolution of governance, and the "final form of human government."[2] Thus the end of history had arrived. Fukuyama's optimism about the combined remedial effects of market economics and electoral democracy was pervasive during the era.[3] Much educated opinion in the West celebrated the end of strategic and ideological conflict, exuding confidence that the question of social organization had been resolved in favor of a clear winner, and thank God, the most virtuous social, economic, and political institutions had triumphed (Landes 1998; Mandelbaum 2007a, b).[4]

Yet even without the World Trade Center attacks of September 11, 2001, the rise of autocratic China as an icon of prosperity challenged the universality of liberal values. The successes of other authoritarian and/or populist models of modernization—for example, Iran, Russia, or Venezuela—suggested that the appeal of market-based democracy for developing countries was far from certain, putting the ideological victory of liberalism into doubt.

No amount of energy and resources dedicated to social engineering has succeeded in bringing about the anticipated great convergence of market economics and liberal democracy. Only the Tigers of East Asia seem to be converging in a manner consistent with the theory, but they are far from liberal, being weak in the rule of law and lax in the independence of the judiciary. Meanwhile liberal democracy has become but one of many attractors pulling emergent states into their orbits. Others have emerged from within the developing world itself. China, Iran, Russia, South Africa, Turkey, and Venezuela are among the new powerful attractors, leading in directions that do not follow the anticipated trajectory of liberal democracy.

To understand the possible evolutionary paths of global democracy, we must first recognize that there are many sources and accelerators of global governance diversity. It is clear that governance diversity in the post–cold war period far exceeds liberalism's expectations. New governments have taken shape at an amazing pace and in amazing numbers. But they are not changing in anticipated ways; that is, many show no sign of transitioning into liberal economies. Regimes in transition are not passive recipients of Western advice. They are living up to the true meaning of the term *third world*, which was not coined to suggest inferiority or an aptitude for mimicry, but to emphasize their revolutionary capacity.[5]

The Age of Liberal Certainty

Fukuyama's timely assessment blended three strong intellectual currents, psychological, moral, and functional, that together form the liberal international consensus dominating post–cold war geopolitics.[6] The psychological slant was recent, involving an individual's quest for existential meaning and referring to a "struggle for recognition," the quest for dignity and equality. The moral and functionalist emphasis on law and materialism was initially conceived during the Enlightenment of the eighteenth century, when it was hoped that commerce and the resultant economic progress would be great regulators that could restrain human passion and erect barriers against despotism. This argument is most typically associated with the writings of Immanuel Kant (1724–1804), who envisioned peace and social progress from the free flow of goods and ideas across national boundaries. Kant further presumed that bottom-up emulation would spread the liberal norms developed by a few enlightened states, transforming international relations.

The natural effect of commerce, wrote Montesquieu (1689–1755), another philosopher of the Enlightenment, is to encourage peaceful manners. In summarizing the utopian face of Enlightenment humanism, the belief that nations linked by commerce would eschew war and that a world of liberal governments would be a world of peace, Robert Kagan writes, "Increasingly commercial societies would be more liberal both at home and abroad. Their citizens would seek prosperity and comfort and abandon the atavistic passions, the struggles for honor and glory, and the tribal hatreds that had produced conflict through history" (2009, 8).[7]

The functionalist dimension of liberalism holds that the universal quest for technological advancement will expand the frontiers of international collaboration. Building highways, factories, and skyscrapers is not sufficient, according to liberal internationalism. Technological determinism impels emerging nations to replicate Western social structures as factories, technical management, and mass communication drive out older forms of organization and communications.

Technology calls for the same occupational structure in all polities, regardless of their original regime type, both to transform society and to eliminate cultural differences (Perrow 1972). Regimes seeking wealth and frontier technology must adjust their contracting norms, protect private property, and adopt the standards of liberal, market-based democracy. Convergence will occur whether or not a nation's leaders desire it; the forces of progress and the desire to amass wealth and the power that only modern technology can bring will demand modernization and economic liberalization. Nations either liberalize or fall behind. Fukuyama related the drive for technology to the homogenization of all human societies:

The unfolding of modern natural science has had a uniform effect on all societies that have experienced it, for two reasons. In the first place, technology confers decisive military advantages on those countries that possess it, and given the continuing possibility of war in the international system of states, no state that values its independence can ignore the need for defensive modernization. Second, modern natural science establishes a uniform horizon of economic production possibilities. Technology makes possible the limitless accumulation of wealth, and thus the satisfaction of an ever-expanding set of desires. This process guarantees an increasing homogenization of all human societies, regardless of their historical origins or cultural tendencies. All countries undergoing economic modernization must increasingly resemble one another: they must unify nationally on the basis of a centralized state, urbanize, replace traditional forms of social organization like tribe, sect, and family with economically rational ones based on function and efficiency, and provide for the universal education of their citizens (Fukuyama 1992, xiv–xv)

However, competition and survival in the global market place have increased variation. The variety of feasible strategies of which regimes may avail themselves in the global ecology is far greater than liberal internationalism anticipated. Dominated for much of its history by the ethos of a military caste, Pakistan is in the forefront of global defense technology, yet the majority of Pakistanis are inadequately provisioned with schools, clean water, and roads. The nation occupies an adaptive zone in the global landscape that liberal internationalism never considered. Is praetorianism intrinsic to Pakistan's culture, or is it a response to a particular set of geopolitical opportunities? During the cold war, renting out their strategic location provided Pakistan's rulers with considerable unearned income that allowed its elite lineages to survive and prosper by forming alliances with elites outside Pakistan. To what is the Pakistani state adapted, its culture or its environmental niche?[8]

Liberal Internationalism: The Normative Voice of Modernization Theory

Western economists rarely use the term *modernization theory*, but they too project a modernizing discourse that perfect competition will produce socioeconomic efficiencies and eliminate many of the injustices and imbalances among and within countries. In a unique look at the intellectual history of liberalism, Albert Hirschman traced the origins of the belief that international economic competition would eliminate opportunities for social misbehavior, such as corruption and mismanagement (1997).[9]

Liberalism anticipated a world in which global economic competition would "eliminate the system's latitude for deterioration" (Hirschman 1970, 7). The mission begun by the Enlightenment, to restrict the discretionary behavior of the absolutist prince, was transferred to managers of the economy. A competitive economy, said Western economists, would bind political power to predictable rule-making and transparent regulation. Concurring with Hirschman, Nils Gilman writes that "the modernization theorists saw their project as the Enlightenment writ large" (2007, 8).[10]

In contemporary social thought, economic development enjoys the status of a universally accepted solution, linked to all of the good features about being modern.[11] All roads to modernization start and end with economic development. It dissolves kinship-based social structures; it fosters individualism and creates a demand for education, expands the middle class, nurtures achievement-based norms, and is the consolidating glue that cements democratic transitions. Modernization theory was the silver bullet that would change the world without inflicting casualties. Today's idolizers of globalization are the heirs of modernization theory. Gilman writes, "I was struck by how much modernization theory's relentless optimism and self-congratulation reminded me of the dominant emotional tone of Clintonian America. I considered Francis Fukuyama's success in reviving modernization theory a result of the theory's comfortable fit with the emotional–intellectual landscape of the 1990s" (2007, ix).

September 11, 2001, gave further impetus to the revival of modernization theory among policy makers. "Now the renewed discourse of modernity became the position of liberal internationalists who hoped to add some foreign policy carrots to the bag of sticks that the George W. Bush administration represented as its main approach for dealing with the post–9-11 world" (Gilman 2007, ix). The US–British intervention in Iraq led many of the thinkers responsible for the revival of modernization theory, like Fukuyama, to wish they had not been taken so seriously.

Liberal internationalism sprang from modernization theory as its normative voice, offering a foreign policy framework of common rules to mediate international conflict via institutions like the United Nations, the International Monetary Fund, and World Trade Organization that share responsibility and power among all actors, regardless of their relative power or ideology. It advocates the avoidance of solutions in which one party gains everything at another party's expense. Its relevance for the post–cold war concepts of geopolitical stability is paramount to the overall orientation of international development policy.

The pairing of democracy and capitalism idealized by liberal internationalists sustained the hope during both the Bill Clinton and George W. Bush administrations that a democratizing Russia would not fear an expanding web of democratic alliances on its borders. "Russia appeared committed to entering postmodern Europe. Moscow no longer defined its interests in terms of territory and traditional spheres of interest, but rather in terms of economic integration and political development" (Kagan 2009, 7–8). Strobe Talbott, a deputy secretary in President Clinton's State Department, confirms that the president was always on the lookout for opportunities to integrate Russia into the principal structures of the global architecture. "Over time, that became a harder task," Talbott concludes (2008, 287). Similar optimism existed that China would embrace geoeconomics and give up geopolitics. Competition with China would be peaceful, dictated by commercial interest. China the spoiler and revolutionary instigator would become China the stakeholder.

Liberal Internationalism and the Challenge of Developmental Authoritarianism: Unwanted Feedback

Globalizing states are assuming ever-new forms and functions. Both democratic and autocratic regimes are reshaping their policies to provide economic incentives to their populations. Democracies are shifting the focus of public policy from traditional nation-state concerns—social welfare and the management of social risk—to the provisioning of market opportunities. Autocracies enjoy many advantages in pursuing the same opportunities. And when it is a matter of reducing the role and cost of government to pursue global opportunity, autocracies do not face the same obstacles; few are encumbered by social welfare mandates to manage the household risks faced by their populations.

A universal consumer culture wished for by modernization guru Walter Rostow alters behavior at both ends of the political spectrum, changing democracy and autocracy alike. The payoffs are so coupled that changes in one entity cause the landscape of the other to shift. But Rostow assumed that the feedback would move in one direction only. Autocrats feed the appetite for low-cost consumer goods among the populations of democratic regimes by keeping their own domestic wages and entitlements down (Fingleton 2008). Nor are they encumbered by costly environmental mandates. Like China, they can curtail the demands of their own populations for both wages and consumer goods. Furthermore, to shift the terms of global trade in their favor, autocracies create barriers to domestic consumption by upholding producer and distributor monopolies, often controlled by regime cronies. Thus consumer capitalism fosters the economic success of democracy's enemies overseas and a loss of democratic functionality at home.[12]

Democracies experience the positive effects of *supercapitalism*, as well. Political economist Robert Reich coined the term to refer to an abundance of cheap, high-quality products created by global supply chains (2007). Before supercapitalism, consumers did not receive the best quality for the best price. Cars went obsolete, repairmen arrived late, investors were passive, and the average citizen had limited direct exposure to the stock market; the volume of shares traded was only 3 million by the early 1960s and did not reach 10 million until 1970. However, supercapitalism produces democratic citizens of two minds. They seek access to cheap goods produced where labor and environmental standards are relaxed, but at the same time they seek to preserve and enhance their social rights at home.

Liberal democracy and global capitalism pull in opposite directions. Citizens pay for the heightened efficiency of global production chains by surrendering political and social rights to corporate and shareholder interests. Well-governed firms place the particular interests of their shareholders over the general interests. Thus supercapitalism compromises the democratic political values of both shareholders and consumers alike, while clashing with accountability to the electorate at large. It democratizes economic opportunity while facilitating the decline of democratic polities.[14] The dynamic properties of supercapitalism are coevolutionary.

Modernization theorists envisioned that a universal consumer culture would change the fundamentals of authoritarian states. They did not consider the dynamic effects when feedback from two systems operates simultaneously. A visit to China's megacities might remind the casual observer that modern values may be ascendant, but that institutions of power that are hidden behind the structures of cement and steel remain unchanged.

Rich but Not Free, Autocracy Is Back

Francis Fukuyama published *The End of History* in 1992, when global communism's strut time on the international stage had ended. Autocracies around the globe were weakend by severe crises of legitimacy and resources; neither the Soviets nor the Americans were eager to countenance their respective autocratic proxies and clients. The decline of autocracy seemed imminent and offered ample justification for believing that the road to economic prosperity ran parallel to that of electoral democracy. Today, however, democracies no longer draw more investment than autocracies. Adapted to changing global norms, autocrats have learned to base their political survival on economic performance and can now match the capacity of democracy for economic growth.[15]

Autocratic polities are learning to control and channel the opportunities from globalization. Instead of unleashing political freedom and social mobility, they are reversing the expected modernization effects that liberal theory had anticipated. They may seek democratic "legitimacy" even as they systematically eliminate checks on executive power and withdraw the rule of law. In a formula for autocratic survival that oil-rich regimes share with communist China, they reduce collective action by their citizens, by concentrating the benefits of market access through channels controlled by state-owned companies that intervene in industries as diverse as banking, aviation, shipping, power, arms, telecommunications, and mining (Bremmer 2010).

With resources gained from global markets, resource-rich regimes can buy off the non-elite population, enhancing social entitlements while clamping down on what Bruce Bueno de Mesquita and George W. Downs call "coordination goods," the free media, or rights to free speech and assembly (2005). Autocrats have learned that citizens who are satisfied with social welfare schemes have little reason and limited capacity to demand political freedoms. Iran's Islamic republic has improved social indicators while suppressing freedom of expression, a formula appreciated by oil-rich polities throughout the Middle East (Dunning 2008). Instead of the anticipated process of homogenization, a nonliberal variant of modernity has emerged, changing the environment of global capitalism.

The Historical Sociology of Liberal Internationalism

Liberal internationalism is generally defined as a doctrine that fosters democracy, human rights, and an open economy, and the promotion of multilateralism. As a system of beliefs, it is frequently associated with President Woodrow Wilson, but its history dates back to the European Enlightenment. In the "Second Definitive Article" of *Perpetual Peace,* Kant expressed optimism that liberal republics would "[p]rovide a focal point for federal associations of other states," and that one powerful and enlightened nation would have an interactive effect on the global system. Other states would then "join up with the first one, thus securing the freedom of each state in accordance with the idea of international right, and the whole will gradually spread further and further by a series of alliances" (Doyle 1986, 1157). Thus the 2010 "Report on Advancing Freedom and Democracy" of the Bureau of Democracy, Human Rights, and Labor of the US State Department proclaims, "The United States supports Russia's integration in multilateral organizations, such as the WTO and the Organization for Economic Cooperation and Development, which will promote rule of law, enhanced corporate good governance and transparency, and the push for greater adherence to international norms of democratic governance" (United States Department of State 2010).

As victors of the Second World War and then the cold war, Western democracies entered the twenty-first century poised to champion the policies that between 1960 and 2001 were so successful that the world population doubled and economic activity increased sixfold. Indeed liberalism's victory over both fascism and communism inspired a triumphalism, and many liberal internationalists still believe that a deterministic logic moves all societies in a linear direction toward global optima. All effectively adapted societies, they argue, will end up with the same sophisticated state structures. The replication of liberal regimes will reflect intrinsic tendencies in the nature of capitalist economies. Hence, they conclude, liberal democracy is the summation of all evolutionary progress in governance, just as private, open economies are the key to growth.

The cold war was fertile ground for the moral and functionalist currents of Enlightenment thinking to merge liberal markets, liberal politics, and the middle classes into a single unifying concept: modernization (Lipset 1960, 18).

Leading liberal internationalists like John Ikenberry maintain that authoritarian political systems are ill adapted to capitalist economics, and that their "deep contradictions" hinder their ability to compete with capitalism. First, capitalism grows a middle class to challenge the vestiges of "closed political decision-making." Second, economic growth requires contract enforcement and independent commercial courts, which autocracies (they incorrectly assert) do not provide. Third, capitalism induces an "intensification of function," producing an "explosion of complexity" that replaces a mass polity with a pluralist one (Ikenberry and Deudney 2009).

Democracy works best as the economy develops because the relationships among state, corporate, and civil society become too complex to manage through centralized autocratic control. The proliferation of interest groups that results from economic growth cannot function in an authoritarian framework. The argument is teleological; China is effectively showing that when decisions are complex, technocrats may have better answers than voters.

The historical sociology in which all three of these assumptions are embedded is refutable. The fundamental dilemmas of historical sociology are not reducible to the adaptive strategies of a single social class.[16] The European aristocracy, not the middle classes, maintained a dominant role over the course of eight centuries, despite dramatic technological change and internal rivalry (Mayer 1981).

Liberal internationalism nevertheless correlates its historical progress to the rise of an enlightened global middle class. Even if the arrival of a global middle class is inevitable, the prospect that it will arrive speaking a universal language of transparency and accountability is not. Milanovic (2005) found that global economic trends do not sufficiently strengthen the global middle as a pillar of the system. Moreover the talent pool in developing nations is more state focused than entrepreneurial. For example, China's middle classes are products of Communist Party policies and are readily coopted as beneficiaries of state policies. Successful entrepreneurs that join the party enjoy a range of selective benefits that cannot be accessed by nonmembers (Dickson 2010; *Economist* 2011).

Second, authoritarian regimes have learned to defend capitalist property rights through a range of policy innovations or commitment devices that protect private wealth against expropriation (Root and May 2008). In many autocracies the head of state sponsors civil service and judicial reforms to bolster central government effectiveness and to defend property rights.

Third, one-party states have acquired the capacity to manage diverse points of interest within the party structure, and can indeed access markets for political gain. Authoritarian France during the eighteenth century matched Great Britain's growth by using collective (i.e., corporatist) enforcement, rather than individual liability to protect property rights. So too did economic growth occur in East Asia without the contract-enforcing mechanisms associated with Anglo-Saxon legalism. Finally, liberal internationalists must acknowledge that the narrative of democracy in many developing nations since 1980 does not replicate the pattern that occurred in Western Europe after World War I, when suffrage extension produced progressive taxation along with enhanced social protection for the weak.

Many of the conceptual weaknesses of liberal internationalism derive from its association with American pluralists who, according to political scholar Theodore Lowi, "had no explicit and systematic view of the state. They simply assumed it away" (1969, 54). In its place, they posit the myth of perfect self-regulation through pluralism, and presume that the push and pull of interests groups is a sufficient basis for public policy. "The corrupting element was the myth of the automatic society granted to us by an all-encompassing, ideally self-correcting, providently automatic political process" (p. 54).

The myth of the adaptiveness of interest-group pluralism complemented the myth of the "total social equilibrium of freely contracting individuals in the market place" (Lowi 1969, 54). It allows interest groups to mobilize public power for private advantage; the public policy that results generates concentrated benefits and diffuse costs.[17] No wonder developing-country policy planners view interest-group liberalism as an incomplete framework for attaining progressive socials goals or building national cohesion. In a weak institutional environment, pluralism facilitates capture of the state by well-organized minorities.

An important subsection of the global development community, most notably the IMF–US Treasury complex, did not recognize the dangers of the unconstrained concentrations of financial power that Lowi's critique anticipated. These organizations transferred financial resources and trained developing countries' financial officials to actively support economic development. Banking systems throughout the developing world mastered the functions of a modern financial system, regulating the money supply and managing day-to-day transactions while global markets ensured a steady flow of capital.

While central banks in the developing world acquired many of the critical functions to mediate financial transactions, the polity lacked the institutions to prevent a concentration of financial interests from distorting the economy and harming the common people. Many developing countries ended up with a centrally controlled, high-powered banking sector controlled by a small elite, resulting in a dangerous concentration of economic and political power. Indonesia's Suharto used the strengthened central bank to provision an inner circle of regime supporters with funds to build factories, entire cities, infrastructure, and to export raw materials overseas. The system attracted international investors who assumed that lending to politically connected locals was safe. Similarly well-connected economic elites with easy access to foreign capital also blighted Russia's chances of becoming an economic democracy.

Liberalism's faith in pluralism was so strong that it neglected the notion that government must protect juridical and administrative functions from well-organized private interests.[18] Where there is an absence of a formal juridical framework to guarantee basic principles and rights, liberalism converts mere ineffectiveness into illegitimacy (Lowi 1969, 41–58). That faith in pluralism resulted in self-defeating policy prescriptions, such as former Defense Secretary Donald Rumsfeld's (2001–2006) belief that once the Baathist party was removed, democracy in Iraq would just happen as a naturally unfolding process. Instead, public authority dissolved.

When Complexity Makes the Landscape Dance

The liberal perspective on the evolution of the international system emphasizes a progressive directionality toward cooperation and interdependence. This optimistic and influential view found expression in Robert

Wright's grand synthesis that integrates the game-theoretic concept of non–zero sum with biological and social evolution into a single analytical framework (2000). Strobe Talbott explains Bill Clinton's enthusiasm for Wright's ideas:

> For most of his time in office, Clinton was equally careful not to broadcast his belief in a version of Darwinism in its most optimistic form: the notion that globalization was conducive to emergence—or evolution—of an increasingly cooperative international system. In off-the-cuff public remarks, in prepared speeches, and in private conversation, I heard him field test the idea that the spread of democracy, open society, market economy, and individual empowerment was the wave of the future. An example came during a joint press conference in Beijing with President Jiang Zemin of China on June 27, 1998, when Clinton ad-libbed, "It is important that whatever our disagreements over past actions, China and the United States must go forward on the right side of history for the future sake of the world. The forces of history have brought us to a new age of human possibility, but our dreams can only be recognized by nations whose citizens are both responsible and free." (Talbott 2008, 330–31)

Clinton idealized a world that, in the words of Wright, would provide increasingly "richer forms of non–zero-sum interaction" and in which "people become embedded in larger and richer webs of interdependence" (Talbott 2008, 331).

Another frequently cited popular expression of the liberal internationalist perspective is the proverbial "flat world" popularized by columnist and author Thomas Friedman, in which business opportunities are as large and as wide as the globe itself.[19] The globalization of production that inspired Friedman's flat world metaphor helps readers visualize a world of opportunities. Indeed transnational production chains have become a driving force of the international economy. But the emergence of one dominant global system seems as remote as ever. Expanding global trade has not facilitated the expansion of the human community in the pursuit of common goals.[20] International financial specialist David Smick explains that "frankly speaking from the perspective of the financial markets, the world is not flat . . . nothing happens in a straight line. Instead, there is a continual series of unforeseen discontinuities—twists and turns of uncertainty that often require millions of market participants to stand conventional wisdom on its head" (2008, 2). Smick concludes that, contrary to Friedman,

> for the financial markets, the world is curved. We can't see over the horizon. As a result our sights are limited. It is as if we are forced to travel down an endless,

dangerously twisting and turning road with abrupt steep valleys and risky moun-
tainous climbs. We can't see ahead. We are always being surprised, and that is why
the world has become such a dangerous place. (Smick 2008, 2–3)

What makes the landscape rugged, instead of flat? From where do
these abrupt valleys emerge? What are the sources of these risky moun-
tain climbs? What are the origins, the causes, and, most important, the dynamical properties of these risky terrains? Interdependency spawned by
the actions of multiple players has made the landscape rugged and pock-
marked. When the choices of numerous interdependent players interact,
they have great difficulty finding an optimal solution. The metaphor of
a "dancing landscape" effectively captures the dynamics of coevolution,
and we will explore its implications for global political economy in chapter 6.

The Coevolutionary Dynamics of Globalization

Modernization theory assumes that as an attractor, liberal society represents a single fixed point approachable from any direction by all other
societies, regardless of their initial point of departure. In coevolutionary
theory, however, no single attractor exists because the action of one agent
causes others to react strategically by changing their actions to seek local
optima. Since selection occurs at the level of individual components, as
well as at the systemic level, in a coevolving system each alteration has
the potential to transform the global fitness landscape even as it reshapes
the fitness of others in the system. Instead, mutually interacting entities
self-organize. The result is differentiation and novelty, in which the relationship between process and outcome is emergent. It is not possible to
design a dynamic process of evolution that can reliably arrive at a desired
fixed point in the environment.

Neither Fukuyama nor Friedman captures the coevolutionary dynamics of geopolitical evolution that occur when global interdependency
catches modern democracies and modernizing autocracies in the same
coevolutionary web. Today's global business landscape is made rugged
and the challenges more daunting by the combined effects of global technology diffusion and global resource dependency. We end up with an
"interacting dancing landscape" in which the payoffs from investments
depend on the actions of many interacting agents.

In a coevolving world, the principles of global order will be very different from one in which they all evolve toward a single designated point that represents either a local or global optimum (Kauffman 1993, 183). The coevolution of evolutionary partners confronting their own local fitness challenges will reshape the coupled landscape.

Landscape models offer perspectives that can help clarify a key lesson about complex systems: success depends less on the attributes of an individual agent than on where that agent happens to be situated in the system. Levinthal explains:

Such a process of local adaptation has important implications for the diversity of organizational forms. It suggests that the diversity of forms is determined by historical affects that influence an organization's form at founding and the topology of the space of alternative forms over which organizations search. An organization's form at founding will have a persistent effect on its future form when there are multiple peaks in the fitness landscape, since the particular peak that an organization discovers is, in large measure, determined by its starting position in this space of alternative organizational forms. Imprinting effects persist as a result of the path dependence of the search process. Local search in a rugged landscape provides an important source of diversity of organizational forms apart from the external logic of ecological arguments or contingency theories. (1997, 935–50)

The adaptive search of newcomers does not begin from the same departure point of the already arrived. Nor can the newcomers reverse paths they already traveled in order to imitate the adaptive search processes of the first nations to industrialize and liberalize. Communism's collapse or Saddam Hussein's fall do not transport the local populations back to where the West started its ascent centuries earlier.

Convergence to a global optimum represented by liberal democracy makes even less sense in the context of the geopolitical landscape of the twenty-first century, when developing nations must first tackle the challenges of their own local fitness landscapes. Countries will seek their strategies for survival within local subsystems and through coevolution with their nearest competitors.

How individual developing countries will be outfitted for adaptive journeys along rugged developmental landscapes will be determined by competition, status, and legitimacy *within a local context*. The larger members of local subsystems will have a transformative influence on the evolution of the subsystem they belong to. Developing nations will face new challenges from the actions and strategies of larger developing nations, and those local subsystems will in turn transform the landscapes of the mature industrialized democracies. In such a world, the economic rationality of an optimal system has little meaning.

Interdependency occurs when a firm on one continent becomes a major supplier for a firm on another continent. When the equity value of the firm on the buy side declines, the equity value of the supplier will move in the same direction. Or when China's state-owned firms target a sector or copy the technology of a US producer, this dynamic alters the competitive environment for other US firms (Bowen and Rose 1998). Yet the greatest coevolutionary impact occurs at a system level, where the rise of China will affect international norm-building. Soft power extends the reach of China's foreign policy to the principles and norms that govern global financial stability, the costs of ensuring peace, the protection of human rights, and the effectiveness of global efforts at emission reductions and the reversal of climate change. According to François Godement, "every issue from trade and the global economy to climate change and nuclear proliferation, as well as every region from Africa to the Middle East . . . will feel the impact of China's revisionist challenge to the international system" (2010, 4).

Liberalism and communism, both products of the European Enlightenment, did not anticipate that increased global interdependency would cause a human complexity revolution. Communism failed to anticipate that individuals have properties and needs that are often greater than those of the collectivity. But liberalism, as the primary ideology of modernization, does not capture or adequately represent the coevolutionary drama that will shape the future of developed and developing nations alike. How can these changes be characterized? Where will global policy turn "to sustain a transforming vision of the future in the absence of a classic progressive belief in the virtue of the people or an Enlightenment faith in the perfectibility of man" (Gilman 2007, 19)?

5

Promises and Pitfalls of New Institutional Economics

In the mid-1970s a group of social scientists, mostly economists and political scientists, began an inquiry to identify the structure of social institutions that made up the building blocks of long-term economic growth. Their program became known as the *new institutional economics*, or NIE (Eggertsson 1990; Ménard and Shirley 2008). New institutional economics emerged as one of the most influential socioeconomic discourses during the eighties and nineties. Alignment with modernization theory, the guiding premise of global development policy, enabled the influence of NIE on global public policy to soar, and its policy implications were easily subsumed within the broader agenda of liberal internationalism. It promised to make economic growth possible to all people by grounding economic incentives in a universally applicable institutional framework of good governance.

After the fall of the Berlin Wall, the new institutional economics became the conceptual workhorse of efforts by liberal internationalists to transform third world economies into functioning market economies.[1] This made NIE instrumental in establishing the centrality of institutions to discussions of economic development. Its practitioners were rewarded with influence in setting the agendas of numerous international efforts to address global poverty (Chang 2011). Multilateral donors, such as the World Bank or the United Nations Development Programme, along with bilateral donors like USAID and the UK Department for International Development, revised their policies and practices, accepting as fact that poor institutions are the underlying cause of economic development. Support for technical cooperation on institution building gushed along with preconditions to encourage aid recipients to adopt the right institutions. The US introduced an independent government agency in 2002, the Millennium Challenge Corporation, to index assistance according to a recipient's standards of institutional quality. By 2012 the UK spent a fifth of its total aid budget on institution strengthening and governance specialists outnumbered the economic advisors in the department of international development.

Yet the economic performance of countries that participated in these programs to strengthen private property rights or accountable governance often made less economic progress than authoritarian regimes that repudiated the advice. Instead of convergence toward the liberal optima proposed by new institutional economics, the agents in the global economy interact in unforeseen ways. NIE may have succeeded in capturing outcomes, but it failed to identify the processes that impel economic change.

NIE inspired a revolution in the diagnosis, prevention, and treatment of poverty that is reflected in more than fifty quantitative surveys and indexes of thousands of institutional variants that classify the determinants of economic performance over time (Besançon 2003; Rotberg and Gisselquist 2009). But being able to catalog the essential institutions has not provided a remedy to global poverty nor has it improved the effectiveness of the assistance specialist practitioners offer to developing countries.

The relationships between institutions and economic development are more complex than economists had any reason to expect, and the challenges ahead seem as daunting as the important advances that were made in the diagnosis of poor governance.[2] New opportunities in the emerging global economy have been exploited by countries like China that ignore the institutional foundations inculcated by liberalism and the NIE. Functional specialization is encouraged by a more competitive global economy, which offers many niches for developing nations to specialize, innovate, and increase technological capacity without adopting Western norms of economic organization. As wealth spreads to cultural zones outside of the West, the beliefs and institutions of developing societies diverge from the institutional models that shaped the fortunes of the first generation of nations that escaped from mass poverty.

The Good Governance Synthesis and Liberal Internationalism

The rise of the NIE in academic circles is related to the expansion of a "good development agenda" in policy circles, in which social planners enjoy the good fortune of seeing their ideas implemented in the context of donor-assisted interventions by a range of multilateral and bilateral organizations (Kapur and Webb 2000).[3] The NIE agenda was elaborated by the OECD (1992) and then the World Bank (1993) and the Asian Development Bank (1995) into a discourse of good governance and anti-corruption. This agenda shifted the international policy debate from getting the prices right to getting the governance institutions right. However, important differences exist between the policy practitioners and academic researchers.

Practitioners call for policy maps that can translate the new institutional research into a set of rules and guidelines to be bureaucratically administered to fill gaps in developing-country capacity, with inputs that can be monitored to justify next year's budgetary allocation. Needing explicit guidelines for when to intervene, policy makers are avid consumers of databases that inventory the factors that cause governments to be trustworthy, reliable, and impartial.[4] The response has been indexes of institutional quality by scholars and organizations that benchmark gaps in global performance (Besançon 2003; Rotberg and Gisselquist 2009). The donor community uses gap assessments between "best practices" and conditions on the ground to determine interventions. A frequently cited institutional database used to measure the institutional gaps is the World Bank's *Governance Matters* website.[5] It measures institutional quality, aggregating primarily subjective surveys of rule of law, efficiency, and integrity of the bureaucracy and the courts, and control of corruption. Gap assessments are then conducted that trace economic failures to specific institutional deficiencies. Once attributions are established then programs are designed offering technical cooperation to close the gap between the institutions of the best and the worst performers.[6]

The Elusive Double Helix of Economic Growth

The new institutionalism's impact on development economics and policy can be compared to the impact of the elaboration of DNA's physical structure, the double helix, on microbiology and genetics (hailed as the greatest triumph in biology since Darwin). The publication in 1981 of Douglass North's *Structure and Change in Economic History* established the centrality of social institutions in debates about the sources of long-term economic growth and the rise of the West. In the decade that followed its publication, new institutional economics became the tool of choice to study the political economy of growth among historical and contemporary societies alike.[7]

Essential to North's approach was the application of Oliver Williamson's ideas about how organizational forms reflect efforts to reduce the costs of monitoring and enforcing compliance (1975, 1985), and Ronald Coase's ideas concerning transaction costs as obstacles to the efficient allocation of resources. Coase states that in the absence of transaction costs, bargaining could allocate property rights efficiently, regardless of the initial allocation (1960). In 1937 Coase explained that the very existence of firms is due to costs associated with market transactions. Institutions, North insisted, influence individual action by reducing uncertainty about the behavior of others, making possible gains from exchange through voluntary agreements that facilitate improved social outcomes.

Many analogies exist between North's influence in economics and the impact of Erwin Schrödinger's 1944 book, *What Is Life?* which became the cornerstone of molecular biology (1944). Looking for the equivalent of chromosomal analogs, or the code scripts, of growth, institutionalists try to decode the "DNA" of economic development by seeking a blueprint for its requisite structures. Several interconnected key concepts that all open societies possess include the rule of law; secure, impersonally enforced property rights; impersonal, competent and honest bureaucracies; an open and competitive economic system; and an open and competitive political system.

But are they formed by incremental changes, or are they the results of a cascade of simultaneous changes? Does sequence matter? What sets of variations are possible, and which are not? How are they connected? The problem for practitioners is that the emergence of this particular cluster of liberal institutions is not reducible to a set of incremental steps. And as a system, a liberal society is not reducible to the behavior of its components.

Like the research agenda of molecular biology, the institutions that form the "double helix of economic growth" are problematic. NIE discovered critical building blocks of economic development, but not the integrative actions among the parts.[8] Thus transferring one successful "master plan" of institutions and regulations conducive to growth to copycat institutions and regulations rarely produces the expected outcome. The pattern or amalgam of components that constitutes the "master plan" can be impossibly difficult to determine—which replicates the "transplanter's dilemma" referred to in chapter 3.

Nevertheless, the race to classify the essential institutional code of economic growth continues, just as it does in molecular biology to break cells into enzymes and proteins. The latter race, however, always runs into an obstacle—"even given the complete DNA sequence of an organism, molecular biologists cannot deduce how that organism assembles itself during development" (Lewin 1992, 166). The faith of molecular biologists that the secrets of evolution were written in genes has proved to be premature. Sharing the same DNA does not produce the same behavior. Cell types differ from one another not because they contain different genes, but because the genes behave in different ways.[9]

What makes a human being more complex than a vegetable is not the number of genes. Genetic codes exhibit limited variability. "Most molecular cellular mechanisms are the same in all organisms" (Mayr 2001, 272). They function as parts of a complex cellular network, and being able to decipher their structure matters less than uncovering their role in the network. The body's organs, its kidneys and liver, for instance, are not constructed from genes—the genes carry the instructions from the chromosomes that design the molecules or proteins that interact with other molecules in a complex network that creates the kidneys and liver. The structure of a cell's genetic network contains considerable uniformity, while patterns of cell activity diverge radically.

Knowing the institutional structure of a regime, like knowing the DNA sequence, does not explain how it was assembled or how it originated. Biologists have begun to think about an organism's genome as a highly interwoven network in which a particular chromosome's catalytic function or capacity can vary significantly. Some genes are simply more central to an organism's regeneration than are others. A small number of genes act as major "hubs" and are involved in a majority of all activities, while most genes are lesser "nodes" that participate in only one or two molecular reactions.

Functionality cannot always be deduced from structure in social institutions, either. Among East Asia's developmental autocracies, it was common for a single ministry to have budgetary control over other ministries, or for one minister to facilitate inter-departmental coordination. In the Middle East, a department of the interior might have the same rank as any other ministry, but in the actual protocol of decision-making, it stands above all others as the all-purpose director. The challenge to understanding regime performance becomes understanding which units are for general purposes and which exercise discretion within a limited scope of authority.

The problem with linking economic growth to a particular set of institutional instructions is that institutions are open and complex systems nested within a web of social networks. Institutions have swarming, epistatic properties—an institution or a contract that records land ownership, for example, influences every other part of a society. Institutions undergo processes, and they themselves *are* processes.

Structural variance in institutions also occurs when formal structures must compete with informal networks, such as *neopatrimonial regimes*, in which residual cognitive and motivational preconditions cause parallel systems of rule-making.[11] A full set of institutions is constitutionally specified in neopatrimonial regimes, but in actuality, the relations between principals and agents are governed by informal roles; so more than one mechanism determines the behavior.[12] The rules that govern economic exchange may be structured among sources of authority at different scales, the formal rules of government occupy only one of the scales.

Again, just knowing the complete set of genes encoded in human DNA does not help us understand the programs those genes specify. Similarly, the "pattern of a system's organization"—the configuration of relationships that make a table a table or a bicycle a bicycle—differs from its physical structure, and does not help us understand the programs those genes specify. Moreover the structure of the actual physical components matters less than the process of change. And in a living system, the components change continually.

Economic development is made vexing by its dynamic and decentralized aspects, in which the function of a particular institutional design will shift from epoch to epoch, from society to society, and even within the same society over time.[13] For example, the level of monitoring and sanctioning of rule observance can vary without rewriting the rule or the structure of the monitoring institution. Many regimes derive resilience from redundancy (Ostrom 1990; Ostrom, Gardner, and Walker 1994).

When power changes hands, the new regime can switch on one set of institutions and reduce the frequency of another without ever changing the institutions.

The best academic work, that of Douglass North for example, recognizes the rupture between the announced, formal goals of policy and the informal behaviors embedded in customs and beliefs. North has observed that not only can an institution produce both formal and informal behaviors but that informal and formal institutions can exhibit complementary qualities (North 2005, 48–64).[14] Nevertheless gaps between the *de jure* and *de facto* distribution of power are difficult to observe or to measure and are not readily recorded in the indexes of institutional quality that guide the interventions of the development community. Societies with the same institutional designs can display many different forms of behaviors, and societies with radically different institutional designs can exhibit similar behavior. Simply changing how a rule is enforced can trigger behavior that diverges from the stated objectives of the institutional design process. By starving the federal oversight agencies of the means to monitor the financial system, for example, the US Congress in the 1990s opened the door to many abuses within the financial service industry. But such qualitative, rather than structural, changes are easily hidden in arcane protocol and budgetary procedures known only to actors within the system.

Assessing the legacy of new institutional economics, Harvard economist Dani Rodrik concludes that beyond "a very aggregate level of generality," these ideas do not provide much policy guidance. In fact, when assessing particular cases, there is wide divergence, and "[t]here is increasing recognition in the economics literature that high-quality institutions can take a multitude of forms and that economic convergence need not necessarily entail convergence in institutional forms" (2008, 52). Rodrik concludes that "there is no unique correspondence between the functions that good institutions perform and the form that such institutions take" (p. 15). We need to know how the different institutions work together; which tasks performed by a particular institution will depend on how that institution is integrated into the larger social fabric.

Even if we succeed at constructing a succinct, complete blueprint of contracting norms, rules, and institutions, understanding the determinants of performance will be incomplete. Social evolution has discovered different solutions to various design problems, and economic institutions are but one component of the social system's network architecture for achieving complex collective asks. Collective learning occurs through feedback within social networks where information travels via links with different degrees of connectivity. With more sources of information, agents with links to the few critical hubs can more aggressively respond to opportunity than those populations on the system periphery.

A Second-Best Path to Institutional Resilience

As of May 2011, nonconformist China is banker to the world's largest capitalist economy, owning 26 percent of US Treasury securities and 8 percent of total US national debt. While most economists underestimated China's growth potential, no school of economics missed its potential to create an effective network of economic relations more than did the new institutionalists of the property rights school.

How did China build a global system of economic relations with manufacturers and suppliers all over the globe, yet without institutions that protect property rights, without independent regulators, and with a government that can confiscate property with virtual impunity? Institutionalist theory makes capitalism without property rights implausible, yet China is the developing world's star performer, not India or the Philippines, both of which have constitutions that replicate Anglo-American institutions.

Chinese economist Yingyi Qian (2003) tries to square this circle by submitting an explanation for China's rise to economic prosperity expressed in terms that rest within canons of neoclassical thought. He specified several key institutions and practices that have been crucial to China's takeoff—all of them, in his wording, "second best," such as no-name bank accounts that attract savings into government-controlled banks and allow the government to steer the economy while sustaining large state enterprises. China also allows private investment into firms in which the government holds ownership through the use of town and village enterprises (TVEs) that align the interests of local governments with commercial for-profit production. TVEs are part of a larger trend in China to make reforms politically compatible with the incentives of the local party officials, a tendency that will be discussed at length in chapter 9.

Dual-track pricing has allowed the government to maintain quotas and price controls while permitting farmers to sell surplus production. The goal has been to create a new commercial economy without making the beneficiaries of socialist entitlements into losers (Lau, Qian, and Roland 2001). The early collectivist stages of Chinese communism established the Communist Party's legitimacy by assuring "rules of the game" that situate the entire population at the same starting place, and this reduced social impediments to opening the market; the party continues to derive legitimacy from its commitment to protecting livelihoods.[15]

A high percentage of China's GDP is invested because of "the expectation of future profits [which] can exert a stronger discipline on the public authority than fear of legal sanctions by an independent third party" (Rodrik 2008, 189). Instead of courts to enforce contracts and protect property rights, the state nurtures a mutual interest between private and public resource-holders to preserve the Communist Party, which ensures its longevity by linking its preservation to the profits from private investment. Thus, without an independent judiciary, investors feel their property rights are protected from political risk.

This linguistically awkward term *second best* illustrates the weakness of economics to explain institutional diversity (Rodrik 2008). The idea of best practices in development assumes the implementation of strategies that will produce an evolutionarily optimal outcome. But China's success is due to a different strategy: instead of building the best model or seeking an optimal solution, China's reformers seek *best fit*. Knowing where to end up is easy compared to finding a way to get there; thus China's search is similar to the evolutionary change processes of other complex systems.

Economic systems are complex systems. By concentrating on the simple "atoms," such as property rights, rather than the network structure of the whole, NIE reflects only a narrow representation of the range of collective behaviors essential to increase the investment rate.

Variety

Scott Page (2010) has observed that interconnectivity and interdependency give rise to diversity, not to equilibrium or global best practices. The competition for resources in a highly interdependent environment gives rise to many strategies, ensuring the existence of groups with well-separated traits, just as nature offers many different species the opportunity to develop a range of variations that ensure survival in a shared environment. These variations arise because agents are interacting with other highly diverse agents: development is an evolutionary outcome of their interaction.

In the same way, an economy is the product of the interaction of highly adaptive groups with distinctive traits and other such groups with different sets of distinctive characteristics. The actors are often networks that respond to each other and that, as a group, react strategically to other networks. These interactions generate their own internal dynamics as well. What results is unending novelty. But conventional economic models typically presume that representative agents act autonomously, interacting with the economy as passive recipients to prices set by the market. Two misconceptions arise as a result. First there is a failure to appreciate that economic agents are linked through networks that communicate and respond to the actions of other heterogeneous agents, the result is a system that exhibits a collective behavior dependent on all of its parts.

The adaptations of the agents as they adapt to their local environments take many forms: competition, cooperation, exploitation, and consumption. Because the local circumstances of one group vary from that of another, there may be reason to optimize one strategy over another. No single strategy is guaranteed to optimize the survival of all the groups that coexist within a given ecology. Interdependence causes a variety of strategies to coexist and coevolve. If all species competed to occupy the same niche, either at the top or the bottom, conflict and extinction would result, and the shared ecology would become unsustainable due to interminable conflict.[16]

Different survival strategies also protect the survival of the ecology. Speciation, the process by which new species are formed and/or stabilize, is one way that nature ensures that different functions will be optimized and that the components of a system will have greater autonomy. The divergent survival strategies of different species may ensure symbiotic outcomes; members of one species do not compete directly with members of other species for the same resources. A rabbit that runs away from a fox does not compete with the fox—it competes with other rabbits. A fit rabbit only has to run faster than other rabbits in order to survive and breed.

In the same sense, developing countries do not directly compete with already developed countries and therefore are unlikely to imitate the socially efficient institutions of the foxes. Evolution increases fitness within a given species without requiring imitation of a rival species. Interdependency may result in synergies, like the birds that relieve an elephant of worms and insects, as well as competition between different species.

Being part of ecology limits the options of any single agent in the system. When one agent mutates, it affects the other organisms in that particular ecology. If one agent moderately improves its fitness, it may find that it has new competitors that may individually be lesser organisms, but that together may unify to destroy the mutation to prevent the more endowed rival from emerging. To avoid being weeded out and replaced by other agents, the weakest agents may modify their strategies by copying more successful organisms, but only enough to survive, not enough to become models of efficiency. After being defeated by the armies of the French Revolution, Prussia did not decree the need for a French Revolution to occur domestically within Prussia; it modified the institutions of the monarchy to better compete, but only enough to ensure its survival, not to set the benchmark for others to imitate.

Interdependency makes it difficult to determine what constitutes progress. This is because of system-level effects. If all organisms that operate far from the fitness frontier were eliminated, the system might be pushed into instability (Bonner 1988). The positioning of one group at the top might require a range of contributions from partners who at first seem unfit. An agent's dependence on a partner may preclude the radical reforms necessary to raise its own adaptive fitness up to its partner's optimal levels.

The overall fitness of the global ecology is a product of the interaction of many different strategies at the individual or species level. Interdependency encourages the elaboration of a variety of products, services, institutions, and organizations that change the endowments and preferences of the agents.

Survival of the Simple: Complexity Increases Fragility

The rise and fall of great nations attract far more attention than the glacial pace of adaptation by smaller, more persistent, and less complex social entities. Our attention is naturally drawn to those societies that are complex rather than to the collectivities that occur with great redundancy. Accordingly, we have numerous studies of the rise and decline of great societies like ancient Greece or Rome, but a Tacitus who studies the tribal clans that have lived in and survived the fall of empires and a Herodotus who actually did travel to a lot of obscure places is rare.

Evolution seems to produce fewer distinct types of complex organisms in favor of the ubiquitous simple organisms. The higher fitness of large complex organisms may be more difficult to sustain, and may be more vulnerable to changes in the landscape. Rome passed, but the tribal subsystems that inhabit the deserts of North Africa survive to the present. The social structures of the Germanic tribes to the north proved more resilient than the sophisticated social hierarchies of the Romans.

What does it mean to speak of the survival of the fittest, and can the question be applied to society? All that we can infer from the study of evolution concerning progress is that the survivors among any given generation are better adapted than the non-survivors. The direction of economic evolutionary selection is determined by the success that economic agents have in finding solutions to current problems. This ensures diversity, not convergence toward a single optimal model. Planes have not displaced automobiles, although they are more evolved. Bicycles, railroads, even buggies and horses all coexist with planes. The simple structures may even turn out to be more resilient.

We frequently presume that evolution means progress. But evolutionary biologists warn us to avoid such simple conclusions. "Indeed, evolution seems highly progressive when we look at the lineage leading from bacteria to cellular protists, higher plants and animals, primates, and man," writes Ernst Mayr. "However, the earliest of these organisms, the bacteria, are just about the most successful of all organisms, with a total biomass that may well exceed that of all other organisms combined" (2001, 278). Many forms of life that survived for over a billion years are static (p. 219). In very precarious environments, no form of life survives better than single-celled bacteria.

Among evolutionary biologists, confidence in the one-dimensional, linear momentum of change toward a single focal point is refuted by evidence that many extinct species, such as dinosaurs, were more complex than those that have survived. The longest continuing species, cockroaches, horse crabs, and sharks, are not among the most complex. "To be sure, natural selection is an optimizing process," Mayr explains, "but it does not have a definite goal." What ends up constituting an improvement in adaptation "is strictly a *post hoc* decision" (1992, 132). The competitive selection processes of evolution do not guarantee the predominance of any one form of social organization. Families and tribes are still the oldest and most robust form of human organization.

If no mechanism in social evolution exists to ensure that complex institutions will emerge from those that are less complex, why do we observe greater complexity? The differences between the most complex and the simplest forms of economic organization increase over time, and this creates the *impression* of growing complexity. The simplest forms of transacting economic exchanges do not necessarily disappear. Derivatives and credit default swaps do not drive out simple loans. As economic interdependency increases, the variety of symbiotic relationships between alternative forms of transacting may also increase. Networks of families still offer an indispensable structure for shaping economic transitions (Greif 1993). While it may appear that more complex institutions are replacing simple earlier forms, this is often an illusion caused by an increasing degree of variation between simple and more complex structures.

Linking Institutional Quality to Growth

In molecular biology, whenever a new protein is discovered, it isn't long before the discovery of another protein, with its own set of genetic instructions, is proclaimed the "elementary particle" of the system. Several generations ago, atoms were elementary constructs; today, physicists believe they are complex systems. Similarly, whenever an essential institution is identified as the critical core of economic growth—Anglo common law versus French civil law, or the number of veto points—it turns out to be a mere subordinate subsystem.[17] But the search for the missing or elementary ingredient has led to continuous variety and refinement. The commitment to engineering governance has spread from Hernando's de Soto's preoccupation with land titling and the formal registration of property rights to independent government auditors, office of the ombudsman, procurement protocol, presidential term limits, multi-party elections, strengthening of political parties, monitoring election results, payroll reform, leadership training for officers that serve the head of state, results based management, tax identification of the entire population, and civilian control of the army. No wonder the budgets for technical cooperation on institution strengthening have surpassed that of economic policy advice that focused on few key officials in a few key ministries such as the central bank or the finance ministry. Each of these institutional concentrations mimics critical areas of competency that are generally ubiquitous among high performing economies. So why do independent evaluations report that most of the efforts failed.

Divergences among the behaviors of individual and of groups do not reflect the structure of the institutions but instead result from the rules that govern the regulatory circuitry of the system. Thus the same structures can be observed where institutional performance varies dramatically. Elinor Ostrom explains that diverse outcomes are due to divergent rules that govern the relationships among multiple authorities with overlapping jurisdictions. "The patterns of interaction and outcomes depend on the relationship among governance actors at different levels" (Andersson and Ostrom 2008, 86). A single institution or system of law cannot function on its own; it is dependent on hundreds of other laws and institutions.

For this reason the many indexes of good governance tell us very little about how institutions actually perform. Divergences reveal themselves only as development proceeds because regulations that govern key functions kick in at different sequences and trigger different functions. In biology the release of catalytically active proteins can trigger one cascade of reactions at one sequence and a completely different chain of events at another. Just as great divergence and specialization can be triggered due to differences in the regulatory circuitry of an organism, variation in regulation can alter the behavior of social institutions.

The Persistence of Institutional Diversity

The identification of the economic logic of institutions enabling global trendsetters to attain system-level dominance has transformed economic research, as well as global development policy. But why do economies that fail to reach their production possibility curve take up so much of the historical record? And why do interdependency and fierce competition for control of global resources intensify divergent patterns of institutional change? To understand institutional diversity, the next generation of inquiry must go far beyond the boundaries set by the founders of NIE. There are eight causes to consider:

1. What is optimal locally may not be optimal globally, and what implies progress globally may be irrelevant locally.

2. Parasites and predators thrive alongside the best designs at the peak of ecological fitness. Synergies link the emergence of dominant forms with the narrative of suboptimal institutional survival. The best moves set up niches that are filled by second-best moves for others to follow.

3. When confronted with similar threats or similar opportunities, some groups will emulate successful governing practices, technologies, and institutions, while others will not. The range of possible best moves depends on a society's historical antecedents. The choice of strategies deepens by reference to the memory of a population's past actions.

4. Alternative institutional lineages may eventually converge to the same or similar outcome.

5. Reform playing itself out may be a very different process from what appears *ex post facto* to have been its deterministic logic.

6. What looks like stagnation may be an illusion, caused by the fact that societies do not all move in the same direction.

7. While it is true that institutions set up the rules of the game, it is also true that the strategies of institutional change emerge during the course of social change.

8. Attempts to transfer globally optimal institutions (which often fail, due to wrong fit) may cause a transitional economy to experience increasing gaps between changing reality and the institutions deemed to be optimal. The gaps between design and capacity to implement may contribute to further inefficiency. An example can be found in the laws in India requiring such high standards of evidence that few criminals can be convicted. China has a larger financial system (as a percentage of GDP) than India, not because of better laws, but because, as Qian points out, it has lower standards, such as no name bank accounts (Root 2005). No-name bank accounts, identified by a number rather than a name and essentially a license for tax evasion, channel the nation's savings into the government-controlled banking system.

The source of the failures to operationalize the NIE rests in the theory of growth to which it has been adapted. That theory is blind to the processes that cause the aggregate environments to coevolve as the agents adapt to each other. The complex interdependencies constraining the adaptive potential of the system arise interactively, as a result of the strategic efforts of agents reacting to and anticipating the behavior of other agents. Each actor adapts to an environment of other agents who evolve simultaneously. Even once we have identified all of the parts, we may still fall short of identifying the essential differences between the behavior of the aggregate and its components.

Systemwide Interdependence

When conservative prophecies about the demise of communism were fulfilled by the fall of the Soviet Union, the NIE was ready with the blueprint to transform the socialist economies into functioning market economies. This gave the NIE a foot in the door of global development policy. But the dilemmas of global policy have become far more subtle and complex. There are basins of attraction besides the West with important lessons to impart about successful industrialization. The catalogs of best practices rarely outperform the progress that is made via myopic strategies of trial and error.

The institutionalists have succeeded in highlighting how economic change is process-dependent. But the formation of economic structures that emerge need not converge to the mechanisms or strategies of the successful and dominant institutional lineages of the past or present. The optimal selection is rarely within the choice set a given population or government faces. Institution-centric explanations of change are limited by systemwide constraints that shape the structure of institutions locally, making the adaptive moves by individual agents depend on the adaptive potential of the system itself.

NIE opens issues that can only be addressed by expanding analysis far beyond the boundaries originally set in the seminal works of Coase, Williamson, and North (Coase 1937, 1960, 1998; North 1981, 1992; Williamson 1975). The NIE framework is good at measuring the gaps that separate practices that succeed in generating economic growth in one society from those practices that encumber performance in another society, but the greatest quandary of economic growth is why the best institutions are rarely copied. The institutional structures that provide a particular regime with effective extractive and mobilization capacity are much easier to explain than the failure of the laggards to emulate the adaptive strategies of the most successful performers. Some states emulate the most successful models, but many fail to do so, even when confronted with threatening internal or external pressures.

The most vexing problem in development is the general drift of institutional evolution in which inefficient institutions are just as likely to survive as efficient ones. Why do so few societies ever approach the global efficiency frontier? Given the human desire to imitate, why do best practices not replicate rapidly? Why is it that all economies do not follow the path that goes in a straight line from bartering to forming listed, publicly traded companies to establishing central banking and labor unions? If good institutions are foolproof ways of acquiring wealth and progress, why does one of the most powerful forces in human evolution, imitation, not work here? If economic prosperity can arise quickly and easily from good institutions, why is wealth not abundant beyond a handful of countries? If good institutions that offer accountability, transparency, and predictability are inherent properties of prosperity, why do efforts to transplant them falter?

Applications to Global Development Policy

The position of the institutionalists—namely that institutions matter—has become the mainstream in discussions of economic development among the international policy community. Still being debated is what comes first, good institutions or growth. Does the direction of causality run in the direction of development to institutions, or institutions to development?

Determining the direction of causality is important because critics of the new institutionalism opine that the West *began* its ascent with the institutions it is now trying to impose on others. The skeptics, like Jeffery Sachs, say that policies that directly stimulate growth, such as infrastructure, education, or industrial subsidies, must come first, and that only after material development is heightened will the demand for better governance increase (Sachs 2005). Institutionalists defend their position with statistical regressions that correlate missing institutions with failed programs, assistance that did not meet its targets, and low growth. Both sides of the debate frame their questions using the same analytical conventions concerning systems, behaviors, networks, and change. The more traditional economists, like Sachs, continue to emphasize gaps in financial, physical, and human capital. The institutionalists emphasize gaps in regulation, participation, and the rule of law, property rights, media freedom, and corruption prevention. Both arrive at their blueprints for success by adding up the variables in order to fill the gaps that are first on their list.

The conventions governing international assistance presume that social systems are closed and that in equilibrium they exhibit "normal" behavior. The key actors, either leaders or elites, are atoms that are internally homogeneous and make decisions independently of what others do, and that behavior is prescribed by formal codes or rules. They presume that the motivational structures that must be targeted are private and individualistic. Change will be proportional or linear, like finding the right recipe and identifying the right ingredients.

Complexity thinking leads us to view systems as open and dynamic, not characterized by equilibrium. Social change is not predictable or additive, it is nonlinear and phase transitions happen. Many interdependencies result in multi-causal and unforeseen outcomes. Macro outcomes emerge from micro behavior and interactions. The actors are heterogeneous; they coevolve, responding strategically to the actions of others. Most important, their decisions are interconnected, adapting to the behaviors of others. They respond to incentives not exclusively as individual actors but as members of networks. Solutions are rarely within the mandate or responsibility of any single organization or individual. Success depends not only on convincing a single decision maker, but on changing behavior by influencing the linkages within social networks. Interventions must target the network. The type of network will matter a great deal. There is no right formula. What works once may not necessarily succeed a second time in a different time or place.

Is It the Politics?

The failures of institutional reform inevitably must trace back to the politics that shape the institutions. Poor countries do not have poor institutions because their leaders do not know what good economic policy is or what good institutional design looks like. In fact, poor policies and flawed institutional designs can be good politics, and may be instrumental in keeping extractive elites in power.

A number of books and articles—including Bruce Bueno de Mesquita and Root, *Governing for Prosperity* (2001); Bueno de Mesquita, Alaister Smith, Randolf Siverson, and James Morrow, *The Logic of Political Survival* (2003); Yi Feng, *Democracy, Governance, Economic Performance* (2003); and Root, *Capital and Collusion* (2006)—have offered a political lens through which the failures of international aid, and the persistence of governance designed to perpetuate poverty and exclusion, can be understood. We announced that regardless of the sector, development is a political process. A nation's politics determine why institutions persist that deprive citizens of economic opportunities.

If the elite politics is the force that shapes a developing nation's institutions, then the missing ingredient of development, we concluded, must be the politics. We demonstrated that politics has always been missing from the "to do" list of the donors, and that the politically motivated selection of institutions explains economic divergence among nations. Once agnostic about the role of institutions, many economists have since joined the choir. Who today would refute the view that poor institutions persist because they make it easier for powerful elites to survive? Or that poor institutions, those that fail to deliver prosperity, are the internally generated results of the politics of elite control?

Does it follow from this realization that the developing community must learn how to influence the politics of developing nations, and that aid providers must learn to think and act politically? A politics-centric view of development, one that acknowledges the institutional incentives of elites to feather their own nests, will not help us distinguish why some nations have stagnated, whereas others adapt. Has there ever been an elite that put the interests of other social strata ahead of its own, or that welcomed a transition to a more inclusive society? It is unreasonable to presume that powerful elites with everything to lose from a process of creative destruction will permit more equal social formations to occur.

Operationally speaking, inculcating powerful elites to accept adaptive transformations that come from the bottom is not a useful role for outsiders. Defining a political role for directing external intervention will inevitably encounter resistance from the targeted populations: it is operationally intractable. Thus from both analytical and operational perspectives, as the latest, all-you-need-to-know variable, politics does not improve upon previous structural/functionalist efforts to identify growth's missing ingredients. We were wrong for the same reasons that earlier efforts to identify an elemental variable, such as better technology or more capital have failed.

Adding political goals to the traditional socioeconomic aims of development assistance will not remove the barriers that prevent external assistance from putting aid-receiving governments on the path prescribed by modernization theory. Neither will it help align the trajectories of developing nations with the paths already forged by the world's high performers.

Political interventions are inevitably biased by the cultural and geographical origins of that intervention. This is one reason why, as a descendant of modernization theory, both new institutional economics and the governance agenda it inspires fail to offer an explanation of institutional change that is applicable to a range of non-Western social development strategies.

Identifying politics as the primordial source of institutional failure is no more correct than prior efforts to name the structural/functionalist characterizations of nations as they develop. We will now proceed to a perspective on the motives and behavior of elites that is much more likely to identify why many nations arrive at suboptimal solutions to their developmental dilemmas. What we will learn is that all the variables of socioeconomic development change in response to each other—they coevolve. Let's see how.

6

Dancing Landscapes: How Interdependency Shapes the Optimization Challenge of Globalization

Struggles in the Captain's Tower

This chapter explores evolutionary concepts and processes that account for variations in governance regimes in order to understand why many countries get stuck at local optima, instead of attaining global optimum solutions. *Fitness landscapes, parallel processing, lock-in, coevolution,* and *epistasis* all help clarify why some complex problems cannot be solved optimally. They force a reconsideration of the optimization challenge posed by globalization to emerging states and policy makers.

Fitness landscapes reveal how interactions among countries change the nature of the optimization problem. No matter how focused a country may be on directing its energies toward confronting its local optimization challenges, the local optima governments aim for are made unstable by the actions of others. To get to the highest point on a given fitness landscape, they must consider interactions that will cause the landscape to shift and change the menu of options. The coevolution of partners confronting their own local fitness challenges will reshape the coupled landscapes.

Interdependency and diversity in a globalized world affect the moves of coevolutionary partners at diverse fitness peaks. The strategic context of Chinese–US relations, for example, has been described as that of two parties sharing the same bed but hosting different dreams (Lampton 2001). Even if they are climbing toward alternative adaptive peaks, their fitness depends on interaction with each other and on interactions with their various partners that inhabit the same landscape. A conflict for local influence over system-level behavior makes the outcome of institutional selection and strategy increasingly complex for both.

The dynamics of global interdependency replicate the dynamics of natural ecosystems in which coevolutionary pressures alter the landscape, as well the organism. Competing agents change the local fitness landscapes for each other; they also create niches in the local landscape for new organisms to thrive.[1] So long as landscapes differ, fitness values will vary and mutations will accumulate. Coevolution does not presume convergence to some global optimum; the adaptive process is always pulled toward local optima. "Mix, intermingle, and become more diverse" is the outstanding lesson of global interconnectedness. This is the lesson that policy planners of the liberal West must learn.

In contrast to the conventional theory of modernization, which assumed that developing countries could attain economic growth and democracy if they imitated the successful institutional frameworks of developed countries, the fitness trajectories of emerging power players depend heavily on the system-level properties of their respective environments, which differ from those of the incumbents who went before them. As a consequence even rising democracies like India, Brazil, and Turkey espouse policy options on key global issues that differ from the consensus views of the West.

Just as the West's planners were becoming comfortable with their role as system managers, they must react to global megatrends, such as changing trade flows, population growth, and migration. These trends are effecting a global complexity transition that reduces the scope, resources, and legitimacy of hierarchical control systems. The geopolitics and geoeconomics of dynamic complexity are not amenable to those control mechanisms, weakening the stability framework of post–cold war liberalism. The global system is already becoming less responsive to directives from the vanguard of industrialized nations; dancing landscapes await those who thought of themselves as the organizers of the dance.

Interdependence and Variation and the Need for Parallel Processing

The concept of the optimal decision will be familiar to economists, as it is at the core of microeconomics as well as of modernization theory. It presumes that individuals have fixed and well-defined preferences concerning the menu of choices available to them. As rational individuals, they will gather all accessible information and match it against their preferences in order to make the optimal decision. In making rational choices, they gather information from the "price system": they evaluate the costs of any given action their competitors or adversaries might take. In conventional models, populations and individuals optimize independently; their choices are not affected by the strategies adopted by others. Once they account for all the options, they make a decision in which the potential benefits outweigh the potential costs.

If each agent (or system component) optimized its cost functions separately, it could obtain maximum fitness in its particular landscape, as the conventional approaches would predict. But it is more realistic to presume that the agents are connected in various ways. They do not act independently; they both generate and respond to changes in the behaviors of the components around them, and to the larger global environment of which they are a part. To avoid information overload, they engage in parallel processing, which changes the very properties of the optimization problem and allows the agents to operate within partially subdivided networks. Parallel processing is an essential evolutionary process in which agents "process" information from different sources simultaneously. The need for such processing increases with the degree of interaction.

Parallel processing implies that each agent acts both independently, in pursuit of its own advantage, and also interdependently, as it reacts to and produces adaptive responses in its neighbors. As these agents and the populations surrounding them, compete with rivals for local advantage in a limited space, they will not all find similar value in the "inevitability" or "effectiveness" of a global optimum.

When multiple agents engage in parallel processing and perform their particular optimizations at the same time, they fundamentally change the behavior of whole system. Parallel processing may also cause conflict over boundaries of interdependency, creating system-level imbalances (Bar-Yam 1997, 421–27).

Take a Hike!

To understand the evolutionary influences that can engender a range of possible institutional variations among newly forming states, it is useful to consider the lessons evolutionary biologists have drawn from studies of landscape ecology. Landscapes have helped biologists think about the multiple factors that combine in the evolutionary process. Using landscape ecology to understand how local circumstances determine the fitness of particular populations, we can reformulate the optimization challenges that globalization poses to emerging and developed states alike.

Landscape models offer perspectives that can help clarify a key lesson about complex systems: success depends less on the attributes of an individual agent than on where that agent happens to be situated in the system. The shapes of a given fitness landscape will determine what its population choses to optimize in order to survive.

Most developing regions face fitness landscapes filled with peaks and valleys, places in which to get stuck or lost, that make which direction to take unclear. The more interactions an agent must consider before initializing an action, the more that landscape can be described as *rugged*. A landscape is rugged when the global peak or optimum is not visible because numerous local peaks block the view. Although an optimal solution may not be visible, a fixed number of solutions, local optima, do exist; rugged landscapes are not problems of unlimited dynamic complexity. Scott Page (2010) demonstrates that solutions are possible even when lots of choices are involved, even for problems as complicated as harnessing nuclear energy; a chess game, despite thousands of possible solutions, is nevertheless solvable.

The more rugged the landscape, the more limited the supply of mutual information about the strategies of other agents, and the more confined a given population will be to local optima. A population whose optimization choices are determined locally is unlikely to evolve with a population facing a different landscape. They may coevolve in reaction to one another, but they will not evolve in tandem. If one landscape is rugged and the other flat, imitation will never be an optimal strategy; the fitness challenges will not correlate. Climbing a rugged landscape requires skills, capabilities, strategies, and adaptations that diverge significantly from those required by the challenges of a flat fitness landscape.

Optimization on a Dancing Landscape

On a rugged landscape, it is difficult to find optimal solutions for any number of reasons. Where one is located in the landscape and where one begins one's search matter. Efforts to replicate best practices of other landscapes will undermine efforts to attain local optima. It is not even possible to reverse one's path in order to imitate the adaptive search processes that worked in a different landscape. The starting conditions of the two must also be the same. Yet even though the choices interact, the landscape is stable, and thus a fixed number of solutions exist.

The global ecology, however, has become what Stuart Kauffman's research identifies as an interacting *dancing landscape*, characterized by nonconvergent variation. In this kind of landscape the frequency of interconnectivity and the intensity of interdependency create an environment of reciprocal instability. In a dancing landscape the fitness for one agent depends on the actions of another, and no agent can improve its payoffs independently of what its competitors do. A small event anywhere in the system can have a large consequence in any other part.

Most developing nations find themselves in a dancing landscape where an optimal solution is not in the choice set the population faces, the combinatorial complexity is intensified by the confluence of many agents acting independently (Bar-Yam 1997, 553), and coevolution causes the very landscape to transform. Dancing landscapes present problems that do not stay fixed and cannot be solved optimally (Page 2010, 93–94).[2] Interdependencies with other adaptive agents are so numerous that the payoffs to any given adaptation or solution constantly shift. The local peaks are constantly rising and dropping, altering the sets of options available to other agents.

When Fitness Depends on the Actions of Others

The measure of success for most polities or firms is their performance in relationship to their immediate competitors. Similarly most actors in the global political economy are overly concerned with parrying the moves of a local rival. They behave as if even a small loss to a local rival could threaten their survival, and they expend great energy to gain leads on political opponents and gain popular approval. The permanent efforts of the Pakistani military establishment to precipitate conflict with India in order to justify its control over state resources and agendas are one example of this. It is a myopic outcome that keeps local elites in power. But, if leadership focuses entirely on the next amount of damage a particular local rival can inflict, a failure to adopt appropriate long-term goals is inevitable.

If actors place insufficient emphasis on the overall state or cycle of the global economy, long-term goal-setting is frustrated.

The ruggedness of the landscape will determine how far into the future local social planners will see. When a society's adaptive search is trapped among low peaks, it will be difficult to attain a future orientation. An extremely rugged landscape is unlikely to produce forward-looking, modern states capable of deferred gains. The best place to find the highest fitness peaks is to already be on one. The view from one peak to another is relatively unobstructed, enabling a view to the other highest peaks in the system. If when they look forward, those social planners can only see the next local peak—in other words, they can look up but cannot see beyond—then they will place less value on the future.

To accomplish the ultimate work of coordinating mutually synergistic collective behavior, social planners have the task "to improve the internal model each entity builds of its world, thereby enabling those entities to co-adapt better" (Kauffman 1993, 645). When fitness landscapes are highly correlated and neighboring points share common fitness values, then "[c]oevolving adaptive agents attempting to predict one another's behavior as well as possible may coordinate their mutual behavior through optimally complex but persistently shifting models of one another" (p. 404). Rich interdependency with other groups in a shared ecology will become possible. But when interdependency causes the landscapes to dance, the combinatorial optimization problems that result makes coordination unlikely. In such cases, synergies will not unfold except randomly. The measure of system interdependency is the correlation of its parts. Correlations must exist in the microstructure in order for the macro structure to retain its structure. When the landscapes cease to be correlated, coordination among the agents diminishes. A loss of microscopic cohesion causes a complexity catastrophe. As the similarity of fitness values recedes, adaptive evolution can no longer take place. At that point a rugged landscape transforms into one in which there is no structure.

Many conflict zones in the world economy bear a resemblance to the problem of randomness that occurs when a landscape suffers a complete loss of structure. As the landscape ceases to have structure and there are no interdependent payoffs, coordination becomes impossible, and the continuity of collective planning among the agents decomposes to produce a pure Hobbesian war of all against all.[3]

When the Local Is the Global Peak: Optimization Challenges in India and China

The economic coming of age of both India and China signifies how globalization is replete with examples of states settling for local maxima rather than global optimum. Both nations ignored the best practice options advocated by international change consultants. Relatively unaffected by donor assistance, both were free to select paths that ran against the grain of development policy. Neither state was the client of a larger power. Their economic landscapes were rugged but were not much influenced by coevolution with partners. Each was led myopically by steps to adapt economic reforms to the local environment.

Landscape theory can be used to predict the level of socially productive investments in China and India, and how they approach their optimization challenges from the perspective of attaining a local optimum. The sheer size of their economies reduces their interdependencies with other developing economies. Since they are not natural resource extractors or cash crop exporters, their exposure to external shocks and disturbances is also minimized. As the two largest emerging economies, they are able to fix their sights on attaining their own local maxima. They enjoy an advantage that other developing nations do not have: the local peak is also the global peak.[4] Solving their own fitness values, they can shape the values of others.

Why Is India Democratic?

In this section we will see how the local fitness landscape was also the source of the resilience of Indian democracy. Standard approaches attribute India's democracy to top-down learning by the nation's elite, and presume that the time spent in the West and their education in British schools produced a desire to carry back to India what they were taught to revere. But, if India's democracy is the result of a top-down emulation imposed from a central location, how can we explain why the founders of Pakistan who went to the same schools and were educated with the same materials organized Pakistan along completely different lines?

The choice of India's Western-trained founders to inaugurate a legislative democracy may appear to reflect their "parallel" search to attain a global optimum, but this was not the case. India's trajectory as a democracy began with partition in 1947; the first elections came in 1951. Democracy was the local optimum for India's elite for a number of reasons.[5]

First, the Indian National Congress (INC) Party had been in existence for more than a century. It led the fight for independence and had been planning for the post-independence government for decades. Although the partition of British India was anathema, it ensured victory in the first national election. The Congress Party preferred to break up India rather than share power with Jinnah and the All-India Muslim League, a powerful coalition that preferred proportional representation and, in conjunction with other minority parties, could have challenged the Congress Party for leadership. Proportional representation that would have reserved seats for key ethnic groups might have reduced Congress chances of forming the first government. Partition eliminated the threat that the League could form a government from among the same competing interests and factions that the Congress, itself highly factionalized, hoped to attract.

With the Jinnah dilemma out of the way, Bueno de Mesquita et al. (2003, 382) report, "The Congress-dominated constitutional convention erected primarily single-member districts with first-past-the-post elections. These elections rules practically guaranteed the Congress coalition members legislative majorities in the absence of popular electoral majorities. Indeed the Congress Party dominated the national parliament, often with around two-thirds of the membership, despite not winning a majority in the popular vote." There were scores of political parties to divvy the vote among.

Thus the formation of Pakistan helped ensure Congress's victory in the first national election, and gave it breathing space to shape India's future in ways that would preserve the party's domination of future national parliaments. In agreeing to partition, both Jawaharlal Nehru and Jinnah served their own ambitions over the interests of the population, and the ongoing claims for territory remain unresolved. Instead of precipitating a "civil war," partition of India and then of Pakistan resulted in major wars and ongoing bitterness between the two nations. The creation of East and West Pakistan offered a solution that ensured both Muslim and Hindu elites the prospect of continuing dominance. If there had been no separate Muslim state at the outset, dissatisfaction among Muslims within India might start a series of breakaway revolts in the regions where they formed the majority, and the spread of such revolts to the Sikhs or the Tamils could cause the newly built national edifice to crumble.

Second, India was a multiparty system at independence in 1947. Even with the Muslim majority regions out of the picture, national unity remained a pressing issue. At the time of independence, only Gandhi had the stature to ensure national cohesion. Internally, Congress was a coalition of coalitions, in the same way that George Washington was the head of a group of contentious colonies. Nehru was one among several leaders of the independence movement, and the many smaller political parties were limited because their support was regional. Each subdivision within the party would have opted out of the coalition if it did not feel there were credible assurances of power rotation. All contending interests and regional representatives could agree that they needed to find a system that ensured that no single political figure would become a dictator and send the country down the path of dissolution and fragmentation. Democracy keeps India together; ensuring that the rotation of leadership helps it avoid the pitfalls of a succession crisis or dissolution through civil war.

The parliamentary leaders of the India National Congress, like Nehru, were mostly "twice-born" Brahmins, a rneligiously sanctified elite.[6] They fully expected to enjoy the fruits of sovereignty. But the subcontinent's large minority Muslim population threatened their dream of unity, power, and wealth.

Third, democracy protected against a military takeover if civil war broke out. While the Brahmins were India's highest social caste, next in the hereditary order was the soldier caste, Kashtriya, and an elite and wealthy subset of it was the Rajput caste, the ruling and military class (rajas, maharajas, and warriors). But many of the rajas, maharajas, and such were not part of India; they still retained their princely states.

Caste-based perceptions blinded India's elite to the social perquisites of democracy. Social status at birth determined in large part access to social assets, particularly health care and education. Social service delivery has since failed, and without educated masses, the result is protection and patronage, rather than policy-based governance. In short, a largely local perspective—a climb to a local peak—has shaped the form of democracy that took root to ensure the continuity of the Congress Party elite. They did not seek global optimum to align India with the industrial democracies in either politics or economics, they needed to solve a local problem, preventing a mutiny of the nation's many divergent parts.

India attained its competitive advantage in the globalized economy by ignoring the advice of global change specialists who advocated privatizing the state-owned industrial sector and removing barriers to labor mobility. Attaining a globally competitive manufacturing capability would have put India's most abundant resource, its large underemployed population, to its most efficient use. But India's leaders have consistently avoided antagonizing powerful unions that defend the state-owned manufacturing sector. Instead, India's producers found a path to the global economy by investing in the service and high-tech sectors. Finding these local optima has turned India into a hub of innovation within the global communications network.

China's Red Queen's Hypothesis: Running Faster to Balance Local Variation with Global Coevolution

Unlike India's leaders, the leaders of China's independence movement did not have to posit national unity as their foremost concern. China already had a long memory of national unification, but almost no history of looking far beyond its immediate borders to a wider world. A cosmopolitan formula of multiparty democracy found few takers; the inherited assumptions from imperial Confucianism were deeply entrenched (Fairbank 1986, 171).

Both Mao Tse-tung and Chaing Kai-shek envisioned a future based on command by a single party in which a government by meritocracy was expected to continue. Legislative powers were unfamiliar; the risk that popular elections would let stupidity govern could deter China's return to great power status. Both rivals sought nothing less than total victory. They only disagreed on the fastest path to catch up to China's rivals and reassert China's stature as a major world power.

As in India, the West touted mass privatization, but Mao and later Deng Xiaoping went after local peaks, not global optima. Mao thought the fastest path to reconstructing China's status as a great power would be to simplify the problem of development by designing a Taylor-like assembly line of mass production for the entire national economy, transferring a system developed for factory-based industrial efficiency to a labor-based economy. During the Cultural Revolution (1966–1976) the entire population, regardless of prior training, was to become entirely interchangeable, like cogs in a giant national system, eliminating all private ownership and leveling distinctions among the private endowments of the parts. This way contemporary China gained distance from pre-modern values and social inequities supported by ancient pedigrees.

Mao's optimal solution of collectivization, however, conflicted with the optimal design of private incentives necessary for economic growth. His successors rejected Mao's experiments for not producing a growing, modern economy. They needed to reconcile the revolution's promise of social equity while attaining the revolution's promise of national regeneration so that China could resume its place as a great power among nations.

Deng Xiaoping followed Mao's example of not seeking to imitate the managerial practices that constituted the global optimum. He refused to turn over the reform process to international change experts. Shut out of donor-assisted intervention, China had to find its own way to global economic integration. Even after becoming eligible for international funding, China rarely responded to international counsel.

Under Deng, officials at all levels of the administrative hierarchy engaged in the process of economic reform.

Early reforms in agriculture reflected local initiatives that proved successful and only later were endorsed by national-level leaders. The reform process has been interactive up and down the government hierarchy rather than following the top-down process in South Asia. The successful examples at the local level influence government debates about general policy. Deng allowed local units to self-organize around problems that need to be solved. (Shirk 1993)

The economic rise of China is frequently but erroneously attributed to its outward orientation. Indeed Deng Xiaoping is known for remarking, "Not a single country in the world, no matter what its political system, has ever modernized with a closed-door policy" (Fukuyama 2011, 98). But the context of the optimization problem Deng tried to solve was local: to attain the highest local peak. In such a context the agents adapt locally and identify solutions through experimentation in a local context.

Many reforms initiated during Deng's tenure were labeled experimental. Successful experiments conducted in the context of simple localized units were eventually applied to larger units. Once a reform was selected, investors were assured that it would be sustained through government backing, further encouraging investment (Root 2006, 190–91). System-wide interactive dynamics emerged through simple rules magnified in surprising ways. The process of learning by doing made it possible to replicate success. Mutations that improved local fitness could be selected because they did not have to meet standards of global fitness set outside of China. The chance acquisition of favorable mutations within a Chinese context could be rapidly replicated. But without opening to the outside, inbreeding could have depressed fitness (since neither parasites nor predators evolve in parallel so as to delete deleterious mutations). By opening the economy, Deng ensured that Chinese institutions would evolve in response to changes in the world economy. The constant race that causes continual coevolution between two species, as between a host and a parasite, is sometimes referred to as the Red Queen's Hypothesis. Deng's recognition that China must run twice as fast to increase its fitness relative to its competitors is Deng's Red Queen's Hypothesis, that China had to increase its fitness relative to those societies with which it competes.[7]

Deng recognized that exposure to forces of global competition was needed in order for China to maintain its relative fitness in the system with which it also had to coevolve. Firms that did not commercialize were likely to see their loans cut off. Even if they remained under government management, they had to show a profit to avoid being reorganized. Commercialization ensured that market forces would select fit local variations and dispose of deleterious mutations.

Instead of dissolving the Chinese Communist Party, the leadership changed the incentives of party members to support economic reform. Ironically, had democratization occurred first, local party members, no longer assured of keeping the advantages of government positions, might have been more concerned with reelection than business development. Local party members used their influence within the government to foster local economic growth, since they were among the principal beneficiaries (Li 1998).

Ignoring Western counsel to promote fast-track privatization, China instead pursued a dual-track strategy, preserving its state-owned sector and adapting it to commercialization, while spawning a new privately managed sector. Instead of privatizing land, the Chinese liberalized agriculture by allowing farmers to sell surplus crops, but only after obligations to their collective quotas were met. China used the same dual-track approach in other areas, such as coal and steel production. Instead of privatizing the nation's industrial assets, China opened town and village enterprises to commercialization, giving the management, namely the local governments, equity in the additional revenues generated. It permitted no-name bank accounts so that money regardless of its source ended up in the state-controlled banking sector. With each of these hybrid or non-traditional arrangements, the government aimed to minimize the adverse social consequences of reforms to ensure that individual opportunity was not attained at the expense of collective well-being (Lau, Qian, and Roland 2001).

Deng allowed foreign investment to abet local learning and permitted Chinese to study overseas and learn from others so that global knowledge could be diffused at home. At last, by the beginning of the twenty-first century, China had joined the global brain (Bloom 2000). But this was the last stage of a process that had begun forty years earlier, with Mao's efforts to ground China's modernity in the culture of its people. China's developmental decisions are criticized for being transitional, but for its leaders, process matters more than the end.

In a sense, the local Chinese landscape was less rugged than that of India because communism removed many archaic cultural practices along with ethnic and class-based divisions. China chose an investment strategy based on strengthening the manufacturing sector because it employed China's most abundant resource, its people, in its most profitable usage. Rather than aspire to excel in world-class technology to which only a small minority of highly trained professionals could contribute, the productivity of China's economy gains most by optimizing the output of physical labor. In the process China has introduced many innovations on the shop floor that make its manufacturers more competitive globally.

The messy trial-and-error process in China differs fundamentally from India's top-down system. Yet the two narratives of institutional selection share one common element: the local peak was the global peak. While greater participation in the global system means heightened connectivity, it also means a more rugged landscape. When there was limited connectivity, if any part of the global system was changed it would have little effect on the local economy. Being a global player makes the optimization problems more complex and more susceptible to variables beyond internal control. Finding solutions locally will no longer be sufficient. An interdependent and interconnected India and China will have implications for the control of the global system as well. A conflict over domination can ensue when two agents are climbing toward alternative adaptive peaks.

Planning or Tinkering

The debate over which model—China's or India's—is better for building a modern economy is essentially an argument over the merits of top-down control versus those of evolutionary learning. From its creation by the Indian government in 1950 through its peak years in the 1970s, the Indian Planning Commission ran a massive exercise in top-down social engineering. Charged with assessing the country's resources and formulating ways to produce a rapid rise in the general standard of living, the Commission instituted five-year plans that specified complete sets of instructions to create an industrial economy. In its highly centralized assault against nationwide poverty, the Commission tried to anticipate all contingencies in the creation of a complex, functioning economy. With this effort, the Commission became the highest-powered, continuous seminar on economic and social development held anywhere on the globe. Many former members of the Commission became celebrated professors in universities around the world.[8]

The Planning Commission's efforts to design an all-encompassing mechanism of national economic coordination trapped India in four decades of mediocre growth rates. Poverty persisted and productivity declined in heavy industry, although it received massive investment. Centralized planning failed to harness bottom-up variation or to capitalize on local diversity to define appropriate local fitness options in India's rugged landscape. A few projects worked according to plan—but an unlimited range of unplanned behaviors arose from the interactions among local social organizations, producing a complex black market economy. Unfortunately for Indian productivity, when business innovation shifts to the informal sector, innovators have difficulty finding resources for increasing the scale or scope of their enterprises.[9]

Chinese planners never attained the celebrity status of their Indian peers, but by trying multiple paths and starting with smaller interventions from the top, they found a better way to determine what worked. After

Deng declared the opening of the Chinese economy, he instituted a multi-level process that facilitated both change and stability, and strengthened social organization and social learning through local experimentation.

The idea behind Deng's approach to expanding regional diversity was to discover, rather than to dictate, what worked. As a stimulant to experimentation, local leaders were permitted to retain some of the surplus wealth they created. This made innovation compatible with their political incentives, stimulating intense competition to find local solutions to local problems. Deng's strategy encouraged different approaches to be tried in different places, with multiple agents each searching for their own local optima. The result was an accumulation of diverse local projects offering different solutions to the problems China faced. Millions of new economic entities were created.

Successful local projects were scaled up, serving as models for larger projects that required more capital. The mainstreaming of the household responsibility system, along with town and village enterprises, originated as local solutions. Successful projects were copied, and replication produced more suitable, better-adapted projects. Each copy changed the conception of the project, permitting variation and improvement over time.[10] Careers in the bureaucracy were built from the bottom up as well. Administrators moved into positions of central command only after they had excelled at local levels and had a proven record of local performance. Success in provincial postings became a virtual requirement for rising to national political prominence. In contrast, recruitment in the Indian system was stratified: entrance exams established status distinctions that took precedence over career mobility. Initial rankings are binding for life, leaving 98 percent of the staff without career prospects (Root 2006, 134–35). China's efforts more closely resembled an evolutionary model in which variation arises from below rather than from an optimal plan that guides project selection from above. In India the black market grew to rival the formal sector in size, but the Chinese model ensured that capital accumulated in state-owned banks, not in black-market activities.

Nevertheless, an appreciation of the evolutionary logic of the Chinese growth model has not pervaded the thinking and practice of the international development community, which has opted for large projects conceived at the headquarters of large international institutions and which pursues best practice rather than maximum variation. As history has shown, competition for donor-funded projects does not optimize the local fitness of the project recipient; instead it causes local organizational capacity to cluster around temporary and informal solutions.

Nor does the record of international assistance to promote economic growth enjoy a superlative record. Rather than helping developing nations find the terms for integrating into the global economy, the top-down approach inadvertently stymies the building of organizational capacity at local levels. The contest to obtain external assistance projects weakens indigenous capacity for innovation instead of strengthening the interactions where most societal cooperation and competition occur. But China's trajectory and that of India do possess one common element. Since India had to deal with poverty on a scale that transcended the capacity of any international effort, and because China was denied access to permanent assistance, both nations developed their own solutions for dealing with the rest of the word in mutually beneficial interaction.

Maturity and Complexity

As the Chinese economy and polity mature and become more complex, "the heights of accessible peaks fall toward the mean fitness" (Kauffman 1993, 52). The effect of future mutation or variation on China's fitness is likely to be harmful because future mutations will disrupt functions that have accumulated during the period of rapid transition that began in 1978. Because most mutations will be deleterious in a complex mature organism, options for change diminish as the system matures. Similarly, in a mature polity, mutations of social institutions will be more disruptive, "the number of conflicting design constraints among the parts increases rapidly" (Kauffman 1993, 53) ; revolutionary long jumps are unlikely to succeed and may produce utterly random outcomes—which leads us to presume that as China's economic system matures, it will be locked into its current institutional arrangements. This process of normalization will likely diminish China's prospects for convergence toward liberal norms. In chapter 9 we predict parallel patterns of political modernization rather than convergence toward a shared global norm.

Lock-in will reduce the rate of China's future growth to levels that resemble the more mature industrial economies it has been trailing, and it will expose future growth and stability in China to new sources of vulnerability, determined by China's interdependence with the economies with which it has become inextricably intertwined. Future growth will be linked to mechanisms that effect systemwide transformations and are determined by the macro-level rules of global trade. Will China's behavior in the international arena change as it becomes more cognizant of the limitations imposed by interdependence?

Lock-in and the Late Starter's Advantage

Are some nations simply more inward looking and less adventurous? Do they wait for change to come while being satisfied with relative self-sufficiency? Landscape ecology offers a way to better understand the dynamic ecological properties of regime change when one part of the environment affects what occurs in another. Understanding the degree of interdependency and connectedness of a system's parts helps explain why, despite the dissemination of information about best practices, the world often changes slightly, but rarely dramatically. The optimization of function is constrained by the interdependence of the system's components (epistasis). Stuart Kauffman ascertains that in biological evolution, a general systemwide improvement is possible only if the improvement of one trait is greater than the negative side effects on other traits.[11]

Like complex organisms, social structures and social change processes function interdependently. Within a single polity or economy, the mutation of a single institution will affect other institutions in differing ways. As an evolving society gains complexity, the trajectories of change are diminished. General improvements obtain only if an innovation in one part of the system does not outweigh the consequences for the system as a whole. A balancing point is reached when the complex structure of interdependencies constrains the adaptive potential of the system, reducing an individual's fitness in relation to the average properties of the system (Kauffman 1993, 644).[12] If, for example, jet planes had wings light enough and long enough to allow planes to land in water, they might not be strong enough to support engines powerful enough to fly over oceans. The social planner's dilemma is like the dilemma of the aircraft designer: to determine under what combination the various component parts will

function optimally. Ernst Mayr masterfully captures this dilemma of correlated evolution:

An organism is a carefully balanced, harmonious system, no part of which can
change without having an effect on other parts. Let us consider the increase in
the size of teeth of horses. These changes require a larger jaw, and in turn a larger
skull. To carry the larger skull, the entire neck has to be reconstructed. The larger
new skull has an effect on the rest of the body and in particular locomotion.
This means that in order to acquire larger teeth virtually the whole horse must
to some extent be reconstructed. This has been confirmed by a careful study of
the anatomy of hypsodont horses. Also, since the whole horse had to be reconstructed, the change could occur only gradually and slowly, over many thousands
of generations (2001, 218–19).

As a country's adaptive fitness increases, its interest groups and institutions become entrenched; changing just one thing accomplishes little.
A "lock-in" occurs and adaptation becomes incremental. Economic historian Alexander Gerschenkron's "advantages of backwardness" is an
exploration of the dynamics of lock-in, in the economics of catching up
(1962). Gerschenkron's theory postulated that how backward a country
is at the outset of its economic development would determine starting
points and should determine the selection of policy interventions needed
to spur its development. Contrasting Germany's swift rise and Britain's
stagnation in the early twentieth century Theodore Veblen (1915) attributes the former's advantage to a backwardness that did not impose barriers to adopting contemporary best practice. During initial encounters
with globalization, the regions or organizations that benefited most were
those whose adaptive fitness levels were low, such as China, East Asian
nations, and India (as compared to Latin America, which after World
War II, initially enjoyed a higher standard of living). East Asia, for example, was able to attain macroeconomic stability conducive to a high
investment rate during the takeoff years 1960 to 1990 because interest-
group lock-in had not yet occurred, allowing the government to adopt
the latest blueprints for planning and resource mobilization. Entrenched
vested interests that delayed the adaptiveness of the first movers had not
yet been mobilized.

Lock-in is also what Mancur Olson had in mind in his account of
why societies victorious in World War II, such as France, Britain, and the
United States, suffered from stagflation, unemployment, and inflation, in
the seventies, while the losers Germany and Japan increased industrial

effectiveness and expanded their shares of world economic growth (Olson 1982). The effect of lock-in on the tapering off of growth rates is the danger China faces as it becomes a mature system.

Dancing Landscapes for All

Increased global interconnectedness means the first tier of industrialized countries are no longer the only systemically important countries. They too cannot escape the greater instability engendered by forces beyond their control. The United States was the quintessential flat landscape during the nineteenth century, able to evolve almost entirely in response to challenges that arose locally. Its populations had the luxury of contemplating and selecting optimal solutions because its ecology demanded relatively limited interdependency with others in a shared environment. Internal disorder did not end in external intervention either; even major instability, such as the Civil War, did not expose the country to intervention by external agitators. Great Britain sided with the confederacy but did not provide military assistance. By virtue of its history and its geography the US enjoyed the rare position privilege of being a global player by choice. It could shut out the outside world when it wanted to and engage according to its own discretion. A flat, uninterrupted view of the horizon makes the US experience difficult to replicate. But its discretionary participation in global affairs is an advantage the US is finding harder to maintain in the current global ecology that its own aggressive globalizing policies have created.

However, since 2003, interconnectedness has increased instability for even the upper echelon of countries. Equity prices of firms in newly paired economies now move together. In 2012, for example, 40 percent of the price movement of private equity in Latin America could be attributed to price changes in equity values in East Asia, but most remarkably, ten years later synchronization of values rose to 82 percent. In 2000, external shocks affected 20 percent of the output of first world economies; ten years later, that impact had increased to over 40 percent. Even the US economy no longer enjoys freedom from interdependency. The world's largest economy must adapt to a fitness landscape it co-inhabits, making institutional change even in the United States a problem of dynamic complexity.

Evolution and the Barriers to Optimization

Fitness landscapes provide a useful perspective on institutional selection in the presence of epistasis. However, landscape ecology shares the limits of evolutionary thinking when considering the extent of variation possible in the environment. Yet, without major transitions that punctuate the environment, the wonderful complexity of life of which we are a part would not exist. Per Bak, a physicist (Bak and Sneppen1993), Stephen Jay Gould, a paleontologist (1982, 1989, 2002, 2007; Gould and Eldredge 1993), and Stuart Kauffman, an evolutionary biologist (1993, 1995) have demonstrated the possibility of sudden shifts in the global landscape that can cause avalanches of change (Bar-Yam 1997, 565–66). To explore the sources of resilience to extreme events, the next chapter shifts the focus from the landscape to the mutually interacting networks of agents that populate it.

7

Accelerators of "Stateness": System Structure and Network Behavior in the Making of the Modern State

Introduction

A great puzzle of history is why China was unprepared to meet the challenge of Europe's industrialization and global domination, despite being unified under a single emperor for much of its history. Why in fact did the Industrial Revolution take place in Europe, and not China? Why did China, where gunpowder was invented in the ninth century, not optimize the explosive in state weaponry until the 1900s, while Europeans in the 1430s were using it to revolutionize siege craft?

Both the Austro-Hungarian Hapsburg and the late Qing dynasties suffered similar slow and painful declines during roughly the same era. Yet the failures of Hapsburg leadership did not keep the rest of Europe from moving forward, while the policy failures of the Manchu leaders, who had established the Qing dynasty, were to set back the development of China by at least a century. What happened? The answers to these questions are found in differences in the network structure of authority that created different paths to state-building. These networks—whether decentralized and broadly distributed, or hub-and-spoke structures—offer clues as to whether a state system will likely show resilience and growth, or calcification and decay.

A systems approach allows us to highlight certain recurrent features in network structure and to determine their importance in shaping the innovation environment. Simple differences of system resilience, caused by variations in the adaptability of differing network structures to change, can help resolve a number of questions about the great divergence of East and West. This chapter will also explore a crucially important property of network structure: the ability to develop and adapt social structures to the accelerations in military technology.

Network Behavior and the Divergence of East and West

In his classic 1992 study of social networks, Ronald Burt assessed the organizational capacity to support effective decision-making. Looking at both *centralized (hub-and-spoke) networks* and *decentralized networks*, he established that the former strengthen the leadership's decision-making capacities.

A centralized network may provide greater opportunities for information access, timing, and monitoring and control, making its management less costly in terms of energy, time, and resources. Fewer redundant contacts increase the efficiency of information flow to the center and require less effort to maintain clusters of influence. This kind of network optimizes effectiveness because instead of maintaining relations with all the spoke contacts, the central decision maker can preserve resources to reward the primary contacts delegated the task of maintaining the total network. The conserved resources can be utilized to expand the network to include new clusters of influence. In sum, a hub-and-spoke network offers its decision maker a competitive advantage over the decision maker in a decentralized network, whose dense connectivity transmits more redundant information that reduces efficiencies (Burt 1992, 17–25).

Common sense would seem to support Burt's conclusions about the advantages of centralized, hub-and-spoke systems. It is easy to assume that network density can impede systemwide coordination, and that the cost and difficulty of maintaining communications between and among potentially large numbers of components would cause both waste and fragility.

However, Burt is only partially correct. A decentralized network comprised of many dense connections is more difficult to supervise and thus may be more prone to disruptive large events. But it can better adapt to a changing environment and is more likely to survive those disruptive events. The vitality of dense networks resides not at a central hub but at the system level. Even if one central router, or hub, is removed, its absence will not be fatal because others can take over.

These system-level properties are what Burt overlooked. A hub-and-spoke network ultimately weakens the system-level properties, making the entire system vulnerable to collapse. Should the center break down, the system may fail. Because the nodes are built to connect to the center, but not to each other, the system will lose cohesion and disintegrate.

This difference in *system resilience* can be illustrated first by the evolution of the European state system after Charlemagne's failed efforts in the ninth century to create a continentwide Christian empire. What emerged instead was a multi-hub structure, an ordering (heterarchy) without a single peak or leading element, although each hub might be dominant at a given time depending on circumstances. The *small-world network structure* of the Europe-wide aristocracy acted as the source of system-wide continuity; in such small-world networks the components (nodes) themselves are not linked, but a small number of connections link most of the nodes to any other. The subsystems, its aristocratic families, could adapt to shock without a loss of systemwide functionality. The system's resilience derived from the density of connections among large numbers of interacting parts.

China, by contrast, was unified in 246 BC under one emperor and remained unified under one emperor until the twentieth century. Its last dynasty, the Qing, lasted from 1644 to 1912. Chinese dynasties came and went, but each new dynasty shared with its predecessors a desire for total central control over the entire cultural space. Early unification no doubt allowed China to achieve much higher levels of commercial integration; more uniform and more advanced technologies, especially for irrigation and textile manufacturing; and higher levels of urbanization than those found in Europe (Pomeranz 2000; Wong 1998). A single written language for all public transactions and an empire-wide system of managers provided the skills of effective public administration to a wider geographic area and to a larger population than in Europe. The periods of territorial sovereignty of the various dynasties, such as the Ming, which lasted 278 years, endured far longer than did any contemporary European polity. This would seem to support Burt's conclusions.

Network Structure and System Resilience

Recent discoveries in the dynamics of complex systems in nature offer a clue to the survival of complex systems in general, revealing properties of networks that were not apparent to Burt (Barabasi 2002; Barabasi and

Bonabeau 2003; Dorogovtsev and Mendes 2003; Ferguson 2013; Jackson 2008; Newman 2010; Newman, Barbabasi, and Watts 2006; Ormerod 2012; Watts 2003). Complex systems in nature share an organizing principle: they are composed of webbed networks that are themselves "embedded" with nodes, some of which have multiple connections to more nodes and hubs of nodes, while others have few links at all. In this sense, any part of the network is a microcosm of the whole. Since there is no intrinsic scale to the nodes, these networks are referred to as *scale-free networks*.

Nature has been ingenious in spinning complex webs that take the form of diffuse scale-free networks. Insect colonies, the immune system, the nervous system, the brain, ecosystems, the weather, oceans, deserts, and biological evolution itself are all examples of scale-free networks that arise through self-organization. Yet they exhibit a degree of robustness because a significant number of components can be eliminated before the system itself will fail.

Scale-free networks can also be human-made. Examples include power grids, airline systems, traffic, and the World Wide Web, in which large disruptive events are to be expected—but because the systems comprise multiple hubs, the networks survive even if a few hubs are randomly knocked out. Adding connections in any network has costs in term of energy, time, and resources needed to maintain connectivity, so human-made systems are never as complex, diverse, or interconnected as those arising in nature (Jackson 2008).

There are also variations of structure and degree among scale-free networks. In China, for example, authority was created by an external organizing principle. The distribution of authority was (and remains) concentrated in a hierarchy, rather than diffused among hubs; the Chinese network model features randomly distributed agents in which the replicator dynamics are centrally maintained. This constrains the transmission path or impact of a single mutation. Nevertheless, the Chinese system still has the small-world properties of scale-free networks. These small-world properties are to be found within the Communist Party elite and include invariance to scale. The extensive, distributed structures of European authority show a much greater resemblance to the scale-free properties of systems found in nature.[1] The remainder of this chapter examines how these differences in social network structure altered the evolutionary dynamics of state-building.

The Network Structure of Social Competition in the West

The European state system, beginning with the dissolution of Charlemagne's empire in 814, evolved without a deterministic, central, or external organizing principle. Over the course of European history, no single national coalition or unified elite dominated the entire space.[2] Advantage shifted from one hub to another, without any one center securing a monopoly on victory; modern Germany's efforts at domination were just the latest in a line of failures. The dynamism of the European state system stemmed from this very weakness of central control.

Diffusion of new weapons technology occurred rapidly in Europe. The adaptation of battlefield technology within one state transferred to the strategies of other states within the system. These feedback loops were tight, like that of the frog and the fly. The fly's legs get longer as the frog's tongue gets stickier. In a similar manner, information within Europe circulated quickly, so that every innovation was quickly parried by a response.[3] Technology change could transform a hub, or add a new one, since no central administrator existed to declare an innovation illegal.

Decentralized economic growth created opportunities for new elite groups like the French parliamentarians, the urban bourgeoisie, and professional associations, such as the Inns of London to coexist alongside feudal control hierarchies. Nonconformist preachers, as well as technologies, such as the printing press, spread ideas that weakened the viability of the central control over ideology by the Church hierarchy.[4] As the economy expanded and new nodes of power and influence made the network structure more diffuse, the European state system became even more resistant to central control.[5]

Yet, the conservative aspects of European social order, characterized by the continuity of elite rule, strike most scholars of European history as noteworthy. In fundamental ways, elite lineages do not seem to have changed over long stretches of time: "the aristocracy successfully maintained its power during all the vicissitudes of three-quarters of a millennium during which almost everything else changed, quite drastically" (Hexter 1961, 19). The British cultural historian and medievalist R. W. Southern concludes that "England, for example, retained its basic governance structure despite radical transformations in technology and in population. The slow emergence of a knightly aristocracy which set the social tone of Europe for hundreds of years contains no dramatic events or clearly decisive moments" (1953, 13).[6] Communications across the continent by intermarried aristocracy ensured that systemwide changes arose abruptly and continuously. This elite continuity persisted over a period of a thousand years because individuals and groups within the aristocracy could adapt to opportunities that in turn caused the system to grow and acquire more resources. The extended, scale-free structure of the systemwide network made the European system robust by endowing it with a capacity for self-organization.

One notices the continuity of law-making, but not a particular law: "The truly formative work of the period was often hidden from the eyes of contemporaries," Southern continues, "and it is doubtless often hidden from ours." The foundational building blocks were laid during the High Middle Ages as order emerged in the wake of slow recovery from the disintegration of Charlemagne's empire after 814: "[t]he pattern of monarchy and aristocracy, at least in their more formal manifestations, of law and law-courts, of parishes and parish churches, are too clearly the work of these centuries for the point to require emphasis" (1953, 13).

So how did the European aristocracy remain intact as a governing class exhibiting both continuity and change? The resilience of a scale-free network can be applied to the European aristocracy, then to the European state system, then back again. The royal houses were hubs within the scale-free system and were scale-free systems in themselves. There were efforts to impose hierarchy among the aristocracy such as the hierarchy of Popes, the Holy Roman Emperor, the anointing of the French King Clovis, but all efforts to establish a European-wide hierarchic ranking of royal houses failed. Europe was highly stratified, but no single lineage or group dominated; a network of loosely connected hubs, with nodes of interlinked noble families, spread from Britain to Russia. The removal of a random prince or duke had little effect on Europe's political organization. The hubs were the princely and royal houses, but the nodes of interlinked noble families did not necessarily follow orders from them.

Technological diffusion that made the growth of new nodes possible was facilitated by the network's scale-free design, which endowed the aristocracy with knowledge of, and control over, opportunities. The aristocracies maintained many avenues of social communication, including intermarriage, but also with the new elites, the parliamentarians, bourgeoisie, and professional associations (Chaussinaud-Nogaret 1970; Richard 1974). Self-organization and distributed authority, rather than human-made cohesion and concentrated authority, prevailed.

The recurrent cycles of innovation that make the European experience unique can be attributed to the small-world characteristics of the competition among the intra-European elite. Europe both encouraged and survived dramatic punctuations caused by the introduction of new technologies or new institutions. The need to embrace innovative technology or be defeated by a rival gave rise to systemwide innovation cycles. Tight feedback among the subsystems enabled the network to adapt to innovation without a loss of system-level functionality. Even when particular dynasties died out or were defeated, system-level resilience was maintained. These properties of European resilience reside at the system level.

Europe's Punctuated Rate of Change: Warfare, Technological Innovation, and the Resilience of the European State System

Evolutionary biologists use the term *punctuated equilibrium* to depict the severe disruption to the global ecology that occurs when a long period of stasis is suddenly interrupted and one set of dominant species suddenly disappears to be replaced by another. This change, at the species level and above, is referred to as macroevolution. Major functional innovations observed in nature, such as the emergence of ears for hearing or eyes for sight, can also punctuate the environment in a macroevolutionary way, changing the rules by which others must play.[7] This is a critical point: punctuation can produce macroevolutionary effects on the system (Gould 1989, 2002, 2007: 58).[8]

A social analogue for the punctuated equilibrium in biology exists in the disruptions to the landscape of the European state system caused by new technology, especially military technology (Hodgson 1996).[9] European military and diplomatic historians have commented extensively on punctuated transitions in European military history—when novel structures arose through cross-system selection. Geoffrey Parker remarks in his military history of the world that "[t]echnological innovation, and an equally vital ability to respond to it," were the distinguishing features of Western warfare (Parker 2005, 2).

The first "punctuation" of Europe's social structure, altering the distribution of resources for maintaining the social order, occurred during the late medieval period and involved innovations in military technology.[10] Medieval warfare was supported by a social contract between one member of the aristocracy, a knight, and his superior in the feudal chain of command. The latter recognized the knight's domination over the manor, the primary means of production, in exchange for military service. Thus the knight held lands in fief from the higher aristocracy. This contract among the elite shaped the social character of the European nobility (Strayer 1970). But the introduction of new weaponry, the longbow and pike, elevated the importance of the common foot soldier and reduced the horse-bound knights' domination of the battlefield.[11]

In the Battle of Poitiers in 1356, a decisive battle of the Hundred Years' War (1337–1453), English infantrymen trained in the use of the longbow defeated the mounted knights of France. By 1360 the infantry revolution helped the English to obtain full sovereignty over one-third of French territory. The French kings responded to the invaders only belatedly and not by arming their own downtrodden peasantry with weapons; they wanted to avoid fomenting class warfare. It was not until 1430 that French cannons made the castle gates and walls of the English indefensible. The artillery revolution overcame the superiority of defense in siege warfare. Between 1449 and 1450, more than seventy English strongholds in Normandy fell. By 1453 the cannons that shattered the castles and fortifications of the English aristocracy on French soil drove the English off of the continent.[12] The French monarchy did not put its cannons to rest but worked to improve their accuracy, range, and mobility. French troops later invaded and aimed their cannons at the walled cities of Italy, ending the independence of the Italian city states and reducing Italy to a backwater of the larger power struggles on the continent.

The use of mobile artillery by the French monarchy was conservative in inspiration, intended to preserve the domination of society by the heirs of the knights. But expanding the organizational makeup of armies had unintended social consequences. Ironically, forging and programming the use of the cannon for the common soldier placed a premium on the skills of the town dwellers, and increased the state's dependence on technically competent urban professionals.

The French monarchy continued to expand its skills at artillery and siege warfare during the early seventeenth century to subdue its own quasi-independent municipalities, like La Rochelle, that derived autonomy from their thick enclosing ramparts. The municipalities were not only quasi-autonomous; many were not Catholic. The educated Protestant merchants and craftspeople of the towns, whose skills had been critical to the development of cannon artillery, eventually became the victims of those very weapons. After France's Catholic kings leveled the fortifications of the urban enclaves the independent, educated business classes associated with the Reformation were eventually forced to convert or leave France in 1685. More than 200,000 chose to emigrate, taking to Holland, England, Switzerland, and the New World the skills in finance and engineering that had facilitated the rise of the French state to preeminence within Europe.

While the French were busy employing cannons within Europe, their rivals started to employ artillery to establish overseas empires. Mastery over the cannon led to mastery over entire peoples, as the weapons were put aboard ships to destroy the fortifications of ancient kingdoms around the world. The period of global European domination and colonialism began in the mid-sixteenth century, when capital ships armed with artillery helped Portugal and Spain establish overseas empires in Brazil, Africa, and Asia (Parker 1996). The seaborne empires established by the English and the Dutch in the seventeenth century were the products of the enhanced naval artillery, as well. Superior naval artillery helped Admiral Lord Nelson defeat the combined fleets of the French and Spanish navies at the Battle of Trafalgar on October 21, 1805. In 1842 British ships armed with canon sent Chinese war junks to their grave in the Yangzi River, allowing the British to gain trade concessions in China. In 1854 the canons on Commodore Perry's ships forced the opening of Japan's ports to American commerce.

Michael Roberts (1956) introduced the term "military revolution" to describe tactical and organizational innovations in "early-modern" warfare, beginning in 1560 and initiated to strengthen monarchical states. The tactical changes in the structure of armies enabled the Swedish armies led by King Gustavus Adolphus (1611–1642) to play a deterministic role in the outcome of the Thirty Years' War (1618–1648).[13] Linear formations of drilled musketeers, dramatically increased the size, scale, and professionalism of the bureaucracies needed to support the troops.[14] The households of the great and mighty were by now transformed into bureaucracies capable of managing the transfer of funds and resources to the provisioning of troops on the battlefield (Elton 1953). Just transporting the bullion to pay the troops on time was a major logistical endeavor.

The military revolution's tactical and strategic implications were most thoroughly embraced by France's Louis XIV (1638–1715), who transformed the resource base of the French monarchy in order to provision, transport, and pay his troops. His streams of victories in the field were largely attributable to his ability to outlast his adversaries because of the managerial systems he established.

According to military historian Clifford J. Rogers, changes in military technology—first the infantry revolution and later the artillery revolution that "altered the paradigm of war in Europe"—had "far-reaching consequences for the resources of social and political life" (1993, 243). As noted earlier, the infantry revolution ended the military supremacy of the knight on horseback, and the artillery revolution emphasized the technical skills of urban middle classes. Nevertheless, the social institutions of feudalism remained intact, even as the technological developments revolutionizing the social order and conduct of warfare nullified the moral and functional justification of those institutions. The full political implications of these developments were repressed until the outbreak of the French Revolution.

The tactical dimension of Louis XIV's inter-European wars during the seventeenth century had an impact on the structure of authority within the kingdom. The nobility's private authority over the peasantry in their fiefdoms was subordinated to the authority of the king's representatives (commissioners), changing the *de facto* distribution of social power without altering its constitutional structure. But the residual privileges (collecting taxes from tenants) of lordship were retained, increasing contempt for the exactions and pretensions.

Meanwhile the monarchy transitioned into the contradictory role of being the font of public authority, as well as the guarantor of the socially antiquated privileges of the feudal nobility. The contradictions of this dual role led to a crisis of legitimacy. The financial and organizational innovations required to mobilize permanent armies elevated the status of lawyers, officials, financiers, and wealthy peasants, all of whom were essential to increasing the state's extractive capabilities (De Tocqueville 1956; Furet 1981).[15] The empowered actors from the lower orders eventually were able to organize and express grievances against the residual powers of the feudal lords.

The repeal of feudal privileges, initiated first by lawsuits, dragged on until the onset of the revolution in 1789. After mutinies in 1791, the army of the old regime led by blue-blooded aristocrats dissolved; almost half of the officer corps were in exile and sided with the counterrevolutionary armies of Austria, Britain, Prussia, and Russia against the French (Archer et al. 2002, 391). The monarch was beheaded on January 21, 1793, altering the basis of state legitimacy within the European system.[16]

The *levée en masse* introduced shortly afterward allowed the revolutionary army to fill its ranks with all single men between the ages of eighteen and forty, and eventually all Frenchmen were conscripted. Mass mobilization was supported by a campaign of nationalist indoctrination that included compulsory primary education and a nationwide propaganda campaign. By 1794 France had nearly 750,000 citizens under arms, with 250,000 more on the rolls, and that army was three times larger than any army fielded by Louis XIV. By 1794 the nobility, which had constituted 85 percent of the army's officers, were left with only 3 percent of the posts.

Merit and seniority became the basis for recruitment to the officer corps. Closing the social gap between the officer corps and the men facilitated a style of decentralized warfare in which the officers and their men fought alongside each other. An army of serfs and mercenaries could not copy the improvement in communication that resulted and transformed the French armies of the revolution into a cohesive force that threatened to overwhelm the capabilities of France's adversaries. Like the infantry and gunpowder revolutions before it, mass mobilization, along with the professionalization of the officer corps, had the macroevolutionary effect of a punctuated change.[17]

Napoleon's 1806 rout of Prussia's army in less than two weeks at Jena and Auerstadt revealed the latter's forces to be deficient in motivation and ability, and at risk of eradication. Only a major societal change in recruitment, training, and command could save France's foes. To improve the core competencies of its military organization, Prussia needed to increase the range of tasks the average soldiers could perform. In September

1807 the Prussian War College was established, and merit appointments ended the nobility's monopoly on entry to the officer corps. Prussia freed its serfs in October of that year and enacted limited municipal self-government the following year. A general staff was installed as a full partner in military decision-making to allow the collective intelligence of the brightest members of the officer corps to counter the tactical skills of Napoleon's corps. After initial reluctance, Prussia's king, Frederick William III, also authorized volunteer battalions, a statewide militia, and formal conscription.

The professionalization of the European state system, beginning with the French Revolution, opened the military to talent regardless of birth and was given its fullest expression by the Prussians. But unlike France, whose revolution came from below and toppled the old order, Prussia saw its change imposed from above to preserve the old order. In sum, the evolution of warfare in Europe reveals a deep, defining characteristic of the European state system—its intensive rate of technological change, driven by the quest for military dominance in a system of dispersed political authority.

Historically, most state systems regress when the centralized control mechanisms are destroyed, usually occurring when the dominant lineage is eliminated. This is the history of China's state system after its dynasties declined. By contrast, in Europe a failure of one lineage did not trigger a systemwide failure. Intra-regime competition among power centers to adapt military technologies and spread them among various social strata created a necessity to invest in the social assets of non-elites. This proved to be a key accelerator of state capacity.

Two Mysteries of European History, One Solution

Our knowledge of network structure and state-building sheds light on two other mysteries of European history. Why did Napoleon risk his army to attack Russia? And why did the English monarchy capitalize on its North American colonies, while the stronger French monarchy lost the opportunity?

Napoleon risked his entire army to subdue Russia in 1812.[18] Did megalomania drive him to such reckless action? This question fascinates diplomatic historians who ask how the greatest military tactician of all time could have erred so completely, risking and losing most of his army, sacrificing all of his prior accomplishments.

In fact Napoleon understood that the command structure of Europe had small-world properties in its networks of royal families, functioning as hubs with connections to subordinate members across the entire continent.[19] Napoleon believed that the only way to preserve the fundamental values of the French Revolution was to destroy this structure in its entirety. If just one hub remained, the revolution would be in jeopardy of reversal.[20] Napoleon was proved correct; a reactionary Russia under Czar Nicholas I became the *gendarme* of nineteenth-century Europe, helping Austrians sustain the Hapsburg emperor by suppressing the Hungarian uprising in 1848. The czar's own empire had a huge Slavic majority, but he identified his interests with the fortunes of a fellow monarch, not with the people.

Napoleon's calculus showed a deep intuitive understanding of the dynamics of scale-free structures. He understood that if the hubs are targeted, all must be eliminated to prevent their comeback. His fear proved correct: the aristocrats regrouped and retook France—and one of these, Prince Clemens von Metternich, foreign minister of the Austrian empire, led the coalition that defeated Napoleon at Waterloo.

The study of social networks helps clarify another question of European history: why did the British, rather than the more powerful and more numerous French, settle North America? One of Europe's great centralizers, France's Louis XIV, missed this system-altering opportunity. Radical Protestants from the British Isles and eventually from all of Western Europe were allowed to settle the British colonies in North America. But the French king barred Protestants from setting up in the French colonies, where stricter doctrinal purity was imposed than in France itself. Louis XIV did not want to give the groups he outlawed in France the opportunity to escape his control by finding a safe haven in the colonies, where they might grow wealthy and increase their independence. He refused to enable economic growth that would have sustained new nodes in the system, preferring to allocate economic opportunities to groups tied into the system of elite exemptions and privileges that the crown could control (Elias 1983; Root 1994).

The radical Protestant dissenters that settled North America ultimately enabled Britain to circumvent French dominance of the New World. But

Britain's monarchs were no more prescient than their French counter-parts; they simply had less direct control over the factions within the population. The more powerful French monarch would not allow devel-opments among his subjects that he could not control.

We see the same pattern followed in both Napoleon's failed strategy for continental domination and France's failure to take advantage of its early lead in the New World and develop the economy, and populate and establish control over its North American acquisitions in Canada and Louisiana. Both made efforts to centralize and control social dynamics by establishing a single hub of command that maintained control over the system. The dynamism of European society followed a different set of principles embedded in the distributed structure of its social networks. Extinguishing the old hubs was never as effective as adding new ones.

Little Germany Fights Big Germany for the Heart of Europe

A convention in contemporary political economy is to presume that elites cede electoral democracy to avoid a graver fate. But this was not the case during the nineteenth century, when state competition in Europe pitted two forms of authoritarianism—one social democratic, the other dynas-tic—against each other. By then the dynamics of European state forma-tion had shifted from the competition between France and England to competition among the states of Central Europe, where the most notable stalwarts of dynastic conservatism, the Austrian Hapsburgs and a socially reformed but autocratic Prussia, battled for leadership. In neither the rise of Prussia nor the decline of the Austrian Hapsburgs does democratiza-tion of political power play a determining role in the formation of the governing institutions.

A generation earlier, Austrian Emperor Francis I (1768–1835) had op-posed widespread reforms to the recruitment system required to match Napoleon's mass mobilization (Goldman and Eliason 2003, 214–15). The Hapsburg rulers of the Austrian empire feared that importing the new patterns of warfare risked also importing values unwelcome in the empire, where the masses viewed Napoleon as a liberator. Ruling over a population comprised of diverse ethnic groups, they were apprehen-sive about providing the population with opportunities to mobilize na-tionalist sentiment against the multiethnic character of the empire. Mass transport and vernacular education were withheld to avoid the dangers of mass coordination. Seeking unity through doctrinal uniformity, the Austrians turned their educational system over to the Catholic Church, which caused a deficit in scientific and technical skills. Deficiencies in literacy and numeracy obstructed Austria's adoption of modern military practices and technology.

After revolutionary violence spread throughout the empire in 1848, the Habsburg rulers continued throughout the nineteenth century to resist universal conscription or open access to military commissions, fearing that discharged soldiers might ignite further popular uprisings, and that returning commissioned officers from minority ethnicities might become ethnic heroes who could lead rebellions. Fear that mobilization in the ranks would lead to mobilization against the empire led the Austrians to keep only enough soldiers at hand during peacetime for routine duties and formal parades. Conscripts were placed on permanent leave and dismissed to their homes as soon as possible after battle, leaving the bulk of the Austrian army poorly trained and undisciplined.

Prussia's military, in contrast, was locally based; organized as *Kreise* (circles). The majority of reservists lived close to their regimental depots so that units could be quickly mobilized and the soldiers would fight alongside their neighbors. Increasing active duty from two to three years meant significantly larger numbers of conscripts were subjected to nonstop training and drilling.[21]

Prussia's societal reforms made it more capable than Austria to adapt the strategic advantages that accompanied industrialization. Its state-sponsored transport capacity provided decisive tactical advantages, and its military strategy was closely linked to its superior ability to transport supplies as needed by the exigencies of warfare. When confronting Austria in 1866, the Prussians could transport two hundred eighty-five thousand soldiers over five railway lines in twenty-five days. The Austrian railway system, which lagged far behind Prussian capacity, significantly hampered military effectiveness. The Austrians, possessing only one rail line despite expansion in the 1850s, could transport only two hundred thousand soldiers in a forty-five-day period.[22]

The rout of Austria in 1866 enabled Prussia to take the lead in the unification of the German states, shifting the balance of power within Europe. Austria's allies within the German states were discredited, and any ambition the Austrians had to be the leader of German unification vanished. The king of Prussia, under advisement of Prince Otto von Bismarck (1815–1898), fathered German unification. Employing a nationalist psychology for mass mobilization, the Prussians "democratized" not the selection or formation of the government, but participation in the army. The German emperor (who was also the king of Prussia) chose all members of the German government until 1918 but placed the state at the service of the people; universal conscription and universal welfare coverage were linked to a program of national industrialization implemented by a merit-based career civil service.

It is perhaps because of their realistic assessment of the threat they faced that a backwater of Europe unified Germany after defeating Austria in 1866 and France in 1871. Prussia's militarized masses were the products of a reform-minded program of social modernization that had begun in 1807 under the auspices of Prince August von Hardenburg and Baron Wilhelm von Humbolt, and fostered mobility into the officer corps and the bureaucracy. Modernization of the political system included granting Jews full citizenship.

Bismarck continued the work of social and political modernization. His creation, the nation-state, was the vehicle to unify the quest for national competitiveness with a capacity for national coordination. It far exceeded the capacity of the multiethnic Austria-Hungary, which was dominated by a minority ruling elite who suppressed the nationalist aspirations of its non-German peoples. While the Germans became citizens of a national state, the Austro-Hungarian empire treated its multiethnic populations as subjects.

The Prussians specialized in technical education as a vehicle for social mobility. By 1875, illiteracy rates among military service recruits in Germany were down to 2.37 percent while they were still 20 percent in France, 10 percent in England and Wales, and 70 percent in Russia as late as 1890. When Germany had attained almost total adult literacy by 1884, the German parts of the Hapsburg empire had reached only 50 percent, and with the exception of the Czech region, which had over 70 percent literacy, the rest of the Slavic regions had under 50 percent, with many regions as low as 10 to 20 percent. By 1883, health insurance was provided to the entire German population, and a state pension was offered to all Germans over the age of 67.

The weakness of the Hapsburg empire was unmasked during World War I, when its inability to stand up against the Russians made it fully dependent on the protection of German troops. Its decline is one historical example among many in which a regime, in the face of threats, does not innovate to parry the thrusts of its rival. Unwilling to risk social and political unrest to become a nation in arms, the empire was dismembered by more socially integrated adversaries. National integration increasingly became the basis for regime legitimacy elsewhere in Europe, but the Austro-Hungarian empire was to die on the battlefield in 1918; the cause of death: failure to establish regime legitimacy on the basis of social integration.[23] That failure caused the Austro-Hungarian capacity for extraction and mobilization to lag behind the nation-states to the west.

The eclipse of the Austrian-Hapsburg empire spanned approximately the same period as the decline of another historical anachronism, the Qing dynasty in China. The decline of both refutes the predictions of contemporary social science that ruling elites will concede democratization only when the alternative is worse (Acemoğlu and Robinson 2000, Acemoğlu and Robinson 2006; North, Wallis, and Weingast 2009). Neither the Hapsburgs of Austria nor the Manchu rulers of China conceded social reform to defer revolution.[24]

The decline of Austria-Hungary can be explicitly linked to the reluctance of the empire's leadership to accept the social prerequisites of modern warfare, causing the empire to fall further behind the rest of Europe.[25] But the failures of Hapsburg leadership did not keep the rest of Europe from moving forward. Even when the individual leaders acted out of local, self-serving interests, the system as a whole exerted a determinative influence causing a convergence to a collective general fitness. These threshold events of punctuated equilibria, changed system-level rules but did not undermine the system's stability and in fact accelerated local capacity-building by magnifying the effects of microevolutionary trends. In contrast, the policy failures of the Qing, like the Austrian-Hapsburg empire, were to set China's development back by at least a century.

China's Transition Syndrome of Dissolution and Renewal

The fall of the Qing dynasty, which ruled China from 1644 to 1912, exemplifies the extent to which regimes will go to resist changes in military organization that could destabilize social, political, and economic structures.[26] Faced with rebellions at home, the Qing were unwilling to risk mass mobilization by putting weapons in the hands of the peasantry and enabling rapid movement via modern systems of transport that could turn against the regime. The decline of the Qing dynasty caused the dissolution of the state system, the retreat of social complexity, and the waning of Chinese culture. It followed the same slow and painful script of the Hapsburg decline.

The collapse of the Qing was also similar in terms of bloodshed to each of the dynasties that preceded it. The Tang dynasty (618–907), widely perceived as the height of classical Chinese civilization, collapsed in blood and carnage after lasting about three hundred years, just as the earlier Han dynasty had collapsed. The period of Tang decline spanned thirty-three years (874–907). Its successor, the Sung dynasty, did not establish stability until 960. The Sung rule ended in 1279, but the Ming did not establish their rule until 1368. The Manchus entered Peking in 1644, but the wars that established the Manchu rule continued until 1683, and the cost could have been as high as eighty million deaths (Finer 1997, 1129; J. S. Lee 1931, 111–63).

Finer notes that in China, "the collapse of each of the great imperial structures ushered in the similar dismal periods of disunion, carnage, warlordism, and court dissension, followed by the predictable barbarian invasion and conquest" (1997, 744). Yet each transition seems an almost perfect replay of a previous one. The new rulers simply refurbished the system of administrative controls and restored the system of centrally administered exams that standardized the rules of public-sector management. The cycle of decay and rejuvenation ended again when total primacy of the center was re-established by control over the appointment, promotion, and dismissal of officials and the recentralization of revenue collection.

A syndrome of "internal disorder, external disaster" (*nei-luan, waihuan*) typically led to dynastic declines. Throughout Chinese history, fiscal capacity was inadequate to defend against interior and exterior threats simultaneously (Finer 1997, 813). The threat of fiscal shortfalls due to the rapacious rule of local gentry or local bandits was a continual source of internal weakness, and like its predecessors, the Qing dynasty did not have the resources to defend both the western borders from nomads while maintaining a navy to defend the east. Every dynasty feared that a diversion of taxes would cause the soldiers to shift their loyalty from the center to the localities. The troubles at home that led to the fall of the Qing Dynasty opened the door to invaders that came from the sea with innovations in armaments that the imperial armies could not match.

The Qing Dynasty came to an end when the last emperor abdicated in 1912 to avoid bloodshed that would deepen China's vulnerability to invasion, but abdication was to no avail; a thirty-seven-year civil war followed. The two factions, the communists and the nationalists, refused to compromise; both believed that only a single party could govern China. Once the communists gained control over the center, they purged society of all loyalties to the old regime, the nationalists, and the remnants of past dynasties. The nationalists had followed the same script during the 1920s and 1930s, when they had the upper hand before the Japanese invasions. The imperial system was eradicated, but the exercise of central authority, once reestablished by the communists, resumed a network structure with many similar features. The script of the Qing decline and fall may explain why the Chinese Communist Party (CCP) today seeks to be as inclusive as possible to ensure that new nodes of power stay within the party, dependent on its patronage and supervision. No wonder Chinese philosophy presumes Chinese history to be circular, a story of ebbs and flows.

On July 14, 1989, François Mitterrand, then president of France, announced on the two-hundredth anniversary of the outbreak of the French Revolution that what had begun with the taking of the Bastille by Parisian crowds in 1789 had finally come to an end. France's blue-blooded nobility were finally no longer in control of the major social institutions. By contrast, no high-ranking member of the Chinese Communist Party is known to trace lineage to the Qing dynasty.[27] When China's dynasties change, they generally try to expunge all linkages to the past: families, organizations, even systems of beliefs that trace their ancestries to a past lineage are expunged; they rarely reemerge. Instead of seeking alliances with the remnants of a previous regime, a Chinese leader prefers separation both from colleagues and from the rest of the nation's leadership.

Thus John K. Fairbank writes of the rise of Mao Tse-tung, "Like an emperor on the make . . . he could have no equals or even confidents. He was already caught in the trammels that beset a unifier of China. If we may look both forward and back for a moment, Mao Tse-tung's rise to power reminds us of the founding of the Han, the T'ang and the Ming" (1986, 235). Moreover he notes, "Since Chinese politics occur in a moral universe, a new regime while coming into power aurally heaps moral contumely upon its predecessor, which had previously of course denigrated its predecessor" (p. 217). Each dynasty consigns its predecessor to history's dustbin.[28]

Control of the Innovation System in China

Between the eleventh and fifteenth centuries, China originated much of the technical knowledge that drove Europe's Industrial Revolution in the nineteenth century. By the thirteenth century, China was governed by a bureaucracy that no European nation could match until the late nineteenth century. Yet a puzzle of Chinese history is why rapid and intensive technological change was so rare in its history. This is sometimes known as the Needham puzzle. China was a "civilization that had held a steady course through every weather, as if equipped with an automatic pilot, a set of feedback mechanisms, restoring the status quo [even] after fundamental inventions and discoveries" (Needham 1969, 119–20). The Chinese rate of technological change was gradual, incremental, and extensive, driven by population growth rather than technology or science (Boserup 1981, 1990). China entered modern times, Fairbank concludes, having "achieved a high degree of homeostasis, the capacity to persist in a steady state" (1986, 50).

Essential to the unity of the Chinese state was the system of centrally administered, standardized exams, which gave the imperial government control over the appointment of high officials down to the county level. Officials selected by the examination process became a select minority initiated into the mysteries of power. The servants of an emperor who himself descended from heaven basked in ceremony and ritual. The social status of the bureaucrats was recognized to be higher than that of the merchants. As perpetuators of heavenly harmony combining Buddhist, Confucian, and Taoist traditions, these mandarins stood above the local gentry in the eyes of a deeply superstitious population. And since the examination system unified the mechanisms and philosophy of governance, the administrators were relatively interchangeable. The examination system allowed the Chinese emperors to establish distinct boundaries that set the apparatus of administration apart from its social environment. The keystone institution, a hierarchical bureaucracy, was established during the Tang dynasty (618–907).

Yet even as centrally controlled education functioned to legitimize the system of controlled governance, ensuring indoctrination, reliability, and homogeneity of rule enforcement, it failed to inculcate functional skills. Modern learning was kept out of the examinations, which until 1905 emphasized artistic and literary culture. This made it difficult for the Chinese to keep abreast of foreign technological innovation or to remedy their deficiency at building firearms.

The continuities of each successive dynasty are always more notable than the innovations, and it can be accurately stated that China was ruled under the same system of regulations for more than 1,200 years. Until the fall of the Qing, the mandarinate was the frame of the entire society, dominating every facet of public and private life from trade and literature to religion (Finer 1997, 764). The central bureaucracy worked with local leaders to identify projects in need of public support, to evaluate proposals for social improvements that came from the local inhabitants, to identify candidates for activities created by government investment, to identify markets for new products as well as products in search of new markets, and most important, to ensure that revenues from the localities were transferred to the center. Nepotism was avoided by dispatching administrative personnel according to the "law of avoidance"—appointments to one's native province were strictly avoided. High returns on social investment allowed China to dominate East Asia, culturally, politically, and militarily for much of the past two thousand years.

But to preserve the network system of central control, China's imperial rulers lost important leads they had over the West in developing military technology.[29] The use of gunpowder, for example, despite its early invention in ninth-century China and employment in bombards and grenades during the twelfth century, was not optimized. It could be used in the manufacture of fireworks, but weapons manufacturing remained under strict central control throughout China's history, even through the last dynasty (Hartwell 1966, 1967; Lin 1995; Needham 1954, 1969). The state held a monopoly over coal and iron, and licensed metallurgy and forge technology, making it difficult for local leaders to develop weapon systems with which they might challenge the center.

Other significant technological innovations, such as the printing press and the compass, would have similarly been thwarted because these keystone innovations could also have precipitated the rise of new social networks. The imperial throne aspired to govern its own possibilities of transformation through a gradual process of accumulating minor modifications (Fairbank 1986, 50). For the same reason instead of exploiting the overseas voyages of eunuch Zheng He, in the 1430s the Emperor banned oceanic voyages to prevent groups like the merchants from acquiring enough wealth to be able to evade centralized control. If this was not enough to discourage future voyages in the 1470s the record of Zheng's voyages were destroyed ending any possibility that the great age of discovery would be Chinese rather than European. Europe's political fragmentation offered options to Columbus when his dream of global voyages was turned down in one corner of the continent; funds were found in another corner (Landes 1998).

Rifles used against renegade Chinese armies were the one Western technology that the Qing rulers immediately embraced. Beginning in the 1860s, after the Taiping rebellion, Chinese officials led armies using Western arms to forestall further rebellion. Possession of foreign rifles gave the dynasty an edge over peasant rebels (Fairbank 1986, 108). During the late imperial period of the 1870s, the Manchus finally accepted the inevitability of industrialization but tried to keep it under administrative control by introducing a system of "official supervision and merchant management." The result was not enough modernization to keep foreigners at bay, but too much independent activity, which stirred the aspirations of new groups at home to be free of the dynasty.

Small degrees of modernization had exactly the social outcome the dynasty feared. The sponsors of textile mills, telegraph companies, financial institutions, and coal and steel complexes eventually formed an alternative source of power, aligning indigenous Chinese industrialists with the spread of foreign influence throughout the last decades of dynastic rule. As the economy diversified, administrative control from the center weakened. Local trade taxes financed regional armies. Movements for revolutionary change could readily enlist frustrated degree seekers who could not find livelihoods suited to their ambitions and ability.

The solution to the Needham puzzle is rooted in China's political centralization, which arrested the forces of macro-systemic change. The exams that recruited the bureaucracy fostered ideological conformity, rendering innovation vulnerable to the dictates of political correctness (Hartwell 1971). The most talented and intellectually gifted were motivated to restrain change that would give rise to new centers of power. Control over social promotion endowed the imperial throne with a loyal group of socially homogeneous senior managers whose promotions depended on the stability of the very institutions that ensured their promotion. The bureaucrats controlled entrepreneurial opportunities, leaving inventors with limited autonomy to diffuse innovations not acceptable at the top. William McNeill explains (1982, 40–41):

Uninhibited linkage between military and commercial enterprise, such as was to take place in fourteenth- to nineteenth-century Europe, would have seemed truly disastrous to Chinese officials. As long as men educated in the traditions of Confucian statecraft retained political authority, such a dangerous confluence would not be permitted. Instead, systematic restraints upon industrial expansion, commercial expansion, and military expansion were built into the Chinese system of political administration.[30]

Thus Chinese history can be characterized by the accumulation of many minor individual variations. Change operated at a microevolutionary level, as in cattle or dog breeding. Local innovations could be scaled up and gradually spread across the entire cultural space. Incremental technological improvements did not alter the properties of the system but led only to qualitative change. China's system of governance reduced segmentation and duplication, and, above all, avoided events that could cause macroevolutionary punctuation and stimulate diversity, disparity, and contingency, the very drivers of European evolution. There were to be no mass deletions of capacity or social strata by abrupt technological transition. The emergence of unwanted novelty was foiled; feedback within the empire was restricted to single-stranded communications between bureaucrats dispatched to the provinces from the center.

Being able to coordinate complex, flexible behavior in response to drastic changes in the system is why Europe, not China, hosted the Industrial Revolution. The Qing dynasty, like those preceding it, had a constant fear of internal disorder and the diffusion of military technology that might enable local entrepreneurs of violence to extort the revenues of the provinces. Evolutionary biologist Stuart Kauffman ventures that modern economic growth results from "takeoffs" in economic systems. Once the system attains a critical threshold, a complexity explosion of new goods and services with exponential impact, can ring out the old and ring in new webs of novelty (1993, 395). Such "avalanches of coevolutionary change" (pp. 370–71) with the catalytic potential to usher in waves of system-transforming innovations could occur in the West, but not in China. China's efforts to prevent the creation of independent clusters of power deprived it of the macroevolutionary stimulus that drove European dynamism.

Japan in between East and West

Before Japan's Meiji Restoration (1868), the elites of East Asia avoided changes in military technology and strategy that would have necessitated a radical transformation of social organization.

But Japanese history does contain a single, brief moment when the diffusion of weapons to non-elites was to threaten the social construction of power. During the late fifteenth century, as the pace of domestic warfare accelerated within Japan, larger armies were employed and this gave a larger role to infantry. Guns had been available since 1543, when the first Europeans arrived, and the Japanese perfected the use of guns and gunpowder during the sixteenth century. For nearly a hundred years, they became expert users of firearms (Perrin 1979). An initial invasion of China was planned and undertaken, which might have stimulated an arms race within Asia, and could have enabled later resistance to European invasions. Regional competition within Asia might have enabled Asia to compete with Europe for global domination.[31]

Instead, Shogun Tokugawa Ieyasu seized control over a fragmented and warring Japan in 1600, unified Japan under a stable dynasty, and ushered in what has become known as the Edo period. He ordered the segregation and eventual expulsion of European traders and missionaries in 1603, and closed the country to foreigners in 1636. A return to more primitive weaponry followed from the same conservative instinct. Japan's armies put down their guns and reverted to the use of swords in the seventeenth century, realizing that while it was less costly to train and equip infantry for the use of firearms than to provision a samurai warrior with armor and years of training, the diffusion of firearms would trivialize their class privilege to bear swords. Equipping the infantry with firearms had democratized warfare and made it more pervasive, causing many

more casualties and threatening to annihilate the smaller samurai population. "Japan was disarmed in order to create a strong central government
without fear of rebellions and at the same time preserving a sharper distinction between samurai and farmer" (Archer et al. 2002, 212).

The shogun, who was technically subservient to the emperor, exercised
control over potentially rebellious nobility, turned samurai warriors into
courtiers and administrators. [32] To restrain the forces of disintegration,
the Japanese emperor required vassals (*daimyo*) to keep wives, children,
and household officials in the capital throughout the year. Japanese feudalism was far more centralized than European feudalism.[33] No single
ruler with continent-wide authority like Lord Tokugawa Ieyasu had ever
prevailed in European power struggles. His shogunate (1600–1867) was
more or less in the same time period as the Qing dynasty (1644–1912).
But because political power and central control were exercised through
the reinforcement of its feudal hierarchy, Japanese subjects did not enjoy
the same degree of social mobility that Chinese subjects enjoyed under
China's bureaucracy and examination system. And an important difference with Europe was that a Japanese vassal could serve only one lord; an
individual could not serve two masters or be the lord in one domain but
a vassal in another. Cohesion was vertical, the system lacked horizontal
dynamics, and every inhabitant was subject to a superior without the possibility of horizontal appeal, up to the very summit of the social pyramid.
Nevertheless, centralization enabled both the Chinese and the Japanese
emperors to control the internal diffusion of military technology.

For the next two centuries, Japan was closed to transactions with the
outside. The appearance of Commander Perry's ship in January 1855, black
with eighteen modern cannons, woke the Japanese from their self-imposed
slumber. By that time, they had no knowledge of modern weapons. It was
long forgotten that they had even gone from guns back to swords.

The "restoration" of 1868 under Emperor Meiji inaugurated a period
of social innovation employing bureaucracy to serve the emperor in the
process of modernizing the polity. Embracing new industrial technologies,
Japan rearmed its population, ended two centuries of self-imposed isolation, and replaced the samurai system, based on prowess, with a massive
army, based on technology and discipline.[34] A general staff drew up war
plans that integrated civilian and military preparedness. War determined
by technology required drilling and long-term service.

While Japan reverted to guns to face the European threat, China turned inward. Having experienced the fourteen-year Taiping rebellion that almost ended dynastic control over many regions, the Qing emperor feared putting arms in the hands of a population that might use them to overthrow the dynasty. Concerned primarily with internal control to protect itself from internal enemies, the dynasty became increasingly insular in the face of external threats. Even after the European seizure of Hong Kong and the Japanese seizure of Taiwan, China's emperors resorted to the self-delusion of invincibility, an illusion the Japanese could not afford.

Twentieth-Century Military Activities and State Formation

The incongruous linkage between mass mobilization for war and social welfare in European history extended from the High Middle Ages through the twentieth century. An example not well understood is the tendency of many Western states to adopt progressive taxation after World War I, and its linkage with wartime activity as well.

Conventional wisdom links progressive taxation to the expansion of suffrage. Political scientists Kenneth Scheve and David Stasavage question this wisdom by examining the linkage between the extension of political rights after the First World War and progressive taxation (2012). It is conventionally presumed that progressive taxation, which emerged during and after World War I, was instigated by suffrage expansion. They determined to the contrary, that large increases in tax progressivity occurred across the continent despite differences in formal governing structures, even among countries that did not expand suffrage. They conclude the increases were payback for sacrifices on the battlefield: "The conscription of wealth in the form of progressive taxation constituted part of a new social compact in which the mass of citizens agreed to fight, while the rich agreed to bear a higher tax burden" (2012, 530).[35]

The organizational requirements of mass mobilization have been an incubator of other societal processes, and the sacrifices exacted from the population during warfare have expanded popular conceptions of the state's social responsibility and the definition of equity. The extent of resource mobilization required during the wars of Napoleon, or by the first and second world wars, changed the definition of regime legitimacy. The sacrifice of life due to mass mobilization for warfare caused more inclusive definitions of social responsibility to be demanded by those who sacrificed for the war effort. Mass militarization of European society led to a massive redistribution of wealth, prompting greater social investments, especially mass education.

Three of the modern political institutions most essential to the accelerated rise of the modern state in the West—the rule of law, which originally designated the relations between feudal lords and the king; the bureaucracy, which arose to manage mobilization of resources for war; and broad-based taxation—each originated in the context of mobilization for warfare.[36] As wars of elite lineages eventually became wars of the state, non-elite soldiers required greater access to training, education, and mass transportation. The result was more inclusive fitness for the population at large.

Conclusion: A System Perspective to State Formation and Development

The diffusion of authority fostered competition among Europe's aristocracy for acquisition of technology, and led rulers to seek citizen support through concessions of authority to representative assemblies. In contrast, China's centralized structure enabled elites to suppress technology cycles before system-altering effects might occur.

China's more centralized authority structure is more democratic, based on meritocracy. This compels China to deter threats that arise internally, even if doing so creates vulnerability to external threats. Today, as in the past, Chinese officials seek to deter diffusion of technology, as well as social capability that might endanger the leadership.[37]

This difference in social network structure explains an intricate and subtle difference between the two civilizations. These differences between expansive, densely constructed networks that diffuse authority and centralized networks that concentrate it may prove to underlie the critical issues that shape the future of global conflict as the two systems that once held regional dominance now compete to be the source of norms within the system of international relations. What preconditions among smaller systems will determine if they are to fall under the spheres of influence of one or the other?

8

Democracy's Hybrid Architecture

Introduction

The processes by which democracies develop or stabilize do not match the expectations of modernization theory. Few seem to be on a trajectory to mature into anything resembling a liberal democracy. Even stable democracies, such as Turkey, India, or Brazil, share few of the values of the liberal West. These countries and others, such as Iran and South Africa, are already substantial powers that have made the transition to "democracy," but they do not emulate the incumbent democracies on a long list of issues, such as the need for legal protections of self-expression and individual free choice. Have these growing powers adopted different types of democracy, or are they still in "democratic transition"? Will their norms ever align with those of the West?

These variations in trajectory were not anticipated by the first generation of scholarship on what is often called the "third wave" of democracy, the transition from autocracy to democracy in the 1970s and 1980s of some thirty-five countries in Latin America and Asia, along with South Africa and Iran.[1] Beginning in 1974 with the overthrow of António Salazar in Portugal, the wave inspired the hope that democracy was a naturally unfolding process that required no preconditions.

Despite an avalanche of regime change in the third world that brought the advent of elections and the creation of legislatures, judiciaries, free media, civil society, and local governments, it seems that the wait grows longer for a convergence to the global optimum of liberal democracy. In nature few avalanches spread far, and as they travel over a greater range, their depth decreases. Similarly the modern "avalanches" that occurred in the mid-1970s in Spain and Portugal have had less decisive results in their former colonies in Latin America, where the demise of successive military dictatorships occurred without establishing democracy on a solid foundation.

Another distinctive wave spread throughout the communist regimes of Eastern Europe in the 1990s and led to the breakup of the Soviet Union. The first to avalanche, Poland and Hungry, remain far more democratic than the countries that followed. With the exception of formerly communist Central Europe, most of the former Soviet Union remains authoritarian. The fall of the Soviet Union was felt among its client regimes in the Middle East, the Palestinian Authority, and South Yemen, and led as well to the softening of hard-core right-wing regimes in Morocco and Yemen. The end of one-party rule in Europe had repercussions that spread to one-party regimes in sub-Saharan Africa, but the democracies there remain of dubious quality, lacking systems and institutions of accountability. Each avalanche has its particular set of defining characteristics, which are rarely replicated.

When the Soviet monolith disintegrated, democracy theorists unreservedly began to chart the evolution toward democracy of its newly independent republics. "Rather than a thousand shoots blossoming into as many different flowering plants," wrote Francis Fukuyama, "mankind will come to seem like a long wagon train strung out along a road" (1992, 338). Some wagons might get stuck crossing over the mountains, but the road had a single end point.

Confident in the homogeneous evolution of global democracy, the conventional social theory of transition anticipated the risk of authoritarian regression—but not of partial democracy, namely democracy without liberal values. Yet an extensive study of democratic transitions (Epstein et al. 2006, 556) has found that partial democracies "account for an increasing portion of current regimes and the lion's share of regime transitions." Out of the 193 countries Freedom House rated in 2008, 121 were democracies, but the inhabitants in 90 of those democracies were judged to be "non-free," the assumption being that democracy is the antithesis of being non-free. The same year, *The Economist Intelligence Unit*'s Democracy Index rated only 30 out of 167 countries as full democracies, 50 as flawed, and the remaining 87 as either hybrid democracies or authoritarian states.

Thomas Carothers estimates that of the "nearly 100 countries considered 'transitional' in recent years, only a relatively small number, probably fewer than 20, are clearly en route to becoming successful, well-functioning democracies or at least have made some democratic progress and still enjoy a positive dynamic of democratization" (2002). Carothers concludes that most of the transitional democracies are neither dictatorial nor "clearly headed to democracy."

Nevertheless, this failure of democratic consolidation does not presage a return to autocracy any time soon. Regression, it turns out, is also far less likely than originally anticipated. But we don't know why. Little is known about "what prevents full democracies from sliding back to partial democracies or autocracies, and what prevents partial democracies from sliding back to autocracy . . . the determinants of the behavior of the partial democracies elude our understanding" (Epstein et al. 2006, 564–65). Turkey and India, which had elections long before the third wave, cannot be considered transitional. Yet they are still out of alignment with the democratic trajectories of the already industrialized democracies. The expectation that mature liberalism would flow once the building blocks of democracy were laid and electoral rules established fails to reflect the unfolding world of multiple partial democracies, a world in which partial democracy has become the norm.

Disparities in the evolution of global democracy are embodied in the rise of Turkey's democracy, which performed exceptionally well in supporting an open economy during the first decade of the twenty-first century. With several decades' experience reconciling Islam with modernity, Turkey is expected to be the crucial go-between for the West with Egypt, Iran, Syria, and Palestine. However, as the indispensible bridge between the West and Middle East, Turkey's future orientation remains unclear. Democracy still conflicts with authoritarianism, and secular nationalism with Islamic conservatism. Modernization theory has failed to identify the specific characteristics that act as "genetic" triggers and constraints on the behavior of young democracies like Turkey. It presumed that the sources of variation in the early trajectories of emerging and established democracies would eventually cease to influence their future trajectories.

The Paradox of Turkey's Drift from the Liberal West

Contemporary Turkey is the quintessential market state. It trades with all partners, regardless of ideology, religion, culture, or geopolitical alignment

(Kirişci 2009). Yet its transformation to an open economy is also a key example of the failure of the liberal internationalist perspective to explain significant global trends. Turkey's trajectory toward an open economy began during the 1980s under Turgut Özal, the prime minister (1983–1989) and later president (1989–1993), as leader of the center-right Motherland Party (ANAP). In its dash for growth across the four decades, Turkey has embraced privatization and economic openness with a vengeance, with trade increasing from 17 percent of GDP in 1980 to roughly 50 percent in 2010. A severe financial crisis in 2001, caused by weaknesses in the banking and public debt sectors, resulted in reforms that helped restore confidence in Turkey's expanding role in an open global economy.

The West assumed that a liberal trading economy and prosperity would ease Turkey's transition into the liberal world order as it came to share the conception of international society with its trading partners to the west. Yet rapid economic growth is not producing parallel social modernization in Turkey and does not align Turkey with liberal internationalist objectives. Its liberal market orientation has not resulted in a rapid convergence toward Western views on judicial independence, human rights, separation of church and state, regulatory transparency, or checks on the power of government. Turkey's recent history, then, presents a puzzle. Turkish political scientists E. Fuat Keyman and Berrin Koyuncu write:

> The last two decades have brought about a fundamental change in Turkish modernity, and have also created a "paradox" in Turkish society, a paradox that has not yet been solved. This paradox finds its meaning in the simultaneous development of the "increasing dominance of economic liberalization" in economic life, whose laws of motion are, to a large extent, dictated by economic globalization that is the economic logic of Western modernity, and the emergence of the politics of identity/recognition that has taken different forms, such as the resurgence of Islam, the Kurdish question, and the liberal claims to rights and freedoms, all of which have become powerful actors in Turkish social and political life. In other words, the formation of Turkish modernity since the 1980s has been increasingly marked by the co-existence of economic liberalization and the resurgence of traditionalism and its appeal to the "return of authenticity." (2005, 108–109)

New trade linkages have redefined Turkey's national identity, paradoxically giving it a more local perspective. Visits by businesspeople to the Middle East and Central Asia to rediscover their cultural heritage develop into opportunities to expand trade. Turkey's successful integration into global trading networks has roused the country's intellectual elites, the Westward-looking modernists, as well as the traditionalists, to affirm their commitment to Islamic identity and culture. This religious awakening goes strongly against the grain of modernization theory, which presumes that as a culture embraces commercialization, religion will become a matter of personal choice, a consumer preference like any other. The belief that gratification of economic and physical security will lead to greater emphasis on self-expression does little to explain Turkey's trajectory.

The awkwardness of Turkey's fit into the global liberal order and the tensions between Islamic and secular factions is exemplified by two complementary but separate components of the modern Turkish conservative movement: first, the Gülen movement (named after its founder, Muhammed Fetullah Gülen), the largest and most influential religious movement in that country,[2] and, second, the Justice and Development Party (*Adalet ve Kalkınma Partisi*, or AKP), which is openly tied to Islam and which has won three consecutive national elections since 2002.[3]

The Gülen movement, which took hold in 1970s, is an alliance of schools, universities, financial institutions, labor unions, charities, newspapers, and radio stations, with no formal organizational structure. In Turkey, Gülen has three hundred schools, and worldwide, it funds at least a thousand affiliated institutions with more than two million students who obtain their education with resources from the movement. As an intellectual and cultural force in Turkey, the Gülen movement has no precise membership but can count on as many as eight million followers, notably students, journalists, businessmen, and professionals. Gülen has also established schools in the West, including more than one hundred thirty in the United States. Gülen seeks to influence not only the Turkish population but also Muslims throughout the world. Through education the movement aims to create a new global middle class with an Islamic focus. It seeks to integrate Western sciences and economic efficiency with Islamic ethno-cultural identity, and to train a modern commercial and scientific Islamic elite. This will require reconciling the profit motive with the ethical standards and cultural values of traditional Islam. While the movement's origins are nationalistic, its founder lives in the United States, where he feels safe from persecution by secular, right-wing nationalists. The nationalists accuse him of using the shield of US power for protection while waiting for the eclipse of liberalism and the end of America's global cultural hegemony. They warn of the movement's megalomaniac aspirations, which they claim it shares with the AKP to assume stewardship of the world as the West falls into decadence and decay. The movement's ambitions do match those of the AKP, in which it also wields considerable influence.

Both the AKP and Gülen try to harmonize change with continuity and provide sociopsychological security to uprooted rural populations. They most definitely do not seek conformity with Western institutions, but they do claim to seek to create ethical, law-abiding societies that anchor the actions of powerful local actors to communal values. They aim to confront the patronage brokers of the republican right who collaborated with global interests to acquire vast wealth, demanding that crony capitalists comply with the obligations of the community.

While Recep Tayyip Erdoğan, AKP's founder and leader, was convicted and imprisoned in 1999 while mayor of Istanbul for being a threat to the republic and its secular constitution, he realized that the business community could only be won over if the conservative Islamic movement could be seen to align itself economically and politically with the West, and in particular with the United States. Having begun his political career as a religious conservative trying to end the secular state, Erdoğan began to formulate a strategy for long-term political power—to unite the only two social forces in Turkish civil society that had an institutional identity: religion and business. These alone among civil society groups were permitted to organize during the sixty years of military/republican rule, and the two groups had grown increasingly distant from each other during the modernization of Turkey under the aegis of the Atatürk's Republican People's Party.

To avoid the fate of earlier Islamic parties, Erdoğan broadened his base to include the restless, economically frustrated middle class (former Prime Minister Necmettin Erbakan's Welfare Party was the first Islamic party to win a national election in 1995 but was driven out in 1997 by the military, which supports separation of church and state). After sweeping nearly two-thirds of the seats in Parliament in the 2002 general election, the AKP became Turkey's first single-party government in nineteen years and proved that religion could both replace nationalism as an ideological tool to mobilize dormant and alienated populations, and to offer a platform to consolidate power. AKP has continued to deepen its social base by spreading the economic benefits of liberalism in order to take under the party's wing other previously marginalized segments of the population, including defenders of Kurdish minority rights and opponents of military intervention in politics.

The two movements, AKP and Gülen, are part of a greater shift toward conservatism; they are the results of tensions within Turkey, but not the cause of them. They arose because of two entirely unrelated "trends." The first was the massive internal migration that began in the 1950s and brought with it a cultural shift. Tahire Erman writes: "The 1980s and 1990s were the years when society realized beyond doubt that not only could rural migrants/*gecekondu* people rapidly jump up to a higher economic stratum, but they could also shape the city by creating their own ways of life and sets of values that were different from those of the modernizing elites" (2001, 987). Former squatters who inhabited the shantytowns of the major cities preserved their own culture even after they moved out. This was contrary to expectations, Erman explains, because the "dominance of modernization theory in the West at the time highly influenced Turkish scholars who, by and large, believed in the modernization of the country following the Western experience. Elitism and the top-down nature of Turkish modernization, as well as the early Turkish Republic's emphasis on the premises of enlightenment and positivism, also played a role in the attractiveness of modernization theory for Turkish intellectuals. Under the influence of this theory, Turkish scholars expected the assimilation of rural migrants into the modern urban society" (p. 985).

The republican nationalists who dominated Turkish politics from 1923 to 2002, when the AKP came into power, offered no easy transition to a secular democracy for the poorer and less educated migrants. Indeed they blocked the formation of the left-center social democratic parties like those in Western Europe that could have championed secular responses to the insecurities of newly mobilized populations. Politicized Islam filled the vacuum, offering a way out of this impasse. It flourished in the enclaves in which the rural poor were clustered, and when they became the up-and-coming middle classes as result of economic growth, they drove the traditional Westernized elites from their dominant position in Turkish society.

Democracy and the Opening of Turkey's Capital Markets
Turkey's political polarization and deep social divisions are exemplified by the clash between the younger, conservative, Islamic movement and

older, republican, nationalist movement. That rift is as old as the founding of the Turkish republic under Mustafa Kemal Atatürk. To understand why these tensions exist and why Turkey's society and culture have not converged toward Western norms, one must know how the Turkish conservative movement gained strength as an unintended consequence of the repeated financial mismanagement of the right, which led to balance-of-payment crisis and the bitter pill of IMF reforms that forcefully opened the capital markets.

The cold war decades had allowed both the West and Turkey's secular, center-right ruling elites to justify crony capitalism and political repression as a means for coping with the geopolitical risks of communism. By the same logic of the period, macroeconomic mismanagement was chalked up to the exigencies of protecting the homeland against external threat. The republican establishment was illiberal both in political and economic terms. Oddly—or not so oddly, in light of who benefited—credit repression and political repression went hand in hand. Citing fears of communism, the government was also reluctant to grant authority to elected parliamentary representatives. To this day, the Turkish Parliament plays a weak role in both policy-making and executive oversight.

Access to loans from abroad allowed the government to avoid its obligations to maintain stable domestic prices and orderly capital markets. Institutions thus had reduced ability to hold the leaders accountable for fiscal excesses. In contemporary parlance, the "bond market vigilantes" were toothless. The financial system under the long rule of the Kemalists was a hybrid of public and private institutions that suffered from significant volatility and repeated breakdowns. Hyperinflation and balance-of-payment crises (in which the central bank ran out of foreign exchange to pay the country's bills) occurred in every decade during the second half of the twentieth century. During the cold war decades Turkey became a frequent visitor to the IMF's emergency room. But its role as a frontline state in the battle against global communism afforded Turkey decades of considerable forbearance.

In 1980, a severe balance-of-payment crisis forced Turkey to devalue the lira, and under pressure from international lenders, the government liberalized trade, investment, and finance. Beginning in 1984, Turkish residents were permitted to hold assets in foreign currencies. Full liberalization of the capital account, the end of controls on converting lira to other currencies, followed in 1990. But the bad fiscal habits that had been treated with forbearance by Turkey's geopolitical allies proved hard to unlearn: government budget deficits persisted and the economy fed on unsustainable flows of foreign financial capital. Inflation went untamed, averaging 50 percent during the 1980s and 80 percent in the 1990s.

When the external threats represented by the communist world waned, Turkey's illiberalism suddenly stood out, especially its weak protection of human rights and freedom of speech and assembly; and *realpolitik* was no longer an adequate excuse for political repression. Islam reentered politics in the early 1980s under Prime Minister Turgut Özal, who was the first Turkish head of state to perform the *hajj* to Mecca. He initiated trade and finance reforms that resulted in the creation of a specifically Islamic business network (in a country that had effectively made secularism a state religion). The domestic debt market he created offered opportunities for business and integrated the rural migrants into urban society.

The emergence of a new business class changed the domestic political landscape as it enabled a larger percentage of the population to engage in trade and finance, and empowered a large interest group, religious Muslims, to increase its voice in national politics. Tahire Erman (2001, 9–10) explains, "Once marginal, they had become an indispensable component of the economy, . . . the shanties they once lived in were replaced by relatively well-built single-family dwellings," changing the position of the newcomers in the city. They began to challenge the center-right coalition and secular republican synthesis that had allowed a Turkish nation to emerge from the ruins of the Ottoman empire. An alliance of Islam with pro-business interests, especially the business elite in the nation's capital, which had been moved from Istanbul to Anatolia by Mustafa Kemal Atatürk decades earlier, ironically helped initiate the collapse of the center-right. It remained for the APK to integrate this group into the political process. The opening of the economy led to an Islamic end because, to become a full-fledged member of the European Union, Turkey had to increase its democratic credentials by ensuring European standards for free and fair elections.

The paradox of Turkey's modernization is that IMF reforms opening the financial system did lead to democracy, but not to the kind of democracy the West had in mind. In Turkey, democracy produced a growing Islamic-focused polity and an idealization of its past as the center of a multiethnic Islamic empire. Prosperity and globalization have also produced a renewed consciousness of the Ottoman empire's glorified past. In that idealized past, a Turkish empire that reached from Azerbaijan to Spain had the political and military capacity to protect the faithful. This newfound self-confidence has led Turkey to reevaluate its ties with the West. Rather than seeing themselves as a mistrusted population on the edge of Europe, Turks increasingly see their future at the center of a revitalized, democratic, and progressive Middle East, where they can be their own masters. This is a far cry from the cold war era, when there were two systems and global security concerns shaped Turkey and allowed its military to play a preeminent role in setting geopolitical and domestic priorities. Pride in that past may well eclipse Turkey's self-identity as a secular nationalist republic, allowing the government to lift the ban on headscarves in public, mandate religious education for Muslims, and vet candidates for state employment by their religious affiliation.

Does democracy represent the "end of history" for AKP's followers, or is it just a means to an Islamic end? Since his third victory at the polls in 2011, Erdoğan seems less disposed than earlier to respecting human rights or religious freedom. His government has brought charges of treason against political opponents, journalists, generals, and student activists. And critics allege that lists of new candidates for state offices and academic professorships are vetted for applicants' religious affinities. Indeed many worry that he meant what he said when he quipped that "democracy is like a bus—once we reach our stop, we'll get off."

Yet the AKP is still very much the champion of modernity. Its leaders embrace industrial policy, sitting down with Turkey's private industry to link private investment strategies with national priorities and helping Turkish business enhance its competitive position in the global economy. To expand its social appeal the party also works closely with the masses, establishing women's and youth organizations.

The party's stated if not always practiced commitment to democracy and its geopolitical alignment with NATO seem to support the liberal internationalist thesis that open trade will produce open regimes. But it is not happening the way those who believe in the end of history expected. Turkey keeps its strategic alignment with the West while its cultural identity and trade shift eastward. Not deviating far from the Western alliance allows Erdoğan to pursue his larger goals of combining Islam with modern management and wealth creation to make Turkey the hub of a revitalized Middle East.

As a moderately conservative force, Erdoğan's AKP can legitimate change and material progress, as its name, Justice and Development, implies. The AKP's success at developing an inclusive coalition, bridging the gap between issues of social equity and those of economic growth, shares one fundamental feature with China's Communist Party: both have used liberal economics to consolidate social and political goals aligned with national history and deeply rooted cultural norms. Their success at economic management will cast a long shadow over future political development. Even groups like Turkey's business conglomerates or Taiwanese investors in China that oppose the regimes' core beliefs are impelled toward cooperation by the expectation of continuous future interactions.[4]

The conservative, communal leanings of Middle East populations have been duplicated elsewhere in states with burgeoning upwardly mobile populations. And a new type of populist leader—Thaksin Shinawatra in Thailand, Hugo Chávez in Venezuela, Evo Morales in Bolivia, and Mahinda Rajapaksa in Sri Lanka—have each stoked populist conceptions of national identity and promised to chart courses more aligned with popular interests and tastes. South Asia, too, is a battleground of competing truths and ideologies, pulled both East and West. The Western-trained post-colonial elites in Pakistan, Nepal, Sri Lanka, and even India are losing status in favor of populist leaders who assert that first world models stymie indigenous transformation. They are increasingly unable to win even local elections or establish electoral consistencies, and frequently hold ground only in technical ministries, such as finance and planning.

Liberal internationalism assumes that lesser members of a trading network will imitate the behavior and rules of their dominant trading partners. This may turn out to be a miscalculation. Trade routes themselves are changing. Globalization is perpetuating the "rule of variety," diverting resources away from globalized elites into the hands of traditional communities that seek their own synthesis of modernization.

Turkey's evolution since World War II suggests that new regimes will not play by the West's rules just because they are democratic. Its recent trajectory suggests that the liberal world order is being transformed by unanticipated, complex change processes. Turkey's rise is also a harbinger of a new reality, one in which emerging economies can adopt the methods of growth used in the West without adopting Western values or foreign policies. Its experience suggests that the regime changes forced by the Arab Spring are not likely to lead to liberal convergence, either. Rather, democracy in the Middle East restores cultural values that are likely to be as alien to the West as those exhibited by the previous generation of unelected autocrats. The religious movements that thrive in the Middle East will rewrite the narrative of contemporary world history in terms vastly different from those imagined by liberal internationalists (Trager 2011).[5] This can lead to misunderstanding on both sides that could magnify mistrust and frustrate reconciliation, leading to an unvirtuous cycle of populist, nativist backlashes in both the West and in Turkey.

The Bifurcation Point for Turkey

The ultimate source of Turkey's bifurcation, and of its political polarization and deep social divisions, has been identified, but with the accompaniment of considerable controversy and a firestorm of discussion. That bifurcation point predates the creation of the Turkish Republic. According to Turkish historian Kemal H. Karpat (2001), it resides in a social learning algorithm in which change is explained as God-ordained. The discourse used to represent the human's relationship to the structure of the physical and metaphysical world diverged from the Western discourse, with which it had once been entwined. Islamic thought did not require the rigor of a system of proofs grounded in human logic, and instead attributed social change to divine will. Karpat explains that rulers in the Middle East disseminated a social philosophy that resorts to divine will without linking cause and effect as a deliberate means to perpetuate the social hierarchy.

Historically, Muslim societies have always changed, but the intellectual assessment of such change—that is, the rational search for its causes—seldom, if ever, properly linked cause and effect. Everything was attributed to divine will, thus avoiding the internalization and understanding of change and the search for corresponding means to cope with its effects. Simply put, the concept of a divine and immutable social order was invoked by practically all ruling Muslim elites in order to perpetuate their own economic and political supremacy, using Islam to legitimize it. (2001, 6–7)

What happened to whole schools of Islamic philosophical thought and study that flourished in the early history of Islam? Early Muslims read Aristotle and studied astronomy. Surely in philosophical circles and theological debates there were discussions about science, nature, and the natural order of things. Karpat does not explain where this huge difference between Islamic and other philosophical schools comes from. Muslim societies are not unique in believing that divine will governs human society even in the face of free will. Even in Judaism, free will is merely a test of faith. The philosophical bifurcation between Turkey and the West must lie in the relationship between secular authority and religious authority. The politicization of Islam caused the melding of secular and religious realms giving Islam and the West different complexity profiles.

In Turkey religion has a long history of being under state control. Atatürk's concept of Turkish laicism placed faith under the control of a ministry of religion, an institution that today is called the Presidency of Religious Affairs. The goal is to enable the state to direct the Islamic understanding of the people. The differences in their political relationship will continue to be a source of tension between Turkey and other Middle Eastern/Muslim states as well as those of the West. The existance of this institution within the state politicizes religion and compels religious groups to target capture of the state in order to control the religious beliefs of the population.

The Source of Variation: The European Awakening

Sensitivity to initial conditions causes bifurcations, minor variations at the beginning that produce large variations at the end. Bifurcations cause lineages to diverge, despite sharing a common ancestor. Differences in development trajectories are the results of bifurcations. In the following section we examine points of bifurcation that influenced the subsequent trajectories of Western Europe and East and Southeast Asia.

Democratization arose in the social systems of the West but was not in those systems' original organizing specifications. So what patterns of collective learning and knowledge transmission were critical to Western Europe's divergence from its tribal past?

No development in European history can "compete in permanent importance with the embracing of Aristotelian logic in the eleventh and twelfth centuries" by philosophers and leaders of the Roman Catholic Church (Southern 1953, 11).[6] Logic became the grammar of law and politics. It steered religious thinking in Western Europe toward reasoned proofs of the role of the divine in human affairs. Latin Christendom inculcated collective learning by the use of logic across political divisions within Europe. The medieval revival of logic, through its diffusion into philosophy, theology, and statecraft, eventually defined the routines of both secular and monastic communal life and organization. Logic narrowed the appeal to the supernatural. It gave order to the chaotic world of nature and politics, making systematic thinking about nature possible, and contracts between men and women the subject of human will, discretion, and agency. It rendered both the sacred and secular worlds tractable to human thought and intervention. The documents and chronicles of Western European statecraft and law embraced Aristotelian logic as early as the twelfth century. The Church banned trial by fire in early thirteenth century in response to the growing rejection of trial by ordeal by individuals (Becker 1982, 1988). Governments began to rationalize their functions using logic to solve problems, rather than resorting to charisma or to divine intervention.

Logic imposed the artificial products constructed by the human mind. It entails recourse to the human skill of creating the artificial. Thus the European state appealed to human design rather than to nature-made order. Secular leaders, for example, who cloaked themselves in the divine and spoke of miracles, hoping to make their authority immune from argument, exposed themselves to great risks of exposure and rebellion.

Law and politics, along with grammar and rhetoric, were among the areas most strongly affected by the pervasiveness of logic, as complex relationships between the ruled and their political masters ultimately came to be expressed in chains of syllogisms that helped transform the privileges of the aristocracy into codified rights. When Chrétien de Troyes in 1170 wrote that the highest learning (logic) had now come to France, enabling it to surpass the civilization of the ancient Greek and Romans, logic had only begun to shape the transmission of knowledge. Over successive centuries, logic continued to give rhetorical shape to the instruments of the state—its legal and fiscal reach over the population, its definition of property, and its preeminent role in defining the crown's subjects' rights of property. It is essential to the statement by French political philosopher Jean Bodin concerning the sovereign's obligations to citizens (1606), and to the *Leviathan* of Thomas Hobbes (1651).

Deductive reasoning supported by logic allows information and meaning to be conveyed in terms of a future orientation. This engendered in rulers an increasing capacity to channel resources into deferred gains that over hundreds of years produced states capable of managing a wide range of risks faced by the population (Migdal 1988). A state can win over the hearts and minds of its population when people know that allegiance to the state will mean better lives tomorrow. Logic also provided the tools of risk management, giving people the confidence to act as free agents. Aristotelian logic allowed European populations to form social associations and culture entirely of human design.

Other conceptions of social order, like Hinduism, with its ideas of social unity and caste, relegate social order to natural forces, which allows social utility to be compromised in the name of divine order. Where nature, rather than reason, is accepted as the principle for social organization, the frontiers of what is humanly possible will not be attained. Human agency will not develop to its fullest capacity. In contrast, the development of logic allowed Western thinking to view society as human artifact. Although one can point to the separation of church and state is a significant bifurcation between European society and others, as this chapter is demonstrating, it is far easier to describe the initial conditions than to determine a point of bifurcation.

Initial Conditions: Democratic Legitimacy in North America

The initial conditions that gave rise to the United States as a nation contrast with the antecedents of states in Western Europe with regard to the democratic legitimacy of the state. In the United States a basic framework of rights for subsequent economic growth was established before industrialization.[7] Property rights were widely distributed when they were established in the Constitution. The rights of corporations were established with reference to their public service; only later did they acquire profit-maximizing goals. Contractual relations were defended in courts, which compelled the government to honor its agreements a commitments that was memorialized in the charter of the first Bank of the United States founded in 1791. Democratic values shaped the legal doctrines that became the foundation of government and business relations.

Democracy was grounded in law long before the authority of the federal government had the capacity to reach into the lives of citizens. This is in sharp contrast to Europe and the developing world today, where a democratic mindset is generally the *end product* of nation-building. Laws in these regions originated to protect aristocratic or autocratic privilege; it was *bureaucratic* authority, not legal authority, elsewhere in the world that laid the foundations of democratic expectations and obligations.

Initial Conditions: Bureaucratic Stability in East Asia

East Asia's "initial condition" was an ancient cognitive tradition inculcated in the population through religion, but unlike religion in Europe and North America, religion in East Asia became a part of the state. Confucianism originated in China and derives its name from a Chinese scholar reputed to have been born in 551 BCE and to have lived in an eastern province of the country. Confucian thought laid the ethical foundations that would later be developed into practical implications for a philosophy of statecraft. It underwent codification and reorientation from the eighth century onward, and culminated in the work of the scholar Zhu Xi in the eleventh century. Confucianism spread to Korea, Japan, and eventually Vietnam, and is the cornerstone of Sinitic civilization.

Confucian humanism shares an important similarity with Aristotelian logic: its doctrines are human-made. It did not claim a supernatural sanction but was called into being by the state (Finer 1997, 821). Like the logic in Europe, Confucianism "pervaded society with a code of social, moral, and civic norms, a pattern to conform to, a metaphysic and cosmology" (p. 811). It initially justified a hierarchical social structure, defined the virtues of loyalty and obedience in moral terms, and required conformity with that morality by both the ruled and the rulers. Like Aristotle's logic, its elasticity as an overarching cultural heritage extends to the present. China has undertaken an effort to reconcile socialism with Confucianism to unify China's cultural history.

A critical difference was that unlike Christianity, which arose from outside the state, Confucianism arose from inside and has always been subordinate to the state, even as it became the basis upon which a state-controlled bureaucracy was constructed. Confucianism based morality on innate virtue rather than rule observance. It is perhaps for this reason that the rule of law does not stand as an independent pillar of political order in East Asia. Nor does the rule of law define East Asian thinking about social responsibility.

The Chinese and Japanese emperor embodied all state institutions, being the head of religion, the realm's high priest, chief warrior, and head of the state. Emperor and state were one, no independent legal realm protected by a powerful and independently funded institution ever emerged to ensure the integrity and independence of justice (Fukuyama 2011). The functions of justice were vested in administrators, but the source of justice was the emperor.

The persistence of Confucian thought has played an important part since the 1960s in the economic trajectories of East Asia's neo-Confucian polities of Japan, South Korea, Vietnam, Singapore, Taiwan, and Vietnam. It helps us to understand how the region's autocratic leaders were able to provide credible commitments even without recourse to a body of commercial law enforced by an independent judiciary.

East Asian regimes have ensured a functioning public sector without worrying about whether the law established it. A strong and independent bureaucratic capacity made state-led industrial policy credible (Campos and Root 1996). The enforcement of rules for meritocratic recruitment and promotion embedded the bureaucracy in the broader society and protected the regulatory hubs of the government from capture by business elites (Evans 1997). Rules of conduct and promotion that limited interference in the performance of governmental routines kept the business elites in line with priorities set by central planners (Evans 1997; Maxfield and Schneider eds. 1997; Root 1996). Without confidence in bureaucratic rule enforcement, the personal rule of authoritarian leadership would have deterred investors who feared executive discretion. As a result East Asian societies have experienced explosive growth without a legal system to protect property rights, and they experienced private-sector investment to a far greater extent than most other developing economies from the 1960s to the 1980s.

Nevertheless, the weak status of law raises two sets of institutional conundrums concerning the future of democracy in East Asia. What will happen when legislative powers over the bureaucracy are expanded, but a weak rule of law will not hold elected officials accountable? How can the financial credibility of the newly emerging legislature be strengthened, and how can the incentives to provide public goods and take responsibility for social welfare be guaranteed?

Are the regimes of East Asia likely to become liberal democracies, or will they remain hybrids? Will they develop independent institutions that can hold executive authority accountable to a rule-based framework overseen by an independent third party?

Initial Conditions: Language Diffusion in Japan and South East Asia

The selection pressure for language uniformity may be a useful proxy for understanding collective learning processes. Populations adapt a unified language to surmount common ecological risks, according to work of linguistic ethnographer Daniel Nettle (1999).[9] Case studies of language diffusion in Africa allow Nettle to offer two hypotheses: "The greater the ecological risk, the fewer the languages there will be in a country of a given size . . . and . . . [t]he greater the ecological risk, the fewer languages there will be in a country of a given population" (p. 83). Cooperative action to overcome ecological adversity creates a common interest in speaking the same language.

Nettle's ideas about language diffusion might help explain the evolution of modern states among the island nations of East Asia, where Japan, the first modern-nation state in the region, developed a national language long before other island communities that span East and Southeast Asia. Not all Pacific Island populations share traditions of coordinated risk management and therefore did not develop the need to possess a national language. Japan's southern neighbors, the Philippines and Papua New Guinea, do not possess national languages. Nor does subsistence-rich Indonesia, an island nation comprised of numerous sub-ecologies that have little interdependence and limited connectivity. Interregional trade was minimal; access to a variety of local food sources allowed each sub-ecology within Indonesia to attain relative self-sufficiency.

Deep-sea fishing is not a livelihood common among Indonesia's populations, either. Perhaps the tendency for some societies to develop cultures of deep-sea fishing reveals the same logic as that of developing a unified language. Living on an island surrounded by the sea is not enough to nurture norms of cooperation sufficient to create a society of deep-sea fishing people. Indonesians live on thousands of islands but are land-focused; they get most of the food from the land and from fish on the shoreline. Their collective identity places little emphasis on deep-sea fishing.

Papua New Guinea, along with the Indonesian province of Irian Jaya, is divided into numerous self-sufficient social groups that have more than nine hundred distinct language groupings.[10] Because of continuous rainfall, yearlong continuous food production enables the tribes that inhabit Papua New Guinea to be self-sufficient and to have little need to import or export basic commodities. Their self-sufficient ecological regimes reduce the need for local populations to have wider communication. The self-sufficiency of microscopic local ecologies may also explain the limited progress New Guinea made has toward becoming a nation-state. Its social structure is centered on "big man" patrimonial redistribution and personalized charisma (Fukuyama 2011). Since eating trumps communication in more southern environments like that of Papua New Guinea, the logic is "I only communicate with the people in my immediate surroundings, so why bother to communicate with my neighbors if food is coming anyway?"

Japan is frequently described as the most integrated of all early-modern nations.[11] Japan's agricultural system had attained significant regional integration by the eighteenth century. An extensive marketing system existed. Interdependent innovations, such as fertilizers, seed selection, weeding, and separating grain from the stalk diffused throughout the Japanese islands: "the penetration of wet rice agriculture promoted sedentary and interdependent communal formation, discouraged the growth of slavery, and disseminated a common agrarian technology across the three main islands" (Berry 1997, 579–81).

Compared to other southern islands, Japan faced greater uncertainty about food scarcity. Did Japan develop a national language long before other island communities of East and South East Asia because localized isolated populations were unlikely to survive on its calamity-prone, overpopulated islands? If having many sources of subsistence reduced the value of perfecting communication, then we perhaps have a reason why early in its history Japan developed a national language. The subsistence of the various subcommunities on its numerous islands was not assured.

Communicating about food scarcity created other network-learning possibilities, facilitating collective problem-solving. With long-established norms of reciprocity, pooling and seeking resources in waters with risky currents, Japanese reformers of the Meiji Restoration (1868–1912) could draw on habits of collective learning to undertake an exhaustive search for a global optimum. Being more integrated than its neighbors, Japanese society enjoyed the benefits of modularity; the pieces were already well integrated, which reduced the steps necessary to reach a higher fitness plane.

How does the logic of group communication shape the pattern of state formation? This brief comparison of the Pacific Island nations suggests that nation-states, like national languages, are more likely to form where a large number of social bonds are necessary for survival in the face of shared ecological risk.

Emerging Democracy as a Complex System

In evolutionary biology, bifurcation describes the process by which new species result from dichotomous branching. Bifurcations result from small-scale differences at the beginning that produce large-scale differences at the end, causing lineages to diverge, despite sharing a common ancestor. The critical theoretical question that lineage bifurcation raises for science is to identify the cause of variation. Was it induced by the external environment or by some internal, initial condition intrinsic to the organism? These same questions are relevant to understanding the rift between the newer conservative Islamic movement and older republican nationalist movement in contemporary Turkey.

In chapter 6 we observed that the ruggedness of local fitness landscapes might exercise a deterministic influence on the evolution of the system. On a rugged fitness landscape, local actors are confined to the most optimal *local* strategy due to the cost of searching. High search costs can make a global optimum, such as political and economic liberalism, unattainable. These costs may favor the survival of regimes with payoffs that diverge from the norms of liberalism.

The analytical literature, along with the indexes of democratic transition that have appeared in the past three decades, presumes "opening, breakthrough, and consolidation" to be a linear sequence. Yet the presumption that successful models will be replicated underestimates the irreversible consequences of sensitivity to initial conditions. In order for an emerging democracy to follow the same developmental trajectory as long-lived varieties, it would have had to develop from the same primitive state and reproduce the same sequence of institutional construction. Even when societies descend from the same fixed point—for example the "natural order" posited by North et al. (2009)—minor variations along the trajectory toward democracy are likely to produce large variations at the end. Because many different variables are essential, we can say that democracy is a complex system. We can only describe its dynamics by describing its sensitivity to initial conditions. Only by looking backward can we locate a bifurcation point, where a fine-scale modification impels a large-scale difference.[12]

Pluralism versus Rationalism in Emerging Democracy

The illiberal variations in the trajectory of democracy were not anticipated in the first generation of scholarship because of a contradiction that exists at the very core of democracy that prompts a divergence from the optimum of liberal democracy. Recognizing this contradiction should enable us to better understand why the evolution of democracy in emerging regions has not been homogeneous, and why the spread of the ballot box has not transformed developing country policies or the well-being of the poor in the progressive manner that modernization theory would have predicted.

Pluralism is the essence of democracy, but it can often arise in conflict with the bureaucratic rationalization of the state. The initial conditions of the pre-democratic environment will often conflict with the ideal of a societal order based on reason. As pluralist practices penetrate deeper into the social structure and as they spread further from the central city, a clash with the particularism of pre-liberal local environments is likely to occur. Concepts like the rationalization of bureaucratic office, the universal and meritocratic exercise of political power, and equality before the law will often conflict with local religious and ethnic norms, as well as with feudal relations of political authority. A pre-democratic community based upon lineages, clans, voluntary associations, religious and cultural communities, and provincial governments may even embrace pluralism in order to protect its prerogatives from the encroachment of bureaucratic rationalism. The result can be that pluralism strengthens local interests that seek to entrench their privileges and status, and to obtain freedom from the rational order needed to implement and administer the authority of the central state. Thus emerging democracy can enable the internal rules of cultural and religious groups to trump individual preferences, and can allow intermediate associations to encroach on freedom of choice of individuals. Pluralism in India and in the Middle East frequently conflicts with consumer autonomy restricting choice in the selection of goods and services. Because emerging democracy can give cause to particularistic interests that seek to prevent the agencies of the state from triumphing over local prejudice, it can lead the polity to diverge from the individualist values of modernization theory. In the next chapter we will see further examples of the divergence from democratic rationality when newly elected rulers support patronage networks to stay in power.

9

Achieving State Capacity: Parallel Political Modernization in China and Europe

State Capacity-Building and Convergent Evolution

The formation of state capacity in different historical environments illustrates how convergent, or parallel, evolution can influence patterns of historical political economy. In evolutionary biology, convergent evolution occurs when similar traits are acquired from dissimilar origins. In a societal context, convergent evolution ensues when solutions to comparable dilemmas of collective action require recourse to institutions of similar functionality, but of divergent origination.

The micro-level parallel evolution of particular institutions, however, does not produce a pattern of convergence at a macro-evolutionary level and may result in further divergences as the environment changes. The emergence of bureaucracy amid autocracy in both China and old regime Europe provides an example: the bureaucracy was strengthened in China to attain regime legitimacy during peacetime; European rulers strengthened bureaucracy to mobilize society for war.

This chapter comprises three parts. The first describes the functional properties shared by all modern states, those that have dominated the world stage during the last millennium and that have been the incubators of world social development. The focus will be on states rather than civilizations. Part two describes critical milestones in the trajectories of France, England, and Germany, and their relations with their overseas colonies. Those milestones of accelerated social development were attained as a result of intense interstate rivalry that eventually eliminated unfit variations. After a millennium of almost continuous warfare, a common Western variant emerged at the end of the cold war with the fall of communism. The consensus on internal governance reduces the likelihood of future European interstate warfare.

Western social development was accelerated by such interstate rivalries, which did not exist in China's trajectory. Part three discusses China's parallel path to modernity, placing its process of state formation in a comparative perspective. China's social development was not accelerated by interstate rivalry; at the end of a two-millennium process of state formation, the Chinese state exhibits considerably less variation from its starting point.

China was caught up in European rivalries that eventually triggered its own modernization. Shipments of Western armies and armaments to China forced the Chinese state to adapt its society to industrial revolution. Having acquired the capacity to compete with the West in factory production, transportation, and munitions, China could resist further pressures to adapt its social system to Western formats. China's adaptiveness went only as far as was necessary to protect its political and strategic autonomy so that it could defend itself from outside intervention. What happens next in terms of normative structures will be determined by Chinese antecedents rather than external pressure.

In fact, family structures, technology, standards of living, and consumer tastes have evolved so that the radical differences between East and West that appeared during the late nineteenth century have disappeared. The remaining major differences between East and West concern primarily the evolution of regime legitimacy—differences that we will explore in this chapter.

Had the Industrial Revolution occurred in China, the direction of norms formation and the definition of political legitimacy might have gone from East to West. Instead, China has become a political outlier. Despite recovering its economic centrality in the world, it still suffers from being marginal in the political order of international relations, and its deficit of political legitimacy compromises its centrality in global politics.

It is widely understood that China's contradictory place in global affairs may be a source of unresolvable friction. In this chapter we will also see why the singularity of China's political trajectory is unlikely to dissipate, despite its economic success in imitating Western formats of manufacturing. In fact, success in the economic sphere enables China to pursue authenticity in political belief and action.

If China maintains its distinctive course, its developmental profile will repudiate a core assumption of modernization theory, that an upward surge in productive capacity requires eventual convergence to identical values in political organization. China's trajectory suggests that political and economic development need not occur at the same rate or end in the same place. Having narrowed the West's lead in economic development, China may choose to avoid political innovations that will disrupt its stable upward economic trajectory, locking into place the institutions that facilitated its economic surge.

Structure and Function in the Building of State Capacity

State capacity resides in citizens' expectations of their government's commitment to future action.[1] Thus it emerges from the processes by which leaders try to make long-term policy credible. A state's ability to administer and mobilize resources effectively and fairly, to steer socioeconomic policy, to legitimate its authority, and coerce compliance all involve its ability to accomplish what it has promised for the future. The problem of *time-inconsistency* occurs when a decision maker states a preference for one position but acts according to a different preference once the time for implementation arrives (Kydland and Prescott 1977).

A government faces a problem of credible commitment, of time-inconsistency, when it has the incentive to promise one future action but then selects another. If social actors do not trust the political leadership's commitment to the stated course, they will act opportunistically themselves, selecting their own short-term opportunities over longer term interests. Thus the government's inability to commit to a long-term action leads to lower levels of investment across society.

Commitment devices are required, such as the separation of rule-making from rule enforcement or an independent state bureaucracy, to dispel the expectation of state nonperformance or opportunism in project selection or personnel recruitment. Without such mechanisms, leadership will not be able to instill the expectation that today's choices will be consistent with its long-term positions.

No single indicator, such as extractive capacity, can describe state capacity.[2] That capacity is a composite of its system-level properties, such as effective administration, legitimacy in the eyes of its people, resilience and adaptiveness to environmental change, along with prescience in recognizing national interest. These macro properties cannot be predicted from the lower level properties from which they arose, and cannot be attributed to the behavior of any single set of decision makers or institutions. The capacity to engender collective behavior consistent with the long-term interests of the polity is a general system property that emerges at some level of institutional complexity. It is derived from the rules of interaction in extractive capacity, planning capacity, coercive capacity, and legitimacy, but it is not reducible to a measure of any single capacity. This makes state capacity a quintessential example of emergence (the acquisition of new structures and behaviors that the individual components did not possess) in social evolution.

We will be looking at examples from the West—England, France, and Germany—as well as postcolonial states in Africa and South Asia, and compare these with China to identify fixed points from which the characteristics of *stateness* emerge. Our intention is to find the mechanisms or points from which altruistic norms from families and kin groups are transferred to non-kin members of the community (Huntington 1996; Fukuyama 2011). This is not to say that various societies all share a common point at which they became states. In nature, for example, the bat, the bird, and the flying insect did not each develop the same anatomical point from which their wings sprouted. There is no common point of departure at which different species became capable of flight. In the same sense, there is no common point at which various kinship-based communities transferred their altruistic norms to non-kin members and thus became states. The results are similar, although the points from which the change arises may not be. Feedback loops, key events, and an assessment of the intentions of individual agents and the unintended outcomes that resulted from their behaviors will all help establish how a leader's political choices or preferences become aligned with time-consistent preferences of the polity.

The Time-Inconsistency of Patrimonial Systems

What differentiates a state from a kinship-based community? As a non-state social collective, the latter is based on kin selection and reciprocal altruism among groups that carry the same genes or that interact repeatedly in the same environment. In a kinship-based community, "selective advantage is due to the altruistic interaction of individuals sharing part of the same genotype" (Mayr 2001, 287).

Political leadership selected on the basis of kinship and reciprocal altruism among individuals sharing a common bloodline is called *patrimonialism*. In its more general use, the term refers to political authority modeled on that of a father within a family. Max Weber refers to patrimonial rule as something that projects beyond the family to an entire society or even a nation. Both ancient and contemporary histories offer many examples of bureaucratic offices filled by a ruler's kin. The domination of Indian politics since independence by the Gandhi family exhibits the power that patrimonial identification can have over an entire culture, despite the adoption of electoral institutions.[3]

Patrimonial rule operates through patronage networks, sometimes referred to as patron–client networks. Patron-clientelism is a form of reciprocity based on dependence and inequality in which power brokers create a following by exploiting control over scarce resources, not only material wealth but also resources that confer status or prestige.[4] The patron gains power by delivering such benefits selectively, according to the value of the loyalty that can be extracted from the recipient. These networks are most durable when the debts of the weaker partner can never be repaid or when the clients have limited channels of communication with the outside and depend on the patron for contact with power brokers in the wider society. The extent of patronage networks has been traditionally limited by the need to maintain face-to-face relationships, but modern political parties allow patronage webs to be woven across entire nations.[5] The patron gains moral authority by being able to represent and protect a local clientele in national or subnational arenas.

Modernization theory tends to assume that patron-clientelism is a residual, or vestigial, characteristic of an older, kinship-based order that state-building should phase out. But this has not happened. The market economy can strengthen the patrimonial order of society. Instead of eliminating patrimonial tendencies, *neopatrimonial* regimes have arisen in which formal institutional structures must compete with entrenched informal networks. Many political parties in recently formed states function as patronage systems; authority is personal and familial, modeled on the mechanics of a household. Again, contemporary India offers an example: the Indian Congress Party in its formative days before 1973 was such a network, and newer political parties that cater to distinct clienteles by offering public services selectively have copied its model of creating vote banks via patronage distribution.[6] Local clientelism is not unique to the trajectory of immature democracies; it is becoming prevalent in autocracies like that of China, as well. The psychological motivations of patrimonial reciprocity are so strong that no society and no form of government can completely eliminate patrimonial tendencies.

The trade-offs that patrimonial rulers make in favor of creating private goods increase the risks of long-term instability; the leaders are vulnerable to political backlash from groups that are not allocated adequate private goods. Saddam Hussein, Muammar Gaddafi, and Hosni Mubarak all seemed invincible, only to end their lives in violence or imprisonment. After Ferdinand Marcos and Suharto were rumored to be ill, the asset values their patrons held collapsed. But a longer lasting consequence of ongoing patrimonialism is institutional regression. Once Marcos and Suharto were toppled, or after Mubarak, Gaddafi, or Yemen's Ali Abdullah Salah were ousted during the Arab Spring, a de-institutionalization and lapse of civil order followed. Yasser Arafat held undisputed patrimonial authority, but when he died, the Palestinian Authority fragmented and dozens of mini-Arafats vied for power. The same process unfolded in Libya after Gaddafi's downfall in 2011. The regression of political routines and deterioration of institutional assets that occur when power changes hands deepens the gap between the quality of governance in state-based and non-state societies. Patrimonial democracies (like India) are less likely to regress when power changes, making them more stable than patrimonial autocracies; monarchy is one way to avoid such ruptures in institutional routines.

Europe and China transitioned from patrimonial domination through dissimilar institutional channels. In imperial China, a bureaucracy recruited government personnel according to a rigorous exam system that weakened kinship as a basis of administrative authority, and enabled higher levels of public provision than were found in other states in region. In Western Europe, states that separated the implementation of law from the exercise of sovereignty found another path toward solving the problem of committing government to actions consistent with their stated longer term objectives. The paths that these societies took to limit patrimonial rules of domination will be explored in the subsequent sections.

Building State Capacity: Credible Commitment and Economic Growth
As noted, an environment conducive to long-term private investment depends on the leader's ability to credibly affirm that when the time for implementation arrives, the policy selected will be the one promised. When commitments are not credible, a government will be unable to generate the support it needs to realize its policy goals. States that possess the institutional infrastructure necessary for credible commitment—an independent court system in which judges are professionally recruited, or meritocratic bureaucracies that ensure the rights of all economic actors—can accelerate capital accumulation and expand the scope for voluntary exchanges. States that provide rule enforcement to protect those citizens who have the best ideas or models for wealth accumulation can benefit by being able to borrow or tax the holders of capital, enabling better-functioning state systems.

Governments will have difficulty making credible commitments to rules over discretion when neopatrimonial systems of social authority circumvent loyalty to formal institutions. When asset values depend on relationships that are impermanent, societal actors sacrifice long-term well-being for immediate payoffs. The result is likely to consist of time-inconsistent preferences for the entire society. In such environments people make poor choices wisely. If resource holders have no expectation that a government will carry out its plans, they will make only short-term plans.

The social capital that forms in kin-based or closely-knit local societies can, by contrast, thwart the formation of civic culture that state capacity requires. When social responsibility and trust depend on kinship and patron–client reciprocity, networks of exchange will depend on personal sources of information. But patronage networks involve significant transaction costs; they are time-consuming, require continuous upkeep, and divert resources from their most efficient allocation. When economic advantages are ceded on the basis of existing social ties, the plans of the best organizers and the projects of the most innovative will fail to materialize.

Bureaucracy and State Capacity Building

In modern states bureaucracy is by far the dominant mechanism for obtaining credible commitment within well-functioning private and public organizations. It is difficult to imagine a function of the modern state, from health care for the elderly to guided-missile systems that is not managed bureaucratically. Citizens of a modern state find nothing exceptional about a system of rational rules fashioned to meet calculable and recurrent needs of a normal routine. They accept without hesitation the idea that governance rests on the right of the principals to issue instructions to agents in a structured relationship that transcends and supplants prior social distinctions. Bureaucratic authority is in fact among the most humdrum of all human artifacts.

Building State Capacity: Bureaucracy as Social Revolution

As prosaic as institutional bureaucracy may seem, the creation of a bureaucratic polity almost always has unintended consequences that can make its impact revolutionary. Bureaucracy has much in common with modern social media, in that it provides quick information flows across large groups that would otherwise be unconnected. Bureaucratic networks redefine the underlying social structure by providing influence and information that enhance the prospects of collective action across groups with weak ties. A bureaucracy can increase identification among inhabitants in the same polity while linking the population's well- being with that of the state. By creating channels of third-party enforcement, bureaucratic networks facilitate coordination of activities and convergence of common expectations among previously unconnected groups. Bureaucracy creates communities of interest based on competence and professionalism that may complement but may also eventually clash with the networks of birth and lineage, creating new networks of status, capability, and wealth.

Bureaucracy also facilitates the use of local knowledge globally and creates channels for global knowledge to reach remote individuals and groups. This can reorganize the network structure of a society and enable networks for complex exchange by making possible associations, affiliations, and connections among groups that never before overlapped. As networks grow, shrink, or reconfigure, the effects of these changes can cause unanticipated responses across the system. New connections to knowledge, influence, and ideas unrelated to prior social ties become possible, causing cascades in the transmission of information, triggering unanticipated social action. As Max Weber notes, "Everywhere the matter-of-factness of bureaucracy has had 'revolutionary results'"(1978, 1002).

The Emergent Properties of Bureaucracy: Adding Complexity to Social Exchange

True bureaucratic effectiveness requires that all social groups enjoy the same protection of the law, and that the demands of elites and those of ordinary citizens are met by the same processes. The authority that bureaucracy lends to state capacity derives from "the definite possibility of separating sharply and conceptually an objective legal order from the subjective rights of the individual which it guarantees; of separating 'public law from private law'" (Weber 1946, 239).

When public office is secured by elections, a similar principle applies: "the individual power-holder, even if he was in the highest position, was obviously no longer identical with the man who possessed authority in his own right" (Weber 1978, 998). By virtue of being elected, the bearer of power is separated from his or her initial social rank. Thus the leveling principles of election and bureaucracy are complementary and can foster Weber's "democratization of society in its totality" (1946). On the necessity for democratic polities to reduce categorical inequalities from everyday political processes, Charles Tilly concurs:

Democracy can form and survive so long as politics itself does not divide sharply at the boundaries of unequal categories. Conversely, political rights, obligations, and involvements that divide precisely at categorical boundaries threaten democracy and inhibit democratization. Democracy thrives on a lack of correspondence between the inequalities of everyday life and those of state–citizen relations. (2007, 118)

The capacity of bureaucracy to enforce rules without regard for persons is essential for democracy to thrive. Bureaucracy can also be put at the disposal of quite varied political or economic interests. It can be a tool of foreign domination, feudal domination, or democratic vitality. "The consequences of bureaucracy depend therefore upon the direction which the powers using the apparatus give to it" (Weber 1946, 230). Bureaucracy, Weber continues, "is the means of transforming social action into rationally organized action. Therefore, as an instrument to organize authority relations rationally, bureaucracy was and is a power instrument of the first order for one who controls the bureaucratic apparatus" (1978, 987).

The evolution of the Japanese bureaucracy illustrates Weber's point about the flexibility of an effective bureaucracy that, once created, is hard to destroy. From the outset of Japan's modernization, the bureaucrats were the emperor's servants. Under the democratic post–World War II constitution, they became servants of elected governments. In both roles, bureaucracy harnessed the best-trained managers to promote national interests. When the source of political legitimacy shifted to the newly created democracy, the bureaucratic organizations were at its disposal to deliver high-quality public goods. After more than fifty years of a functioning democracy, most Japanese still attribute their high standard of living more to the quality of their civil service, while attributing to political parties patronage, governance failures, and corruption.

A European Menu of State-Building Options: France, England, and Germany

The following section establishes in relative detail the case of French state-making because its patterns of cronyism and ministerial venality highlight the risks facing contemporary Chinese strategies. The English case is the most antithetical to China's current trajectory. The rise of imperial Germany has the greatest similarity, but China's Communist Party will seek to avoid its militarist excesses. The roles of nepotism and patron-clientelism in the selection of leadership among former European colonies reveal some surprising commonalities with the vulnerabilities exhibited within the upper echelon of the party hierarchy.

Creating State Capacity: France's Bureaucratic Path to Social Revolution

Historically the great obstacle to the unification of the French nation was the fragmentation of political power. At the close of the Middle Ages, France was a mosaic of conflicting and overlapping jurisdictions added piecemeal during several hundred years of conquest, marriage, and inheritance. As part of their efforts begun by Louis XI to unify their fragmented kingdom, French kings after François I (1494–1547) began to recruit, through the sale of offices, officials who did not have ties to the great aristocrats who, as feudal magnates, were the realm's "patrimonial" leaders. The monarchs hoped to create an officialdom, generally recruited from among the lesser nobility, whose status they could control. But the process they initiated of coopting, non-noble families created a demand for greater access to public office that the monarchy did not have the financial capacity to fill. Nor could the Monarchy afford to buy back the authority it had alienated from the sale of offices.

The French monarchy had tried to rein in the threats of the contentious and fractious aristocrats that insuccessfully rebelled in the Second Fronde, 1650–1653, by usurping their powers, while still granting them access to unearned income at court. An expensive apparatus of rent extraction was constructed to align the interests of the landed aristocracy with the monarchy. Honors, lands, pensions, appointments, and exemptions disbursed at court became vital to their survival. Provincial governorships, often awarded to the high nobility, became hubs of privileges, disseminating minor appointments, such as lucrative posts in the army and in the clergy. Local elites, the seigneurs, were given the prerogative of tax exemption. The non-noble elites, especially the merchant classes, could also exploit the redistributional income stream by purchasing tax exemptions and buying and selling government offices and tax farming. As a result the once-proud aristocratic barons took few measures to restrain the arbitrary power of the crown.

Over the course of the seventeenth and eighteenth centuries, the kings appropriated the public rights and functions of the seigneurs, creating a powerful bureaucracy, new tax systems, and civil courts. The liberties once enjoyed by the hereditary nobility were codified into public rights. State authority—the strengthening of royal justice and taxation that supplanted the private authority of the local nobility with the public—was facilitated by resorting to logic embedded in Roman law that presumed a unified state (Root 1985). But appeals to the unity of the French nation under law eventually rendered the concept of *l'etat c'est moi* itself into a target. The crown's claims to exercise personally the rights that belonged to the state were challenged by the same legal logic used to level the privileges of the feudal nobility. Change in France ultimately came as an unintended outcome of mobilizing the non-noble and peasant classes to serve the needs of the state.

The narrative of French democracy began during the old regime with the reign of Louis XIV in the seventeenth century and the transformation of his bureaucratic agencies in charge of resource mobilization for war. The king's problem lay with the fractious nobility that was exempt from taxation. The crown institutionalized state power through bureaucratic mechanisms because it could not depend on loyalty from local aristocracies to manage the expansion of the royal armies. The feudal nobility had rebelled against the monarchy during the minority of Louis XIV, forcing him into hiding for fear of his life. Once crowned in 1661, Louis was determined to weaken the nobility, and he began by selling offices, a tactic to which his predecessors, Louis XIII and Richelieu, had frequently resorted, but once in possession of their offices, office holders might place their own interests above those of the crown. Unable to count on the loyalty of office holders who could not be dismissed from offices they held as private property, the French crown resorted to relying on salaried bureaucratic commissioners, or *intendants*, sent to the provinces, often against the wishes of local groups and existing office holders. (Root 1987, 15) Royal officials, called *intendants*, had long been in use by French kings as their representative in the provinces, and over time the role had slowly changed. Louis XIV expanded their power, and through them, his own. As the king's representative in the provinces *intendants* became the principal instrument for extending royal control into the provinces. (Root 1987, 38).

Under Louis XIV, selection of *intendants* did not depend on their having a local clientele or a base of local patronage. They served on a commission basis and did not own their offices; the crown could revoke their powers, unlike those of the aristocracy or the purchasers of offices, at any time. The intendants were dispatched to regions where they had no genealogical origins. Louis had closed off such positions to members of the ancient nobility. Only careers in the army and in the domestic service of the king were available to the old feudal aristocracy (Root 1987, 25)

During the eighteenth century the successor to the throne, Louis XV (1710–1774), went further and codified the decision-making functions of the village assembly, transforming the formerly ad hoc assembly meetings into a legally binding statement of the village's general will, making it easier for peasants to organize and influence governmental decisions. Making the peasant communities an integral part of the crown's system of fiscal credibility opened new venues of national politics. The peasants no longer depended on the nobility for representation before the king; their fortunes now included three groups: the crown, its officials, and later the lawyers who petitioned the crown on behalf of the peasantry. The strengthened village communities encouraged by state officials increasingly initiated litigation against the lords to improve their economic condition, disputing in court the legal basis of feudal dues they owed to their lords (Root 1987, 87).By interposing its justice, its taxes, and its bureaucracy between lord and peasant the monarchy was transforming the local governing authority of the *seigneurie* into an anachronism (Root 1987, 65). The *intendants* now assumed responsibility for revenue collecting, and through them, Louis XIV was able to erode the lord's customary legal authority. By the mid-eighteenth century, the seigneur as a governing authority was on the defensive. One of the underlying justifications of the manorial system and of seigniorial privilege—that the lord's possession of land carried with it the right and the duty to govern and to protect the village was under attack as well (Root 1987, 65).

A resurgent peasant community increasingly asserted independence from both the seigneurs and the crown. This assertion could only be rationalized by the proclamation of a new form of legitimacy, the state/nation, in which the state was responsible for the nation (Bobbitt 2002).

Thus, with the process begun during reign of Louis XIV, the crown strengthened village communities against the seigneurs and allowed the kings to protect peasant property from seizure by local powers. In an exemplary court case in Burgundy in 1756, a royal tribunal during the reign of Louis XV did not sustain the claims of a lord who wanted to name a village schoolmaster.[7] This stood in great contrast with the practice of law in Britain where the justices of the peace were unpaid members of the local gentry. The British enclosure movement (1760–1820) and the allocation of grain bounties to large estates transferred income from the poor to rich, impoverished the peasantry, and expropriated peasant property.[8]

Court cases initiated by villagers over payment of feudal dues, payments that the crown protected, increased dramatically in the two decades before the French Revolution. Recognition of assembly decisions gave the village as a collectivity increased access to credit, which made the wave of litigation possible. The number of cases kept increasing. Although the peasantry lost most of the cases as their local management roles increased, they gained resolve.

As Alexis de Tocqueville elucidated in his classic *Old Regime and the Revolution*, the centralizing process in France deprived the *seigneurie* of its governing function. The protection extended by royal bureaucracy to peasant communities and urban communes conflicted with the authority of the feudal class to manage local resources, and had a corrosive influence on hereditary power. Institutionalizing the collective decisions of the village had a revolutionary influence on the expectations of the population.

As a lucrative vestige of an earlier order that no longer served a useful purpose, feudal rights came to be despised (De Tocqueville 1856). In the Constituent Assembly (1789–1791), the majority of the representatives of the commoners (the Third Estate) were lawyers who demanded the elimination without compensation of dues owed by the peasantry to their feudal lords. As the discourse of egalitarianism and rationalism became more enflamed, the hereditary, God-given rights of the monarchy were to be its final victim.[9] Little did any of these groups anticipate that the path on which they had embarked would lead to the demise of the kingly state in which the monarch personified the state.

To further wipe out all traces of feudal authority, the new revolutionary government divided princely realms like Burgundy, Normandy, Brittany, Languedoc, and Provence into administrative units. The newly formed state was to serve the nation, but without taking direction from the common people. The state's authority was vested in the bureaucracy, which was responsible for the people. Although of Greek etymology, the word *bureaucracy* derives from the French *bureaucratie*, which came into use shortly before the time of the revolution.

Bureaucracy improved resource mobilization but delegitimized the aristocratic character of authority by depriving privilege of social utility or responsibility. This extension of bureaucracy into the administration of a peasant kingdom had exactly the revolutionary impact then that it later ignited in the thinking of Max Weber. It reduced the value of the patrimonial ties between lord and peasant that had shaped relations among the social orders since the Middle Ages. As France democratized over the course of the nineteenth century, the bureaucracy transferred its loyalty from service to the crown to service to the state/nation, and eventually, to service to the people, in a manner similar to the evolution of the Japanese bureaucracy after World War II.

As Weber noted, even when bureaucracy starts out with a conservative objective of protecting social privilege, it may end in promoting new conceptions of public order, modifying the cognitive classifications of status and social responsibility. Social networks constructed by the bureaucracy first redefined but ultimately disabled the dynastic structure of power in old regime France. Having undermined the governance function of local lords, the bureaucracy discredited the traditional elites by rendering the dues and rights of the feudal order residual. In this sense, the information it created was channeled into new categories, creating new social understandings that substituted administrative order based on rational hierarchy for dynastic authority. The wars of Napoleon aimed to safeguard the French Revolution's accomplishments by restructuring the rest of Europe into the image of revolutionary France.

Modern France was born of the unintended outcomes of strategies designed to protect the monarch's narrow, sectarian, class interests but which instead became the framework for reforms that supplanted the dynastic order. Initially bureaucratic agencies created by the crown reinforced noble status, but offices such as the *intendants* eventually acquired autonomy from the social status of the individuals who served. Long-lived institutions, such as the royal exchequer and the École Militaire, ensured the state's independence from the founding social groups. The École Militaire, which had been designed to train the cadets from poor noble families, eventually trained non-noble officers under Napoleon I.

Law and Limited Bureaucracy in England

Unlike France, England transitioned into being a full-fledged modern state with its ancient aristocracy fully functional, having evolved into a governing class that championed the process toward *stateness*.

The French crown had created an independent bureaucratic authority to circumvent the powers of the feudal magnates and refused to abdicate its power over the collection of taxes and credit. Yet this appearance of strength only weakened the crown's ability to attract financing; being above the law, French kings were famous for reneging on their debts. The British sovereign, in contrast, failed to establish bureaucratic primacy over the dukes and earls, who along with landed gentry dominated local government. The monarchy lost any hope of controlling taxation after the late 1600s. However, a monarchy that ceased to have any real power was hardly a target worth overthrowing. England's great barons put their efforts into increasing the wealth of their own domains rather than seeking to capture a monarchy without resources.

The trajectory of royal dependency on the Parliament for taxes began with the Magna Carta in 1215. To obtain an independent source of revenue in the 1530s, King Henry VIII (1491–1547) confiscated Church lands but ended up by awarding those properties to elite families, hoping to obtain their loyalty. But Henry's successors were left with limited resources with which to coopt local nobles into obedience. A cash-strapped monarchy had difficulty securing the services of a paid bureaucracy and depended on the local gentry to maintain law and order in the districts. To protect their prerogatives, and to be sure that the crown would not step in and rescind their decisions, the local nobility demanded courts with juries that were not representatives of the crown, one reason why they led the fight to defend the civil rights of citizens from incursions by the crown.

When James I (1566–1625) and his successor, Charles I (1600–1649), tried to rule without Parliament by creating a system of patronage similar to that of their French counterparts, their plans to coopt the aristocracy into a relationship of dependency failed. The crown's search for revenues turned its relationship with the nobles into a zero-sum game. The grandees could not be subdued with the meager resources left at the king's disposal; they defied attempts to entail their estates, restrict trade opportunities, and promote monopolies to favorites of the court.

During the revolution of 1641, the Parliament wrested control of the military from the crown by refusing the king both money and the right to maintain a standing army. As part of the constitutional settlement often referred to as the Glorious Revolution of 1688, the principle of parliamentary consent in all matters of taxation made Parliament responsible for repayment of all debts. As holders of the debt, its members had an incentive to ensure the credibility of the government's fiscal position. Kings with a history of reneging on their creditors had to pay a higher rate of interest than did financial intermediaries subject to the law.

British Parliamentary Institutions, the Public Debt, and Public Interest Rates

The constitutional settlement of 1688 gave the government increased power to borrow, which was essential to war financing. At the outset of the War of the Grand Alliance against France in 1688, the British crown was able to borrow £1,000,000. By the end of the war in 1697, the government had borrowed nearly £17,000,000, and a GNP estimated to have been no larger than £41,000,000 supported this. Government debt grew from between 2 and 3 percent of the GNP to about 40 percent in less than a decade. According to historian P. G. M. Dickson, this spectacular increase in war finance was brought about by the creation of the Bank of England in 1694, which permitted a new system of government borrowing based on long-term loans, as well as the establishment of a permanent national debt (1967).[11]

The bank's charter gave it a monopoly on loans to the government. Since common law courts were independent of the crown, the Bank of England could call on them to block the government from seeking alternative credit sources. Small independent lenders and investors were thus barred from competing with the bank or among themselves, leaving the crown without alternative sources of funds. Weingast (1991) explains that centralizing the kingdom's loan decision in a single intermediary had an additional motivation: it allowed the Bank of England to enforce a credit boycott, greatly increasing the penalties the government would experience if it defaulted. By reducing the likelihood of default, this arrangement increased the credibility of the government's commitments to the bank. The crown's defeat actually increased Britain's financial strength and allowed it to conduct wars through access to long-term credit at low interest rates.

The British government's creditworthiness expanded further with the creation of funded debt in 1715. A political agreement with Parliament established that specific loans had to be secured by Parliament's vote of a specific tax designed to fund the loan's repayment. As a result of Parliament's backing of the public debt, the interest rate on government bonds fell from 10 percent in 1689 to 3 percent during the eighteenth century, greatly expanding the government's capacity to use the nation's savings. The lower interest rates reflected the fact that loan repayment had become more probable.

A perpetual public body—rather than the individuals who comprised it or a monarch who was above the law—became responsible for repayment of these obligations. As representatives of the government's creditors, members of Parliament had more to gain by increasing taxes to honor the nation's debt than by repudiating part of it, since taxes were spread to a broader segment of the population than was the debt. The taxes an MP (or his constituents) might pay to support the debt were likely to be smaller than the costs of defaulting. Moreover MPs might also be indirectly hurt by repudiation, since friends and relatives might hold public securities. Certainly an important part of a member's political support came from individuals who held portions of the debt. Following the creation of a funded debt controlled by Parliament, English investors recognized that the government's incentive was to repay rather than renege, and hence interest rates no longer needed to reflect a default risk.

Britain's war-making capability emerged from Parliament's credibility that allowed it to obtain funds at lower rates than other European governments. Those funds were invested in naval superiority, which created opportunities of wealth acquisition for merchants and landlords alike. As the empire expanded across the globe during the late eighteenth century, new nodes of wealth and innovation flourished alongside the old orders. Diversity in the social tapestry was reflected in social institutions and forms of civic association, such as the coffee shop, the daily newspaper, and the learned society. The uniquely British creation, modern civil society, with its sharp emphasis on institutions that mediate between state and society, contrasts starkly with much of the contemporary developing world, where state power is employed to "marshal the primitive force of community against the individual" (Becker 1994, 1). The habit of bargaining in parliament contributed to the forging of a national political culture shared by a broad segment of the nation's wealthy, which enabled the British elites to develop a more nationalistic and unified political culture capable of cooperation in the face of crisis. Learning to view their private interests in terms of national or public goals, a more open political culture emerged in which those representatives that participated in the negotiating process by which English public law was created became more aware of how their interests corresponded to those of competing groups. An emphasis on consensus over command as a method of conflict resolution, and a belief that public law should be based on a shared community of understanding spread among the nation's representatives (Root 1994, 55–56).

Bureaucratic Inclusiveness in Imperial Germany

Political economists Daron Acemoğlu and James Robinson contend that political reforms aimed at developing democratic processes are a strategic response to revolutionary pressure (2000). From this perspective, extension of the voting franchise is an effective means to avert a revolutionary event. However, democratization can take other forms. A theme of

German unification under the auspices of Prussia was to build a merit-based bureaucracy to mitigate revolutionary pressure that had erupted in the unsuccessful revolution of 1848.

German unification, which culminated in the German empire (1871–1918), reveals that ballot box democracy is not the only form mass society can take, and that an alternative path to citizen fulfillment and social recognition exists in which mass literacy, education, and the possibility of mass mobilization for war can occur without mass democracy (Buzan and Little 2000, 254–55). The Second Reich's strategy of cooption was to open the civil bureaucracy and the army to recruitment by merit. The imperial state guaranteed free public education and social security policies, and promised to guarantee the welfare of the people without providing universal franchise. Welfare programs were expanded to include old age pensions, accident insurance, medical care, and unemployment insurance to stem the tide of migration to America and channel rural migrants into industries protected by high tariffs. Substituting bureaucratic inclusiveness for multiparty elections, Prussia opened its bureaucracy to ambitious and capable people of low rank, and this served to diffuse discontent and reduce demands for opening political institutions to electoral mechanisms. Hoping to stem demands for an electoral franchise, Imperial Germany transformed its subjects into citizens through sweeping political and military reforms, democratizing social access to essential state institutions.

The democratization of state services began after the Kingdom of Prussia's defeat by Napoleon at Jena-Auerstadt in 1806. Embracing the ideal of a career open to talent, Napoleon's foes turned the principles of France's revolutionary armies against their creator. An army that could engage the dedication of the common soldier was the goal of a series of reforms initiated under Frederick the Great that included the emancipation of serfdom. These reforms also opened the officer corps to "all persons of knowledge during peacetime and to all persons of bravery during war." Prussia's military reforms included the creation of an institution to train officers regardless of their birth. Prussian reformers understood that winning the loyalty of the common Frenchman enabled the Republic to entrust him with arms. Imperial Germany ultimately militarized the entire social framework but ensured that the executive branch of government was not subject to the foolish whims of the electorate.

Finally, the Nazis created "the most democratically minded military classes in the world" (Knox and Murray 2001, 71). Nazi officers were given training to make a wide range of decisions on the field without having to depend on central command. The nationalist Socialist People's Army of 1939 to 1945 was the "final lineal descendent of the reformed Prussian army of 1811–15" but realized "the Prussian reformers' career open to talent in ways that would have filled them with horror" (p. 72). The German officer corps was the social revolutionary *sans culottes* of the Second World War (Knox 2000; Knox and Murray 2001). The autonomy of the German officers on the battlefield contrasted with the centralized control of every minor deployment characteristic of the French army. Faster, more localized decision-making allowed the German armies to take advantage of every opportunity on the field of battle, while French officers depended on communication with the center, which was compromised early on when France's communication infrastructure was destroyed.

Reinforcing Patrimonial Authority in Europe's Former Colonies

European powers like France, Britain, Belgium, and the Netherlands failed to undertake efforts to establish legitimate state-based forms of authority in their colonies. Instead, they empowered local aristocrats ("big men") and established systems of linkages with client rulers, often playing local rivals against one another. To save on the costs of direct administration, colonial authorities depended on coopting the powerful elites and clans, rather than on channels of accountability to the population at large. Whereas the English and French kings coopted the nobility and the Prussians the lower classes, the colonialists coopted the indigenous social elites, turning them into client-rulers bolstered with private goods and decorated with titles, enabling the colonialists to obtain local influence at minimal cost.

State-building trajectories of the European colonies have rarely replicated the colonizers' own experiences of state-building because they lacked a well-resourced indigenous bourgeoisie. The business elites were expatriates, and when they departed they rarely left behind an indigenous source of private capital. Capital accumulation depended on the state, which was then captured by the political elites. In some newly independent colonies like Cote d'Ivoire, Morocco, or Madagascar, French expatriates remained to manage external trade. But these were the exceptions.

Without resources, the indigenous bourgeoisie was typically too weak to seize control or to decide the developmental priorities of the postcolonial regimes. With no capital of their own, the middle classes in many former colonies, such as Egypt and Yemen, looked to the state for jobs and became advocates of socialism and state-based industrialization.

Kin-based selection and reciprocal altruism associated with the "big man" legacy still thwart the formation of civic culture that state-building requires, and impede the consolidation of democracy in the former colonies. Patronage-based domination over the local population circumvents loyalty to formal institutions. Social organization stays centered on kinship and reciprocity. This is the same low-cost, low-impact solution to governance that facilitated the integration of the colonies into the colonial economy and eventually into the world economy. But as a result the power brokers in many postcolonial societies, especially those of the sub-Saharan societies, came from the pre-independence elites who collaborated with colonial rulers. These same indigenous elites still resist efforts to build the capacity of postcolonial modern states to prevent tax evasion and rent extraction (Van de Walle 2001). Unlike the mother country, where social authority became vested in state-based forms, formal rules and informal behavior did not align in the colonies after independence.[12]

Building State Capacity: Modern China and Authoritarian Inclusivity

The answer to the puzzle of why authoritarian rulers in Europe developed bureaucratic systems usually leads to one key impetus: mobilization for warfare. European state expansion advanced by resource mobilization for the conduct of war, made possible by a broad tax base and extensive credit. By contrast, wars fought in Asia have generally been short and labor-intensive, rather than capital-intensive. Historically Chinese armies were enormous by Western standards, relying on swift and conclusive results; "with so many mouths to feed, no time could be spent on arduous preparatory bombardment, trench-work, and mining favoured by European commanders" (Parker 1995, 390). This emphasis on augmenting numbers of combatants rather than harnessing industrial power, technology, and discipline has enjoyed great continuity over time. When Chinese troops intervened during the Korean War, their strength was in their numbers. A massive movement of poorly supplied troops was able to encircle

Allied forces, causing many casualties on both sides. Mao even boasted that he was prepared to sacrifice millions of Chinese if it should come to a nuclear attack.

The domestic policies of Mao Tse-tung and the Gang of Four during the 1966 to 1976 Cultural Revolution, designed to remove revisionist elements from all segments of government and civil society, reduced China's logistical abilities and rendered it vulnerable to external threats. Bureaucracy especially was rebuffed in favor of the people's power at a time when Chinese security was tenuous. There were tensions with the Soviets, with India, and with the West because of the Vietnam War. Yet Mao saw China's strength in its sheer numbers rather than its capacity for effective organization.

So the puzzle of China is why its bureaucracy underwent a huge expansion not under Mao, but under successor governments, and to meet the needs of peacetime mobilization.

After Mao's death in 1976, the Soviets under Mikhail Gorbachev grew less menacing and the United States was no longer viewed as a direct security threat. Yet Mao's successor, Deng Xiaoping, who ruled during a more secure period, from 1978 to 1992, added layers of bureaucracy that compromised his ability to wield power as paramount leader of the party by the force of his personality. He institutionalized internal party procedures and limited party interference in government and in the management of state enterprises (Nathan 1997, 59–62). Deng followed the example set by China's smaller neighbors, Singapore, Taiwan, and Japan, that integrated into world markets by relying on technocrats, regularizing procedures, rationalizing regulations, and making bureaucratic recruitment more procedural.

Faced with a hostile external environment, Mao, and not Deng, should have placed high value on strengthening the bureaucracy. Why did Deng weaken his ability to exercise personal discretion and turn to bureaucratic reform after external threats had subsided?[13] Remember, East Asian leaders in South Korea, Taiwan, and Singapore imposed constraints on their personal discretion because they needed to mobilize the state to protect against insurrection and aggression sponsored by revolutionary China.

Deng's primary goal was economic growth. Chinese history suggests that expanding the economic base of the society would increase the demand for appointments in the government structure, a good reason for

Deng to pursue reforms that made the bureaucracy more rule bound and open to managerial talent. Many examples of peasant protests led by socially frustrated local elites excluded from the bureaucracy system exist in China's history (Fairbank 1986, 27–32). For example, barred from entering the bureaucracy after failing the imperial examination, Sun Yet-sen (1866–1925) fought for democracy. A government that seeks to use the bureaucracy as a source of job creation must be able to expand its revenue base without crimping the economy.

It is a cliché in Chinese history books that trouble came to the Qing (Ch'ing) dynasty (1644–1912) because many more exam takers existed than posts. Due to economic expansion during the dynasty's golden century, demand multiplied, but the number of positions, along with the salaries, remained at Ming dynasty (1368–1644) levels. And as the society became more populous, the small number of officials became even more isolated from the people. Fairbank observes that:

One contribution to the Ch'ing Government's downfall was its failure in the early nineteenth century to keep up with the growth of population and commerce by a commensurate growth of government structure and personnel. For example, the government did not raise the provincial quotas of successful degree holders who could emerge from the examination system. . . . But as the number of talented men capable of achieving degree status increased, the rigidity of the quotas closed the door to many of them in their effort to join the government ranks. One result was an increasing effort to attach such talent to the government in the form of advisors (*mu-yu*), deputies (*wei-yuan*), and expectant officials (*hou-pu*, "waiting to be appointed"). But this only increased the competition for preferment without increasing the efficiency of administration. The institutional structure of government failed to expand until later in the century. One effect of blocking upward mobility was that a myriad of young literati seeking office became frustrated hangers-on of the government offices, or *yamen*, where staffs were swollen and job competition induced all sorts of bribery and corruption. (Fairbank 1986, 63–64)

But Deng's desire to open the economy encountered ideological opposition from conservative party members who feared, based on Marx's prediction, that open trade could create an independent bourgeoisie to challenge the status quo. American sociologist Barrington Moore sums it up nicely: "No bourgeois, no democracy" (1966). To avoid the possible buildup of resistance to one party rule, Deng initiated promotions in the civil service that persist to today. The Chinese Communist Party now follows rules that reduce political selection in the recruitment of senior administrators and reward the performance of effective managers. Today the party seeks to become even more inclusive by encouraging successful entrepreneurs to join it and offering commercial opportunities it controls. The goal is to align the interests of the most capable managers and the top graduates with the interests of the state, thereby weakening demands for pluralism.

The result is a transition to meritocracy that is consistent with the traditional Confucian concepts of dignity and self-worth from living harmoniously in a social hierarchy where uniformity and common ideals are more important than self-expression and originality. The party's most important decision-making body, the Politburo, is meritocratic by the standards of most developing nations, although party elders, mostly former leaders, make many key decisions behind closed doors. Of twenty-five members, seven are scions of previous members, but the rest are appointments that result from a highly competitive process. The party attracts the top graduates from China's best universities, making it far more meritocratic than the power elites of virtually any other developing nation, including India. The word "autocracy" does little justice to the complexity of governance in China after Deng.

China's Information Problem

Deng's reforms have transformed the Communist Party, making it capable of managing the fastest-growing economy in the world. But the party is poorly served with mechanisms to detect malfeasance at local levels. Corrupt officials can gain considerable power at the local level before their malfeasance becomes known at higher levels of the central bureaucracy. Without competitive elections and a free press, political officials have no reason to take complaints of the population seriously, but they also have no fire alarms to signal when abuses are accumulating at the local level. This makes it costly for the center to monitor lower level officials, and to assess which local groups are politically dangerous.

Deng succeeded by making economic reforms compatible with the incentives of local officials whose support he needed during the process, but he also compounded the risk of lower level malfeasance. Each opportunity for opening the market was treated as a particular event for "buying in" the support of the local officials, allowing them to take private shares in the commercial economy, but the result was an absence of uniformity in the law and administration. Managers of state-owned enterprises now enjoy a multitude of independent contracts with the center, and particularistic contracting gives governmental officials at every level the opportunity to gain political support from subordinates through generous and unregulated contract terms. As a result, from the bottom up and from the top down, Chinese government officials enjoy a vested or encompassing interest in economic reform.[14]

The webs of exemptions and special treatment create unlimited opportunities for exploitation by local officials to transfer company revenues to private bank accounts, and to transfer the land of farmers to developers. These particularistic arrangements constrain tax collection, reduce fiscal transparency, and create unfair competition between enterprises. The resulting malfeasance can reach extreme levels before central party officials can obtain information.

Accountability in the party is upward, and local officials have little concern for what local people think of their performance; opportunities for self-policing by the community are as remote as they were during dynastic times. Lower level bureaucrats take advantage of their greater knowledge of local affairs to commit abuses, such as collusion in the theft of peasant properties, and they frequently resist requests from the center to comply with international production and labor standards. The lack of responsiveness to local abuses can tarnish the reputation of the regime and threaten it with a loss of legitimacy.

Ironically, since the party has inadequate means to monitor compliance or to monitor corruption and opportunism among lower level officialdom, protests and public displays of discontent must solve informational problems. Mass political mobilization helps the center to obtain information about local abuses within the party and within the bureaucracy. Thus public demonstrations actually help the authoritarian regime to consolidate its authority because they offset the breakdown of central party supervision over the local level and provide sources of much-needed information (Liu 2012). In 2010 there were some 180,000 protests in China, but officials believe that since these are typically local protests that occur after mine disasters or chemical plant explosions, such events do not pose a larger existential threat to the government. The central leadership permits the demonstrations; the people who vent feel that they effect change to the system through their demonstrations. Nevertheless, mass mobilization has the risk of snowballing into a massive, prolonged popular movement that can turn against the regime itself, as did the protests at Tiananmen Square in 1989 or those of the Falun Gong in the late 1990s.

Outbursts of popular discontent at the local level have resulted in purges and procedural reforms that improve accountability and scrutiny. Yet the Chinese Communist Party seems to be following a contradictory strategy: while bureaucratic expansion and mobilization balance each other, they do so at great risk to social stability. Dependency on mass mobilization weakens bureaucratic capability; the long-term risk is that systemic change and necessary reforms are postponed. Even if mobilization may promote authoritarian stability, the underlying social tensions caused by local cronyism and poor local governance remain unresolved (Pei 1997).

Bureaucratic Inclusiveness as China's Answer to Liberal Democracy
The efforts of the old regime French monarchy to coopt resistance among the nobles has many parallels to the current political environment of China. China is a one-party state in the same way the government of monarchical France was a one-party state—and both states employed methods of cooption to diffuse dissent. China's particularistic contracts that bestow exemptions and privileges on party officials are analogous to the fountain of privilege at court where the French grandees sought their fortunes. Bringing China's emerging class of private enterprise managers and professionals into the communist party is akin to the process by which non-noble French mercantile elites were allowed to trade in the sale of public offices and purchase exemptions from taxation. Both regimes engage in policy transfers to groups that are potentially threatening, coopting threats by preventing undue concentrations of private wealth that are independent of the state. Currently the Chinese Communist Party views rural riots as less threatening to the state than the rising bourgeoisie. But there is a price in the fiscal health of the state to be paid for expanding elite privileges. On the eve of the French Revolution state expenses grew more rapidly than revenues, partly due to the burden of supporting a large cadre of elite, tax exempt, office holders (Goldstone 1991).

Another local level similarity between old regime France and contemporary China can be identified. The Chinese are experimenting with village-level "deliberative democracy" to overcome informational dilemmas to win the hearts and minds of the community. Farmers are permitted implementation of simple democratic procedures at the village and township level for the management of local resources. These "incubators of democracy" are assisted by access to newspapers, radio accounts, and information about market opportunities to make farmers aware of national policies affecting their well-being. The experiments resemble the efforts of the French monarchy in the forty years before the revolution of 1789 to employ *intendants* to supervise village deliberations and elections, making residents responsible for local infrastructure. The French monarchy also improved peasant community access to royal courts. But measures to use deliberative democracy can build expectations in local populations while giving them the channels and mechanisms to connect with other discontented groups. Inculcating norms in the population and extending their links to bureaucratic networks may cause unexpected shifts in public opinion that the center will be unable to control. This could shift the scale, speed, and structure of collective action with unanticipated long-term risks.

England's state-building path by which the government's purse strings were moved from the crown to Parliament has evolved into a competence for managing global financial technology. As a result the United Kingdom is a hub of the international financial system. China would also like to become a hub of global finance but cannot follow the English path. The same forces that rendered Britain the pivot of the global financial system make it the antithesis of the China model. If China had transitioned to a modern state as England did, with its old imperial elites intact, it would have left no place in history for the Communist Party to emerge.

China has a principal–agent problem, a conflict of interest between the center and local governments over the transfer of revenues to fund central government activities.[15] Local governments use resources they already control to acquire additional resources. If the extensive extra-budgetary funds siphoned off by local governments are taken into account, the central government's share of total budgetary funds is weak, diminishing the capacity of the central government to attain national priorities. China has no equivalent independent national body that speaks for the national interests and has a vested interest in the overall strength of central government finances. China's weakness in extractive capacity was Britain's strength. The failure to resolve the conflict between central and local extraction has contributed to the decline of every dynasty in Chinese history, and the waning of the state in the midst of a prosperous society continues to be a risk that the current regime has not found a way to surmount.

Of any European analogue, imperial Germany bears the strongest resemblance to the Chinese strategy for building state capacity. The Chinese Communist party, like the emperor of nineteenth-century Germany, seeks to neutralize the political threat of a rising bourgeoisie by creating a professional class with a vested interest in the status quo. However, a militarized population in the Prussian model is not something China seeks because it would lead to outcomes not in the interest of the party. Confucian ideology and religion elevated literate culture above physical force, and held bureaucratic control in higher esteem than military ideals. The mandarins placed themselves above the military and the emperor feared that commanders with loyalty built up within the army might challenge the state.

Finally, China seems at first glance to have little in common with the neopatrimonial tendencies of developing governments, it has enjoyed state-based governance for well over a millennium. The gap between premodern, pre-state social collectives like Somalia and bureaucratically administered states is so great that Pritchard and Woolcock (2004) claim that closing the capacity gap between state based and non-state based societies "at current rates of institutional reform will require another 6,000 years." However, China is starting to show signs of regressing to patrimonial norms in the recruitment of the senior party bureaucracy and at lower levels of authority in the local party complexes.

Without a legal system that stands above the party, elite politics risks becoming increasingly patrimonial (Wong 2012). Office-holding is becoming increasingly dependent on patronage, and there are no strong independents forces, such as a legal system to prevent this tendency. The party wants to be sure there are no such independent enclaves of authority, but this leaves it with insufficient capacity to police itself and prevent office holders from seeking power for the purposes of self-aggrandizement. China may regress to a patrimonial state in which political patronage is the crucial factor in ascending to the top—which reinforces prediction based on Max Weber's criticism a century ago, when he pointed out that although the Chinese bureaucracy is bound by the law, there is little to distinguish between the office and the person or to prevent the use of office for private gain. It is difficult to break the link between state power and private aggrandizement, but if this tendency is not contained, China could end up with a "big man" problem that threatens the party with a loss of legitimacy and efficacy.

China's Search for Political Authenticity

The influential social philosopher Francis Fukuyama warns that China's future transition to democracy is inevitable and claims that the rise of a middle class creates grave vulnerability for one-party rule (2011). The desire for political liberalism is not an artifact of culture, he stresses; even if an autocracy succeeds in gratifying basic material needs, it can never gratify the deeper craving for personal autonomy and social recognition. No other ideology is better suited than democracy for gratifying the existential quest of individuals for mutual social recognition and confirmation of human worth.

Elections have been introduced even in authoritarian East Asia, first in Japan and then among the region's other high-performing economies, Taiwan and South Korea, after a certain level of material gratification was attained. Will China be different? Yes, because the desire elsewhere in East Asia for recognition as a democracy reflected the influence of the region's principal benefactor—the United States. China's security does not depend on an American umbrella and its leaders refute any notion of debt for their economic success to the liberal world order constructed by the United States and its allies after World War II.

Moreover Chinese history offers the Chinese Communist Party a different playbook to ensure continuity of one-party rule and avoid convergence to the "end of history." Economic expansion is currently straining China's governance structures, but the country's autocratic heritage is rich in governance alternatives that can forestall democracy for long periods of time. Just as the emperors used meritocratic recruitment into the bureaucracy and mass participation to counter the threat of a powerful nobility, today the party can use the same carrots to counter threats to state authority posed by the growth of a class of private entrepreneurs and a middle class with professional qualifications.

The Communist Party's solution is not to terminate one-party rule, but to make the existing institutional structure of government more inclusive. China's Communist Party seeks inclusiveness by integrating key economic actors within the state to avoid negotiating with any powerful independent group. The art of contemporary governance, as during dynastic times, resides in controlling the bureaucracy and ensuring that all private interests and interest groups are subordinate to the state.

Many of China's main institutional features were derived in relative isolation from the West, and even though the two may cope with similar domestic and economic challenges, such as dependence on the larger global economy, China will not replicate the governance trajectory of the West. It may display analogous traits arising from the need for adaptation to similar global contingencies but will remain on a fundamentally different trajectory that continues to diverge from that of the liberal West. Marvin Becker, a historian of civil society in Western Europe, concedes, "Numerous models of civil society can and do exist and flourish under a variety of regimes distinct from liberal democracy" (Becker 1994, xix). In its search for political authenticity, China's response to liberal democracy is bureaucratic inclusiveness.

Conclusion: Seeking Political Authenticity in a Networked Global Economy

Long before France, England, and Germany, China acquired state capacity by providing the social mechanisms and symbolic references needed to extend the altruistic basis of human sentiment to non-kin members. The properties of trust, cooperation, and social coordination were ethically and politically defined. Key long-term investments to ensure the collective good were routine.

Yet, China had and continues to have weak taxation capacity. Today it compensates for fiscal weakness by controlling the banking system and using state-run industries to provide many essential social services. These policies may help avoid the chaos of a domestic power transition, but they compromise economic efficiency.[16] Policies that permit state-owned firms with low productivity to have access to government-controlled credit markets produce waste and inefficiency, and circumscribe entrepreneurial opportunities.[17]

In the face of these weaknesses, Western policy makers and social change experts like John Ikenberry (discussed in chapter 4) assert that interest-group competition played out in electoral democracy is the optimal device to balance the conflicting practical, political, and moral complexities of managing a modern economy and that in the end the Chinese too will find that democracy is the only efficient way to manage the complex interactions of the modern and globally integrated economy they hope to construct. This approach overlooks the extent to which China is operating with a different playbook, a playbook that contemporary Confucian political thinker Jiang Qing calls China's Confucian constitutional order (Qing 2012). It is likely that policy makers will consult this playbook, which has enabled China to endure civic strife and to dominate its neighbors for more than a thousand years. It is unlikely that China will consult the West's playbook for ways to remedy China's current crisis out of fear about what will happen if traditions of duty, rights, obligations and roles that have a thousands of years of tradition are dismantled. Thus Jiang Qing, along with Jisi Wang believes that China's evolution will be strongly dependent on a menu of options rooted in the nation's Confucian texts and heritage and that its development model will be the alternative to Western democracy that will align with history and traditions of other non-Western societies. Nonetheless, there is a reason why those texts and traditions might not be sufficient to chart China's future course. In the past the only pressures for change that mattered were local; today China must adjust its behavior in response to global interdependencies that will be discussed in chapter 11.

At the core of what China seeks for the well-being of its own population are opportunities that it must access in the world outside of its own borders. It can no longer cling to concepts that were proclaimed when China was the center of the universe. In its struggle to survive and prosper China too must adapt to the changes of its coevolutionary partners. It will have to make choices by understanding the game it has decided to enter and coordinate its own best efforts with the laws of complexity of the world it has joined. However, China stands outside powerful global trends in the global economy, where the fraction of economic activity controlled by government or large corporations is shrinking. In many of the countries with which China hopes to compete, smaller firms are becoming more important generators of new products and new employment. Corporations are no longer national; they depend on global outsourcing, selling, and manufacturing. It is inevitable in such a highly decentralized global economy for managers to make errors, which is why central control structures are dissipating. This is a global phenomenon for which China's history does not prepare it well. Will the Chinese Communist Party be able to buck the tide and change the global environment, or will it give up its ambitions for greater central control in order to integrate itself into a global economy it cannot control?

In the final two chapters, we will explore whether the future of the international system will be characterized by the competition of two network systems, of East and West.[18] Will they seek to preserve and enlarge their respective spheres of influence, making the politics of global integration categorically antithetical? Or will differences recede as China and the West confront common problems? We turn to the question of global stability and the struggle to determine the future form of the international system.

10

Does China Challenge the Global Legitimacy of Liberalism?

Introduction

One of the key questions of growing global interconnectedness is whether systems remain stable as their parts are altered. How, for example, will changes occurring in what were once peripheral states in Asia or in the Middle East affect the system of international relations?

China's behavior mattered little when it operated in relative isolation. This is no longer the case. Since the early 1990s, one of the fastest-growing features of global trade shifts has been China's economic interdependence with other countries of the former periphery. China's ascendency is already creating fissures in the liberal international regime. Its expanding commercial network is transforming into a political and intellectual network that transfers its model of developmental authoritarianism to trade partners. Will China redefine system-level rules, changing not just the strategy of the players but also the behavior of the system of international relations?

China's relations with other nations are conducted under strict cover of secrecy. The government does not make public the amount, designation, or results of its overseas assistance or investment budget, and any Chinese citizen who inquires into the effects of Chinese overseas assistance is committing a felony.

A leak has occurred in China's efforts to prevent information diffusion about its overseas investment, revealed in its dealings with Sri Lanka, a small country of 21 million people in one of the most densely populated corners of the world. A democracy since its independence in 1948, Sri Lanka has a long pro-Western history of parliamentary debate, a well-organized opposition party, an independent media, and an articulate, internationally educated, and well-traveled middle class, unlike most of China's developing world partners.

China's growing presence there provides an opportunity to explore microscopically what happens when a systemically important country emerges that does not share Western ideals, and gives a perspective on some large questions about two key aspects of China's challenge to liberal internationalist agendas. The first concerns its ability to alter the regulatory role of international institutions on such issues as the rule of law and its relationship with the polity, the limits to state sovereignty, the international community's rights to humanitarian intervention and responsibility to protect. The second concerns the possibility that China may construct an alternative international regime.

To observe these larger trends, this chapter examines the origins of populist opposition to Western models of development in Sri Lanka exemplified by the "sons of the soil" movement. During in the Tamil war, the West, pushing for settlement, spurned Sri Lanka's requests for the weapons with which to gain a total victory. Sri Lankan leaders turned instead to China and found a willing arms supplier. China's rapid transition to a full-fledged supplier of loans and its use of direct "secret aid" have engendered the top-down flow of rewards, and leveraged anti-Western populist resentment into a rejection of the Western discourse of good governance. There are implications both for international liberalism as a global norm-setter and for global development policy.

Geopolitical Divergence

Sri Lankan disaffection with the West has been a persistent theme among the Sinhala-speaking intelligentsia who blamed foreign influences for the island's economic difficulties long before China extended its reach into South Asia. But a critical transition point occurred when that disaffection coalesced into a new political force during the presidential election in 2005. The intelligentsia's dissatisfaction merged with the rhetoric of populist leader Mahinda Rajapaksa, who campaigned against proposals by the liberal West to end a twenty-six-year civil war by devolving power to separatist Tamil regions.[1]

After his electoral victory, the West repeatedly turned down Rajapaksa's requests for the weapons that would inflict a decisive defeat to the

Tamil uprising in the north. The West had long emphasized the need for a balanced approach through devolution as a way to attain national reconciliation, and drew attention to fanaticism, dogmatism, bigotry, and the denial of opportunity on both sides. The Western recommendation of offsetting secessionist demands by offering devolution was viewed by the Rajapaksa administration as a first step toward the loss of land. His government was able to rally anti-Western sentiment by arguing that Western proposals were being shaped by the Tamil diaspora.

By 2008 Rajapaksa found China willing to provide arms, including the fighter jets, antiaircraft guns, and radar equipment he needed to pursue submission of the rebels in May 2009.[2] When Western nations raised concerns over high numbers of civilian causalities and mass killings, China defended the Sri Lankan government in the United Nations from the West's censure, demonstrating what a valuable and rich friend it was to have. Having learned during the cold war, and again in the early nineties, to specialize in high-obligation relationships with the leaderships of countries estranged from the West, the Chinese government saw the Western censure of Sri Lanka's government as an opportunity to protect sea lanes that are critical to its access to resources. The UN Sri Lanka report of massacres and human rights violations are disregarded in China and Sri Lanka where they are viewed as Western propaganda.

Sri Lanka was not China's first such relationship with a county that had strong colonial ties with the West. It had already succeeded in Zimbabwe, which has vast deposits of minerals and precious metals, and is playing a role in the geopolitical repositioning of a number of other countries on several continents, including South Africa, Pakistan, Peru, Venezuela, and Bolivia, to name just a few. China's scheme for geopolitical positioning focuses on securing its access to essential resources that its economy depends on. China's greatest opportunities to get around the West's grip on the big export countries for natural resources arise when Western censure gives resource-rich nations little negotiating space; then since China does not fear being replaced, it can aspire to reaping a long stream of benefits. The resources African and Asian autocrats receive from China not only assure those governments of the means to evade compliance with externally imposed conditions; that assistance also enables them to bypass accountability to their domestic constituencies.[3] In Sri Lanka, for example, China gains political leverage by ensuring that Rajapaksa's government has the financial means to reduce the effectiveness of the opposition, the media, and civil society.

Unlike China's other partners, such as Myanmar, where the military junta in 1988 refused to accept the electoral mandate of its voters, or Zimbabwe, which suffered international censure in 2005 for the torture and murder of journalists by government-hired assassins, Sri Lanka was one of the few developing countries that has remained a democracy without interruption since independence. We shall examine how *positive* forces of attraction drew Sri Lanka into the China camp, which raises questions about how many other regimes are susceptible to the pull of China's emerging network.

A British colony, Ceylon (as Sri Lanka was then known) began its journey into independence and dominion status with a Westminster-style multiparty democracy that progressively democratized as elections were held for officials at the national, provincial, and local levels. The Donoughmore Commission in 1927 introduced a constitution in 1931 and a legislature, the State Council of Ceylon, elected locally. In 1947 the Soulbury Commission expanded the State Council into a parliament with the prime minister at its head, and in 1948, political power was transferred by Great Britain to the indigenous middle classes, many of whom were educated in English and had British training in bureaucratic management and administration. In 1972 the island became a republic and changed its name to Sri Lanka. A president with few real powers replaced the queen as the ultimate authority and head of state; in 1987, Prime Minister J. R. Jayawardene expanded the power and authority of the president. Today Sri Lanka remains a member of the British Commonwealth of Nations.

At independence, many international observers considered Sri Lanka to be one of the newly independent countries with the greatest likelihood of being an economic success. However, the country's post-independence economy faltered; consistency in economic policy was absent in the agendas of changing governments' subsidies and price controls, and until 1978 there was no direct foreign investment. For most of its post-independence history, increases in gross national product were modest, per capita incomes stagnated, and formerly robust educational indicators (education was free) declined. Plummeting prices for tea, the country's principal export, drove up the costs for imported food and machine goods, triggering a crisis in the balance of payments. The central bank inflated the exchange rate of the currency, which encouraged unsustainable consumption and discouraged investment in agriculture, while penalizing exporters. By the early 1970s Sri Lanka was among the many highly indebted developing countries that turned to international organizations like the International Monetary Fund for rescue from fiscal collapse. Economic stagnation continued throughout the seventies and eighties, and overvaluation of the currency made exports uncompetitive. Yet the socialist intelligentsia identified Western policies and conspiracies as the cause of the country's poor economic performance. They complained that key sectors of the economy, notably tea and rubber production, were controlled from abroad. In addition the rural poor were alienated from the managerial classes, whom they accused of being subservient to neocolonial international interests. The British are believed to have favored the Tamils in the civil service, which also alienated the rural Sinhalese population (about 80 percent of the Island's population is rural). A Marxist revolution in the spring of 1971, led by the Janathā Vimukthi Peramunṇa (JVP, or People's Liberation Front), expressed that alienation. Some 15,000 young people reportedly died before the uprising was suppressed. To diffuse further insurrectionary influences, the government expropriated mines and private agriculture, including tea and rubber plantations, but stayed on the parliamentary path. In order to access loans from the industrial West, Sri Lanka's leadership balanced nonalignment with a strong adherence to electoral democracy.

The economic frustrations of being unable to break dependency on unstable world markets for key natural resources shifted Sri Lankan sympathies away from the West. Frustration grew as ethnic tensions flared in the form of the Tamil insurrection of 1973, and required the purchase of weapons to deal with secessionists, which led to further dependency on the goodwill of the West. In 1983 civil war erupted. Successive leaders advocated winning the war through economic integration of the Tamil north, a plan their Western donors wanted to hear, but the majority Sinhalese population maintained that the rebel Tamil Tigers exhibited little interest in carrying peace talks to a conclusion. The war continued as a low-intensity but unremitting drain on the economics of the nation.

Despite deregulation, privatization, and international competition from 1977 onward economic growth lagged and in 2001, Sri Lanka faced bankruptcy, debt reached 101 percent of GDP, and growth was a negative 1.4 percent. Even after growth resumed the following year, steep defense expenditures caused deficits to accumulate. Disillusionment with Western-oriented economic policies was compounded by disappointment with Western recalcitrance toward supporting the resumption of the civil war. Beginning in 2005, many Western donors reduced aid due to the increased violence, China emerged as the largest bilateral donor.

Enter the Black Knight from the East

The West had repeatedly turned down requests for the weapons to defeat the Tamils, and disillusionment with external efforts to mediate the conflict propelled the careers of a nationalist "sons of the soil" movement. Mahinda Rajapaksa, elected in 2005, was the first president to openly challenge the status of the traditional elites. Rajapaksa represented a new-style, populist leadership, claiming to bridge the material and social divides between the Western-influenced upper social strata and the remainder of the population.[4] His father was a parliamentarian belonging to the high-caste rural elite of the south; hence his ability to connect with the rural population and lower middle classes who saw him as one of them.

The election produced policy reversals in the war against the rebels, in internal governance, and finally in electoral strategy. China became a major supplier of arms by 2007, providing the government with the weapons to annihilate the Tamil forces. The destruction of the Tamil Tigers and the death of its leader, Velupillai Prabhakaran, in May 2009 made Rajapaksa a hero among the Sinhalese. His harsh disregard of civilian casualties—forty thousand have been alleged, according to UN sources—put the international community on alert.[5]

After the defeat of the rebels, government rehabilitation and relocation of civilian populations lagged, and numerous allegations surfaced of its involvement in the killings of journalists who reported negatively on the conduct of the war and the stalled rehabilitation programs that followed. EU member states repeatedly called for the UN Security Council to put the safety of Sri Lanka's civilian population on its agenda, and by early May 2009 seventeen countries (including Argentina, Bosnia and Herzegovina, Canada, Chile, France, Germany, Ukraine, Uruguay, and the United Kingdom) asked the organization's Human Rights Council to investigate war crimes in Sri Lanka. In defiance of the EU initiative, the

Security Council, led by Russia and Iran, passed a resolution on May 27, 2009, that ignored the alleged violations of human rights and humanitarian law by the government and instead commended its action and condemned only one side in the conflict, the Tamil Tigers.[6] The rebuttal of the Western initiative by Cuba, Egypt, Pakistan, China, India, Russia, South Africa, and Brazil in support of what Sri Lankan labeled anti-terrorist operations explicitly separated responsibility for human rights from the priority to maintain public order.

Western nations responded by asking for the appointment of a UN panel of experts in June 2010 to advise the organization's secretary-general on accountability issues relating to allegations of violations of international human rights and humanitarian law. The Sri Lankan government protested the subsequent appointment of the panel, calling it "unwarranted," and denied the panel permission to enter the country.[7] Nevertheless, the panel released a report on March 31, 2011, citing jarring examples of misconduct and human rights violations by both sides and asked the Human Rights Council to reconsider its earlier resolution. But the bid for reconsideration failed. Since then, the Rajapaksa government has used the report to rally support and justify its view that China, and not the West, is Sri Lanka's real friend in times of need. The local media have attributed the actions of the West to the lobbying of Tamil populations overseas. The emphasis of the Western media on war crimes, along with its prompting of UN action, hastened Sri Lanka's turn away from the West (Perera 2010). The Sri Lankan response to Western efforts to protect its civilians reveals the importance of having a rich friend like China. Although the Europeans can put human rights issues on the Security Council agenda, enemies of liberal internationalism determine the results.

The Dragon's Gift?

Growth returned to Sri Lanka at the end of the civil war in 2009, and along with the positive macroeconomic trends came a windfall of loans from China for project financing. Chinese businesses descended with a vengeance, finding no pushback from the West, which stayed away. China's engagement escalated from a few million dollars in 2005 to almost $1 billion in 2009 and more than doubled again in 2010. By comparison, the United States gave $7.4 million and Britain just £1.25 million in 2009. The most notable Chinese project is the construction of a new port in

President Rajapaksa's home province, near his hometown of Hambantota on the southern coast of Sri Lanka, ten miles from one of the world's busiest shipping lanes (Page 2009). China says that Hambantota is a purely commercial venture, but US security specialists regard it as part of the "string of pearls" strategy that includes upgrading ports at Gwadar in Pakistan, Chittagong in Bangladesh, and Sittwe in Myanmar.[8]

Before independence, the British military bases in Ceylon created jobs for workers and opportunities for local entrepreneurship. The new ports can offer similar opportunities if they become home to Chinese naval activities in the Indian Ocean. A new airfield has been constructed in the vicinity of the port. Chinese loans are financing a series of roads around the capital city and a series of ring roads round the island.[9] Some estimates put the sum total of all Chinese projects in Sri Lanka at about $6.1 billion, and estimates of the number of Chinese workers range from 14,000 to 25,000, mostly blue-collar labor, of which 40 percent are alleged to be prison labor. A US Senate Foreign Relations Committee report on Sri Lanka notes that Chinese bids are grossly inflated (US Senate Committee on Foreign Relations 2009).

Chinese projects are not grants; they are commercial projects, "which are highly inflated to make allowances for kickbacks. It is not creating livelihood in Sri Lanka. A lot of money is rechanneled into China via labor and import machinery" (US Senate Committee on Foreign Relations 2009). Rumors circulate that Iran also issued credits allowing Sri Lanka to delay repayment for six months for consumption of petroleum worth over $1 billion dollars.[10] Chinese-funded projects in Sri Lanka are awarded to Chinese contractors that import Chinese labor.

Labeling Chinese financing of Sri Lankan projects is not easy. The Chinese loans evade the categories generally used by the international community. It is not bilateral assistance since aid to Sri Lanka is minimal. It is not direct private investment. When asked by an international official representing one of the international financial institutions (IFIs) in 2010 why China does not participate in donor coordination meetings in Sri Lanka, Yang Xiuping, then China's ambassador to Sri Lanka, responded, "China is not a donor." She was correct. China's official development assistance (ODA) is less than that of other donors.

By its unconventional way of dispersing funds, China has effectively evaded international mechanisms of oversight, avoiding collaboration with other donors in such forums as the Paris Club. This means the loans are made without reference to a debt sustainability framework shared with other lenders, which creates the risks of contingent liability. When asked why China does not attend meetings of the bilateral lenders, its ambassador responded, "China does not lend to Sri Lanka."[11] Again she was correct. China's projects in Sri Lanka differ from those generally recognized as aid by other countries. China's giant infrastructure financing in Sri Lanka is undertaken by the Chinese Export-Import (Exim) Bank and need not be classified as direct transfers from the Chinese Treasury or Central Bank to the Government of Sri Lanka.

The loans support Chinese firms that have obtained contracts in Sri Lanka. To solicit business in Sri Lanka, some Chinese firms have launched online campaigns to reach influential Sri Lankans, offering cash payments in exchange for contacts with government officials. The Chinese government takes no responsibility for these solicitations since the government does not make them. But the government is a shareholder that appoints the management of these primarily state-owned firms in alignment with the wishes of the Chinese Communist Party. The officials who run some of these firms, such as China's oil companies, are reputed to enjoy a higher rank than the foreign minister and thus cannot be held to account by China's diplomatic services.

China's direct investments are lower than those of the United States, Japan, the United Kingdom, or the European Union. A state-owned bank that lends to state-owned firms enables China to act freely in Sri Lanka without conforming to the international covenants that govern bilateral aid or government-to-government transfers. The nexus of lending from the Exim Bank, an agent of the government, to state-owned firms operating overseas allows the government to promote the interests of Chinese companies as if these companies were private, even if the beneficiaries are typically firms owned by the state and managed by Chinese government officials. It is presumed that these resemble Chinese loans to other developing countries, which are typically commodity-backed infrastructure credits at market rates tied to export credit. There is no way to determine if these loans are subsidized or whether they comply with rules established by the international financial institutions in which China holds membership. The terms of the loans from China have never been fully disclosed.

Should the Sri Lankan government be unable to repay the loans, it might seek an IMF program, in effect using multilateral financing to pay off its loans to agents of the Chinese government. Thus China has spun a web that circumvents international financial safeguards. By transforming private commercial transactions into government-to-government negotiations that exploit the concept of sovereign guarantee, the Exim Bank can evade the normal set of liabilities of private investment while evading the normal rules of government-to-government financing.

The New Rules of Governance

The Dragon's financial gifts changed Sri Lanka's political landscape. The new form of obtaining credit enables the government to evade accountability to Parliament, the press, and to voters. For example, many Sri Lankans question the commercial utility of both the port and the airport far from the nation's manufacturing and commercial center Colombo. A member of the opposition party who is from the same district as the president alleges that he was denied access even to a feasibility study of the project. Several MPs who are also unable to obtain information from the government have corroborated his concerns. The terms of repayment have never been disclosed, encouraging rumors that the interest on the loans exceeds commercial rates. Even the currency that the loan repayment requires is not public information. Unable to inspect the loan terms, the Parliament is unable to uphold its responsibility to audit the feasibility of government fiscal liabilities. It can make no assessments of the future risk to the current account balance. Flush with Chinese funds, the government can maintain widespread subsidies, a bloated public sector, transfers to loss-making state enterprises, which causes Sri Lanka to enjoy a low rating from international markets. This makes it unlikely that Sri Lanka can find alternative loans from international markets even if it wanted to. And since the head of the opposition United National Party (UNP), Ranil Wickremasinghe, has said that his party will not repay the Chinese loans if elected, China has a strong incentive to ensure the continuity of Rajapaksa's rule and to close its ears to any criticism as to how the Rajapaksa family manages the country's internal affairs.

The loans give the president ample off-budget funds needed to orchestrate loyalty shifts among the opposition MPs and buy off opposition members so the ruling party will wield a supermajority. When the 2010 election denied him the two-thirds majority needed to amend the constitution to eliminate presidential term limits, the government allegedly offered bribes ranging from $600,000 to $1.2 million to holdouts for the necessary votes.[12] Fourteen opposition MPs reportedly accepted the offers, ensuring the amendment's success. One member of the opposition believes the tactic of enticing people to "cross over for personal gain corrupts the entire political establishment." He stated that the undisclosed slush funds allow the government to circumvent the national treasury and essentially buy off enough members to ensure the success of any legislation it seeks (Wijedasa 2010).[13]

The president also serves as the finance minister, and he has appointed one of his brothers the secretary of defense and another the cabinet minister of economic development. The former also acts as the city manager of Colombo, making him the czar of urban construction. The president's son, Namal Rajapaksa, is often the only MP in attendance with the president at high-level international delegations, which is why in diplomatic circles, Sri Lanka is referred to as the "Land of the Rising Son." The president understands he extracts more loyalty from his patronage if recipients believe that his son will follow him in power.

With the erosion of fiscal accountability to the Parliament, the rights of speech and assembly have also withered. The challenger during the 2010 elections, Sarath Fonseka, was arrested February 8, 2010, and sentenced to three years in prison by a military tribunal for corrupt practices.[14] Rajapaksa's critics say that the president disregards due process in prosecuting critics, and that Sri Lanka was a democracy in name only when in September 2010 he took the final step in removing the substance of Sri Lanka's parliamentary democracy, amending the constitution to grant himself full presidential immunity and final authority over all appointments to the civil service, judiciary, and police.[15] He commands the armed forces and ninety other institutions. When *The Economist* opined that the additional powers were unnecessary and dangerous, he banned the offending issue. A Sri Lanka no longer dependent on Western funds can ignore Western covenants on internal governance and due process.[16] Western disapproval hardly matters now that alternative sources of international financial assistance exist.

The ruling party has cultivated its own historical narrative to explain its shift, asserting that the country is simply becoming more Asian. A 2010

New York Times article reported Sri Lanka's foreign secretary, Palitha Kohona, saying that Sri Lanka's "traditional donors," namely the United States, Canada, and the European Union, had "receded into a very distant corner" to be replaced by countries in the East. The new donors were neighbors, he said. They were also rich. And they conducted themselves differently. "Asians don't go around teaching each other how to behave," he added. "There are ways we deal with each other—perhaps a quiet chat, but not wagging the finger" (Sengupta 2008).

The ruling party has twice voted against legislation championed by the opposition for improved standards of transparency. Rajapaksa's spokespersons say that the subservience of previous governments to Western models is why, since independence, Sri Lanka has not done as well as its neighbors to the East that have embraced authoritarian developmental models. According to this narrative, Parliamentary bickering and electoral zigzagging of policy has sent the country on a path to nowhere. Western style adversarial parliamentary politics fails to resonate with the needs and realities of the impoverished populations of South Asia that seek to emulate China's urbanization, mass literacy, industrialization, and its acquisition of wealth.

The shift of influence in the local political economy toward the sons of the soil and away from the Western-educated traditional elites is refocusing Sri Lanka's geopolitical orientation, making China, and not the West, into the center of gravity. Having secured China's guarantee of support, the regime's plummeting status in the West is not a political liability when ample slush funds flow in through Chinese-invested projects. Western censure actually strengthens the president and makes the West look hypercritical. Rajapaksa does not have to explain why his government has transitioned from being a swing voter in the United Nations to being aligned with regimes that vote consistently according to the principle of nonintervention in the affairs of other nations.

Sri Lanka now seeks its partners among other global outcasts, including Iran, Zimbabwe, and, before his ouster, Muammar Gaddafi of Libya. When these regimes acted in isolation, they could be pressured into extinction, but no longer; as a group, their prospects of long-term persistence improve. The patterns of governance transformation that occurred in Sri Lanka are repeated in China's relationships with other Southeast Asian countries—Myanmar, Cambodia, Laos, and Vietnam, where Chinese project financing helps governments escape the safeguard requirements and standards of procedural transparency required for multilateral guarantees. What began as a congruence of national interest is becoming increasingly a convergence of beliefs. Escaping the pressure of international censorship, the leaderships of Angola, Myanmar, North Korea, Pakistan, South Africa, Sudan, Turkmenistan, and Zimbabwe can contribute to an aggregate pattern. As the group controls more resources, incentives for other countries to join also increase. This raises the question of whether a cohesive alternative to Western views on modernization is emerging that can inculcate shared behavior and validate shared values (Newman 2010).

Chinese Soft Power: Enough to Construct an Alternative International Regime?

No direct indication exists to correlate China's diplomatic relations with Sri Lanka as part of a deliberate effort to scuttle international agendas and norm-building along principles it opposes (Gowan and Branter 2009). After all, China's immediate goals are to firm up its commercial relations with Sri Lanka and to secure access to vital resources that flow through the Indian Ocean. China's role can be categorized as providing positive feedback or soft power.[17] Yet even without any aggressive effort to challenge the ideology of liberalism, China's growing influence raises important questions about how strong the integrative logic of liberal internationalism will remain (Ikenberry 2011b, 56).[18]

Belief diffusion among its trading partners is affected by the pull of China's soft power as an exemplar of the virtues of growth under authoritarian rule. "Rajapaksa and his party are positing that economic development should take overarching priority over a discussion about rights and governance" (Arnoldy 2010). They claim that China's Communist Party has contributed more to the welfare and dignity of its people than have the parties of many emerging democracies. Clients like Sri Lanka and Cambodia simply view China's economic success as proof that an authoritarian state facilitates economic growth and is a better model for economic growth than democracy. They see China as an example of modernization that benefits the working majority because it defines social responsibility, justice, tolerance, and democracy without subservience to individual rights. Above all China is admired because it gained incorporation into the world economy while maintaining independence from Western powers.

As a new basin of attraction, China can accelerate the rate of divergence from Western norms. The web that China is weaving does not alter the historical DNA of its partners or cause shifts in their patterns of self-organization. Nepotism and systemic corruption were already endemic in Sri Lanka, and no government has been able to resist its appeal. That susceptibility resides in the persistence of Sri Lanka's patrimonial social structure, which has coopted its democratic institutions. Chinese financial assistance did not introduce the nepotistic tendencies of the governments with which it transacts. Nepotism at the highest levels was the rule in both of the major political parties, the United National Party as well as the Sri Lanka Freedom Party. The first president after independence was D. S. Senanayake of the UNP. After his death in 1952, his son Dudley replaced him, only to resign one year later. His successor was his uncle, John Kotelawala, causing the UNP to become known as the "Uncle Nephew Party." The Bandaranaike family has led the opposition party since its creation. After S. W. R. D. Bandaranaike's assassination in 1959, his wife, Sirimavo, became prime minister and ruled until 1977. Her daughter later became president and ruled until 2005. Neopatrimonial domination of national politics has resisted six decades of electoral democracy.

Chinese aid and influence are not the only factors behind the domestic changes in Sri Lanka. Nor is Chinese influence the determinant factor in pushing Angola, Myanmar, North Korea, Pakistan, Sudan, or South Africa toward autocracy. The illiberal trajectories of these countries are due to internal factors that have deep roots. What China has done is give developing countries a new collective identity and a new framework for regime legitimacy based on copying China's path to worker prosperity. China's soft power validates behavior that diverges from the Western discourse on rights, and as a network it facilitates the spread of information, helping members copy behavior from other partners that experience the same vilification from a disapproving West.

Eclipsed by China, the West is no a longer a meaningful player in the competition to influence Sri Lanka's domestic policies or geopolitical orientation. A similar challenge to Western models is now spreading across countries once considered supportive, such as Pakistan, Nepal, and even

India. China's nascent middle class has much in common with the new middle class of Sri Lanka. Both embrace the cosmopolitan consumption patterns of the West but reject Western protocols for protecting individual rights. Western-trained postcolonial elites who administered those countries after independence are losing status in favor of populist leaders. Western-trained policy specialists are increasingly unable to win local elections or establish electoral consistencies, and hold ground only in technical ministries, such as finance and planning. Thus South Asia is a battleground of competing truths, with their political ideologies and their geopolitical sympathies being pulled both East and West.

Policy Implications: Applications to International Development Policy

This assessment of Sri Lanka's susceptibility to China's influence has important implications for global development policy. In the mid-1990s, Western donors collaborated with Sri Lanka's Western-oriented ideological leaders, such as then President Chandrika Bandaranaike Kumaratunga (1994–2005), to meet the Millennium Development Goals (MDGs) posted by the United Nations Development Programme. The key to meeting these goals was good governance: improving the quality of key institutions, such as judicial and regulatory independence, along with pay systems within the civil service. Low salaries, patronage-based recruitment, and the use of public enterprise as an employer of last resort led to massive demoralization and huge government deficits. But the effort at institutional reform did not supplant the informal patrimonial rules that allow nepotism to flourish.

How could Sri Lanka's current trajectory be more different from that of the high-performing East Asian nations—Japan, South Korea, Taiwan, Singapore, and Malaysia? Their leaders recognized that if plans for social investment were to succeed, first the relationship between the ruler and the system of public administration had to be transformed so that rules would take precedent over discretion. Governance infrastructure was augmented so that bureaucratic, rather than patrimonial, norms could be inculcated. Meritocracy in senior appointments to the economic bureaucracy and a rule-based criteria for policy interventions protected the economic rights of both investors and citizens, and ensured policies were heeded that could contribute to general well-being (Campos and Root

1996). Since powerful budgetary and financial powers were assigned to the bureaucracy, including the allocation of credit to gain compliance from the private sector, it was crucial to ensure that bureaucratic discretion did not degenerate into bribery and corruption. Key policy makers were insulated from elites seeking extractive privileges. To improve transparency, a state–society interface comprised of representative councils enabled communication and coordination between the private sector and the policy makers. The effect was to stigmatize nepotism and influence citizen behavior and values. A cycle of positive feedbacks continues to express itself in civic activism to combat corruption.

The high performers exceeded all developing country rivals by the intensity of private investment funded by national savings. That surge of private investment would not have been secured without governance infrastructure that reduced the temptation to expropriate private investment and without sound fiscal policies to ensure the value of future returns from investments made in the present. By contrast, Sri Lanka went from one crisis of fiscal irresponsibility to another, caused by currency inflation introduced to wipe away the debts accrued by injudicious government spending and patrimonial distributions. Optimal plans for long-term growth will not be heeded without credible mechanisms to limit the ruler's discretion over public administration and over fiscal policy.

Policy Implications: China and the Future of the Liberal World Order

Resource interdependency best describes the imperatives that motivate China's economic policy, which relies on distant and diverse inputs of energy, manufactured parts, raw materials, and energy. Its voting record in the WTO in terms of trade rules makes China seem like a status quo power. It depends on open markets and votes with the developed world against the developing world on issues of trade openness. China enjoys many of the global public goods that economic liberalism provides, such as secure sea-lanes and the WTO's open trade protocols.

China's leaders have shown sensitivity to the growing role they play in global economic stability, especially in macroeconomic performance. They have exhibited an understanding that the Chinese financial system influences the health of global finances and are well aware that the health of China's own economy depends on the health of the economies with which it is intertwined.

Nevertheless, China prefers that liberalism's international component be limited to the interconnectivity of the global markets. Its embrace of economic openness does not lead it into alignment with the core values of liberal internationalism. China's repudiation of democracy, human rights, the responsibility to protect, and the role of global civil society renders it the "single most serious challenge to liberal democracy in the world today," warns Francis Fukuyama (2011, 56–57).

Its influence and evolution are a far cry from the West's expectations that China could be led by trade openness to become a responsible stakeholder that would play a constructive role in international affairs. This view of China's inevitable evolution into being a responsible stakeholder is based on two key assumptions of liberal internationalism: that isolating China from development and collective security was a source of great potential instability; and that the best path to mitigate that instability was to expose China to the benefits of globalization. The West believed that China needed more incentives in order to become a responsible stakeholder in collaborative engagement with other nations, and that greater integration into global commerce would eventually reorient its relationship to the world. It was a course predicated by China's economic linkages with the West, and on this basis, liberal idealism said that China would inevitably accept democratic reform, despite the wishes of its senior leadership, and would converge to liberal principles. Economists constructed a similar future scenario, believing that once a global market for all goods and services was fully constructed, the utility of all market participants would converge.

However, the liberal order that China was invited to join was already organized around US alliances and technology (Hecht 2011). When China went from being an oil exporter to being an oil importer in 1992, most of the world's suppliers already had partnerships with the West. China's need for oil and the West's monopoly of sources led China to develop relations with "rogue" players in order to obtain resources. Its foreign policy prioritizes the desire to escape markets dominated by players that can interfere with the flow of resources on which it depends.

Managing the Risks of Complex Interdependence

China's current trade policies and its relationships with censured partners underscore that it will continue to choose its alignments based on its needs for identity, security, and resources. It will also compete with the West over the benefits of relationships with emerging partners by specializes in high-obligation relationships with the leaderships of countries estranged from the West. This behavior can cause greater divergence within the global system and peril for the liberal system if China's growing share of global trade will make it harder for the West to alter the internal politics of rogue regimes via censure or trade sanctions.

What the West should want is not to force change within China, but to work with China to mitigate risks that global outliers pose to system stability. Walking away from Libya empty-handed after its embrace of Gaddafi should serve as a warning of the danger of being too close to regimes that abuse their own people and of investing in leaders, rather than in the well-being of the population. China evacuated 35,000 workers, and abandoned more than fifty projects that were worth more $18.8 billion and involved seventy-five Chinese enterprises, including thirteen firms owned by the state. This will make Chinese firms more aware of the need to guard against political risks. A lesson China can draw is that if it were to bid through fair tendering in a more transparent environment, its cheap labor and comprehensive experience at building infrastructure in difficult environments might make it a more competent bidder than Western countries. But to encourage China to cooperate on the quarantining of rogue regimes, China must not only recognize the risks it faces through such economic linkages, it also must obtain something that will alter how it is recognized within the international system.

Several key precepts of liberal internationalism—democratic community, shared sovereignty, and the right to protect—pose threats to China's security. China's territorial claims to Tibet, Taiwan, and the South China Sea are not recognized, making it the only member of the UN Security Council whose territory is still contested and not under a unified central government. Theoretically, if China does not adhere to strict protection of sovereignty, it too could be subject to interventions on territories that it claims. Its form of government is out of alignment with the objective of global democratic convergence. Changing China's behavior requires an approach that recognizes the risks and apprehensions that China faces. It will not be won over to a set of values that views its form of government as illegitimate and transitory. Yet few developing country governments have done more to enhance the welfare of their populations, boosting the respect its population enjoys in the eyes of the world at the same time. No wonder China prefers a narrower definition of regime legitimacy, "ruling responsibly" by its own standards rather than being a responsible stakeholder by Western standards. Moreover China believes that history has yet to determine whether its way of managing social and economic affairs is not the better example of building a market economy for other developing countries to follow.

The issues concerning belief transmission and the integration of China are part of a much larger set of policy dilemmas that arise as a result of growing global interdependency. We will turn to these issues in the final chapter.

11

No Captain at the Helm

Policy Diffusion along Global Trading Networks

Liberal internationalism has been the West's foreign policy agenda since the cold war. But being at the top rung of liberal internationalism's hierarchical ladder is no longer enough to ensure that the West will hold sway over the system of international relations. The most popular metaphors of socioeconomic change—the end of history, the flat world—have failed to capture evolving trends in world politics that are dissolving the top-down structure of traditional power relations.

We are witnessing a complexity transition, triggered by new flows of global resource dependency and resulting in worldwide trade and power shifts. The average number of countries each country exports to have been rising steadily since 1976, increasing from an average of twenty to ninety different trading partners. These shifts are dislodging the liberal West from its role at the focal point of global trade and weakening its credibility as a model of modernization and governance. New players have emerged from the global periphery, and their interactions with each other and with existing powers contribute to an evolving ecology in which policy preferences will no longer emanate from Western models. The dispersion of connectivity is causing a global preference gap to grow wider.

In a world once dominated by vertical trade flows, it was natural to presume that belief transmission would move from the West. But changes in the global trading system are resulting in the formation of new networks and the inculcation of norms unique to these patterns of exchange. Local cultures and values are becoming global information sources. As the hierarchical order of global trade decomposes, the new global diversity will run contrary to the laws of most dominant international relations theories. Instead of top-down emulation and inculcation of norms, diverse agents will redefine the optimal strategies for one another and, through feedback loops, for themselves. Institutional structures will arise in the context of both myopic local contests that recombine traditional practices and beliefs, and coevolutionary pressure induced by the environment.

Scenarios of Global Transformation

Nor will the novel strategies for survival resulting from this global complexity transition fit conventional conceptions of geopolitical change found in the metaphors coined by Thomas Friedman, Walter Wriston, Samuel Huntington, or Francis Fukuyama, some of the most influential thinkers in recent history. All four pass over critical feedback loops between the interacting agents that will determine strategies across environments and ultimately reconfigure the system of international relations.

In a world speeding along multiple paths to modernity, perpetual novelty arises from feedbacks, networks, nonlinearity, and path sensitivity. The result is not the homogenized "flat world" envisioned by Friedman, in which global economic opportunity spreads without interruption for all to access (2005). Advances in communications and logistics have lowered the barriers to entry for markets around the world, and portions of developing societies have benefited. However, many developing societies face rugged landscapes, where developmental challenges are extreme and only local options, not flat horizons of unlimited opportunity, are visible. There is no reason for societies facing different landscapes to evolve toward the same end. On a rugged landscape, one society's fitness challenges differ from those of another, so that a variety of strategies are likely. Some societies, like Afghanistan or Pakistan, might choose dependence on another power in order to use that dependency to extract resources, renting out their strategic space in lieu of producing economic surplus. So long as landscapes differ, fitness strategies will vary, leading to more sharply defined but separate traits.

The "twilight of sovereignty" predicted by Citibank's visionary Walter Wriston and other prophets of global capitalism presumed that the reliance on universal systems of communication and information processing would allow multinationals to eclipse the power of nation-states to control the world economy (1992).[1] The state, Wriston predicted correctly, would no longer be the all-purpose unit that shaped the identity and the strategy of the key global actors. World politics in the twenty-first century would be shaped by a plurality of actors: firms, civil society, political parties, and social media. He also understood that these actors would interact through adaptive social institutions, such as networks and markets, without a system of centralized control or organization.

But in 1992 Wriston could not foresee that the state would remain essential to the ends of the more sector-specialized networks. The impact of multinational firms, banks, and other non-state actors on the global order was apparent during the 2008 financial crisis, when the excesses of private markets placed whole governments at risk. But many emerging economies are state-centered, and they hope to avoid problems they associate with the power of private firms in the Western world. They believe the activities of private finance have compromised US global leadership. To make the most of their growing power, some emerging powers, such as China, Russia, and Brazil, use their growing share of international trade to transform ordinary commercial exchanges into assertions of sovereignty. They employ government-to-government channels to transact with overseas clients and use trade to gain geopolitical compliance from weaker partners. The evolving global power shifts strengthen the sovereignty of the nation-states in global affairs. And the 2008 financial crisis has stiffened their resolve to keep it that way.[2]

Among scenarios for future stability, global optimists roundly support the liberal vision based on modernization theory. This vision, captured in Francis Fukuyama's "end of history" metaphor, misconstrues the optimization challenge of global interdependence (1989). As the global economy becomes more competitive, there will be no convergence to liberal democratic norms; no single strategy will optimize the preferences of all the nations within a given ecology, much less the preferences of the subgroups within nations. Just as unfilled niches in ecosystems are rare, the global race for wealth and power is creating an unforeseen range of governance variations. Elites who seek to maintain and enhance their power against local competitors will alter their strategies as the international system into which they try to integrate their economies becomes more competitive. Many will seek leverage over those they rule by pursuing self-preserving alternatives rather than prescriptions for liberal democratic growth (Bueno de Mesquita et al. 2003; Bueno de Mesquita and Root 2000).

Samuel Huntington is the pessimist among this group of prominent global thinkers. He argues that identity politics will strengthen, leading to a "clash of civilizations" in which conflict and alignment occur along civilizational lines (1996). His view draws support from some realists and postmodernists, but it underestimates the transforming effects of new patterns of resource interdependency. His characterization of global alignments as civilization-based does not explain China's linkages with culturally dissimilar Sri Lanka, Pakistan, Peru, Iran, Sudan, Syria, Zimbabwe, South Africa, or Angola.[3] His misgiving is based on the fear that regional, cultural, or mercantilist alliances, even as they fragment the cohesiveness of liberal internationalism, do not offer an effective alternative world order.

These authors' visions, for either stability or instability, do not reflect the global transformation under way or the multiple versions of modernity that lie ahead. Most reflect the traditional political economy of the cold war that conceived of stability in terms of polarities when a world divided into clearly defined zones of influence made system-level properties relatively easy to predict. At the 1975 signing of the Helsinki accords on human rights, for example, six of the 35 signatories were in the Soviet bloc and all were Western.[4] Today's increased complexity of the interactions among the parts that constitute the system results from many divergent patterns of interdependence; and the networks that form can determine the system's resilience.

Both the end of bipolarity and the rise and fall of empires can be seen as shifting internal and external dynamics, as well as responses within a shared ecology across time. A world yielding to its laws of complexity will render any hegemony and polarity transient. Geopolitics will be multidirectional, as partners large and small grow more dependent on one another for their own progress and stability. In this environment, they must assess and adapt the strategies of their competitors, either firms or other nations, and update their overall strategies to consider how every agent in the global economy is connected to every other.

Premature Convergence: Racing Economies, Lagging Polities

Liberal internationalist versions of modernization theory maintain that sociopolitical convergence toward global cooperation will follow trade and fiscal reforms that bring developing countries into the global economy. However, the search for a peace underpinned by a "global civilization" is not unique to Western liberals; emerging states have their own discourse on the values of globalization and seek to contribute their own content to global debates.

Singaporean diplomat and author Kishore Muhbubani (2013) envisions peaceful coexistence attained by a "great convergence" toward a global civilization without the inculcation of Western values, practices, and institutions. Muhbubani's path toward a global civilization avoids the contentious issue of governance. Democracy is not out of the picture, but it is not a prerequisite. He posits instead that consumerism, not economic or political liberalism, is sufficient to create a unified value system that will be more inclusive than Western conceptions of modernization. He views the unprecedented merging of middle-class economic aspirations as the impetus for a more inclusive civilization that would encompass not only the West but also authoritarian regimes ranging from Russia and China to the culturally conservative Islamic states of the Gulf, where many people enjoy high standards of living but live in fear that democracy will upset the stability they enjoy.

The logic of one world that the Singaporean diplomat celebrates is an undertaking of transnational executives and their like-minded peers in central banks and finance ministries, as well as politicians, technocrats, and consumer elites represented by the international media. Like Walter Wriston, Muhbubani makes the point that these transnational actors, "the best minds all over the world," share a common aspiration to educate their children to conduct their business and their governments' according to the same precepts taught in MBA programs around the globe (2013, 83). By managing the spread of global consumerism, they will patch up centuries-old ethnic and cultural estrangements and make obsolete the clash of civilizations.

Indeed considerable evidence exists that material aspirations across different cultures have already converged. Metropolitan centers in China, Australia, the United States, and the Gulf tend to resemble one another; an inhabitant from one can live comfortably in another. But does a desire for better infrastructure, more access to education, faster roads and railways, improved sewerage, vaccinations for infants, and holidays on the seashore produce homogeneous cultural outlooks that lead to a global civilization?

This conception of modernity in which the melding of middle-class values will produce a global convergence disregards two powerful sources of divergence. First, it is disconnected from the heritage of individual rights and constraints on government that lies at the core of liberalism. Material aspirations, as this book has emphasized in its examinations of Sri Lanka, Turkey, China, India, and other countries, are not sufficient to build a consensual platform for a rights-based, liberal political culture.

Second, transnationalism is already finding resistance to its monopoly of the symbols of modernity. While the middle-class inhabitants of the world's capitals may congregate in similar places and dress and spend according to the same sets of preferences, the inhabitants of rural towns and cities of the hinterland rarely do. These are populations that hold on to more parochial aspirations and who distrust global benchmarking. Yet they too benefit from the spread of foreign direct investment and the practice of global production and marketing. Economic growth has enabled the populations beyond the world capitals to invest not only in scientific education and management training but also in cultural authenticity, and to emphasize their cultural and ideological differences—not only from other cultures but from their own leaders in the urban cores where the global trendsetters hold sway. These groups are challenging the efforts of the globalizing elite in the political spheres. Fear that Westernization will dissolve the glue that holds their society together motivates them to use their resources to bolster local cultural values. Such trends can complicate the policy goals of the globalizers and make the resort to illiberal political devices more likely, fostering political instability within newly emerging polities.

Recent politics of European enlargement—a goal that motivated the political elites of both Europe and Turkey from the late 1980s to advocate the latter's eventual accession to the European Union—exemplify these cultural–ideological trends that divide the local and transnational middle classes.[5] Technocrats may argue that a strategic partnership linking Turkey through collaboration on security, commerce, and technology with the West will strengthen both spheres, but this does not mean it will happen. Even as the government of Turkey maintains institutional progress toward ascension, popular support for EU membership has lagged since 2001, checked by the wishes of the new middle classes from the small towns and countryside of Anatolia, where the majority of Turks have their roots.

Groups that place a premium on cultural authenticity have become more outspoken, making it difficult for politicians in both Europe and Turkey to gain domestic consensus on full EU membership. Turks in fact are demanding cultural commodities that recall the former grandeur of Ottoman sultanates, when Turkey was its own master and the center of its own empire. Political leaders in Europe and Turkey have taken notice of the growing strength of the new factions that seek to bolster traditional values, and this diminishes their enthusiasm to spend political capital to champion the EU enlargement project. The spread of voting rights has made the current cohort of politicians more sensitive to local opinion than were the technocratic initiators of the enlargement project. Ignoring these new voices can be costly for national politicians. How ironic that the efforts of rural factions to deter the cultural and political spread of Western values are by-products of democracy, the democratization of the policy process, and the spread of the ballot that has empowered them.

The powerful elite who favor globalization are not the only significant actors emerging in world politics. Rising populism is not unique to Turkey. In Venezuela, Zimbabwe, Sri Lanka, Pakistan, Russia, Thailand, and India, nationalists seeking to reinvent traditional identities have stymied globalizing urban elites through the ballot box. The quest for cultural authenticity among the rising middle classes in these countries makes the hope of global cultural convergence on Western terms seem naïve. In China the nationalistic impulses of the emerging middle classes are being held in check by the technocratic impulses of the leadership to avoid turbulences that may divert the nation's attention from the goal of economic growth.

As a more educated, complex, and diverse body politic takes shape, disputes within countries over the form that modernization will take have been intensified by the spread of prosperity. "How to consume wealth can prove more controversial than how to produce it" (Campos and Root 1996, 177). Once fundamental issues like mass poverty are settled, small differences may end up being deeply contested. After achieving a fairly high standard of living, the governments of East Asia's high-performing countries had to learn to manage the divergent ambitions of populations in which a clash of tastes and preferences arose from the spread of affluence. Thailand, South Korea, Taiwan, Malaysia, and the Philippines have all experienced significant societal friction concerning conflict over such practices as nepotism and corruption that were acceptable or at least ignored during the period of high growth.

Today, with more at stake—and more surplus to fight over—both the local Westernizers and the traditionalists are often impelled to use illiberal tactics, such as the formation and support of militant groups like the Zimbabwe African National Union, the United Socialist Party of Venezuela, or the Thailand's People's Alliance for Democracy. This resort to illiberal tactics in an environment of increasing factionalism is reflected in the regular assessment of democracies conducted by the Economist Intelligence Unit, which reveal that during the first decade of the twenty-first century many emerging nations, Turkey included, have been downgraded to the status of hybrid or "flawed" democracies. In categories such as the treatment of minorities, limits on executive power, and press freedom, they are diverging from liberal standards.

Globalization entails a policy environment that differs significantly from both the predictions and aspirations of liberal internationalism. Transferring global consumer rhetoric from the market to the polity is not a straightforward process. Cultural identity is often constructed politically rather than economically (Lars-Cederman 1997). As a result shifts in global trade can have divergent as well as convergent impacts, fostering polarized political cultures in many of the fastest growing emerging economies.

Even where a common set of material aspirations has emerged, it has seldom produced a middle class with common outlook in matters like individual rights or the role of the state. In China, for example, the middle class that identifies its fortunes with state-owned enterprises and state-led economic development places a premium on being absorbed into the one-party state. This makes increasing the supply of elite positions essential to regime stability. Western liberal political rights do not spread as quickly as fast-food chains. Polities do not move at the same pace as the commodities of economic exchange, and civil rights are harder to obtain than refrigerators or cars. The progressive reduction of national differences in the realm of economics does not automatically translate into social and political realms. Moreover economic interconnectivity among nations has heightened disagreement on issues of managing the global commons and the rights and responsibilities of global citizenship. Racing economies are producing lagging polities, and this dynamic of premature convergence is making globalization harder to manage.

Global Preference Gap: The Sovereignty Network

The West's post–cold war conventions of security face a challenge some-times referred to as the axis of sovereignty. The axis comprises govern-ments that seek an international order in which the state possesses in-violable political authority over the management of its domestic affairs. It considers the leadership role of the liberal West similar to that of the evangelical missionary activity and trade consortiums associated with co-lonialism. The divide between a vision of the future that stresses state sovereignty and a government's right to be the sole authority within its boundaries, and that which stresses interdependence and sovereign rights derived from the rules of international society, polarizes current discus-sions about the future structure of the global system.

After the fall of the Soviet bloc, Western democracies were ready to embrace a post-Westphalian age in which their "responsibility to protect" would mandate international law and supranational institutions, and en-gender cooperation along the model of the European Union. Examples of such mandated interventions include NATO's 1999 intervention in the Balkans and its 2001 introduction of coalition forces into Afghanistan, the removal of Saddam Hussein in 2003, and the establishment of a no-fly zone in Libya in 2011. International NGOs were invited to play cru-cial roles in fostering global civil society by acquiring and sustaining local partners for such tasks as the monitoring of electoral, environmental, and human rights violations.

Since the late 1990s European nations have grown increasingly consis-tent in their voting patterns at the United Nations, exhibiting unanimous cohesion on human rights votes between 2005 and 2009. This solidity has triggered what looks to be, from a European perspective, a backlash: non-European nations that align with the European Union more than half the time shrank from 44 to 32 by 2009, according to reports by the European Council on Foreign Relations. Swing voters who sided with the European Union shrank from 86 to 77 countries. The greatest shift came in the number of countries that support EU human rights positions. Strong opponents, those that support EU human rights positions less than 35 percent of the time, expanded from 19 to 40 states.[6]

Like China, many upwardly mobile states, including Venezuela, Cuba, Egypt, Pakistan, Philippines, India, Iran, Russia, and South Africa, op-pose efforts to make liberal international agendas a global norm and have legislated strong barriers against the operation of global NGOs within their territories. China is consistent in defending its overseas clients from the need to comply with humanitarian safeguards or other conditions imposed by multilateral organizations. It does not allow those organizations to monitor compliance within its own borders either.

Many emerging powers share an apprehension about joining a global system based on Western values. These new global players do not reject the potential benefits of a rule-based international system. Nor do they refute the advantages of international law and organization. What they contest are liberal international values—multiparty elections, labor rights, and Western definitions of human and civil rights—as the system-wide standards of regime legitimacy. They assert that the rule of law need not be characterized solely in terms consistent with Western democracy. They adhere to the conviction that the rights of individuals are forfeit to the collective. They resist incursions on sovereign policymaking, including the international community's right to humanitarian intervention. Thus democracies like Brazil, India, and South Africa, along with non-democratic China, have not supported UN Security Council measures to protect Libyan (2011) and Syrian (2012) civilians from violence fostered by their own governments.[7]

The members of the sovereignty axis all have some definition of human rights, but it is not the same as that of the signatories to the Helsinki accords (1975) on human rights. China, for example, advances a vision of a stable global civilization in which the boundaries among trade, commerce, and culture are explicit, and in which meddling in a partner's internal affairs is checked by mutual self-interest. Moreover they are determined to keep trade and social values separate. These countries prefer the values of a pre-modern international system, when regime type did not matter and the international community refrained from influencing what happened within the sovereign borders of states. This thinking is akin to the classical liberalism articulated by the political economist David Ricardo (1817), which assumes a web of complex economic interdependence free from political intervention and which occurs on the basis of relative advantages in economic activities.

Western globalists fear that the classical model is flawed—and indeed warn that an insistence on the overarching authority of sovereignty paved the way to World War II and the horrors of the Holocaust. To accept the sole authority of sovereignty would be tantamount to appeasement, to renouncing the historical lessons and recollections gained from the many hard-won battles waged both internally and abroad against the sources of disorder and tyranny. Will a full-blown crisis of authority unfold as the universality of liberal internationalism becomes a more fractious issue?

Past changes in systemwide legitimacy were generally an outcome of war. It is for this reason that the rise of the sovereignty network is a dark apparition for those who believe the future for global stability depends on the ascension of liberal democracy as the global norm of domestic and international politics. But as a directive for an alternative world order, the sovereignty network may be a phantom with few prospects for coalescing around a common set of values. Its appeal is largely to nations who maintain that they must find deliverance from Western domination. There is also concern about the future direction of global democracy: many of the members of the axis, like Venezuela, Iran, and Bangladesh, are actually emerging democracies. How likely are they ever to construct an alternative world order when they lack a source of positive attraction?

European institutions, norms, and practices of modernity have spread unevenly among and within countries. As we saw in the previous chapter, European laws and institutions are enshrined in Sri Lanka's constitution, but the values they represent are unevenly diffused among the populace. Are countries not evolving in the direction of Europe moving away from modernity? The core of the international system is no longer rooted in a single civilization; the prosperity of East Asia has expanded the global zone of power and influence so that now several continents and more than one civilization constitute the core.

The rise of the sovereignty network is but one of many global trends that make current models of globalization obsolete. Its emergence challenges the faith of liberal internationalism that common cultural norms can arise anywhere or be transplanted to where they are missing. But neither the axis of sovereignty as a whole nor its prominent individual members will supplant the Western model of political development. In fact, the cohesiveness of the sovereignty network emerges as a critical pattern only if one looks at a narrow range of UN voting on issues that cluster around liberal international themes, such as human rights and the right to protect. For example, after the fall of the Berlin Wall, between 1991 and 2001, the preference gap between the United States and the rest of the world widened at a constant rate, long before the axis was observable (Voeten 2004). If one looks at the larger timeline of UN General Assembly voting since 1946, one will see that the salience of overall voting bloc influence has diminished since the end of the cold war. If one considers a more comprehensive spectrum of voting within the United Nations, the cohesion of the sovereignty axis recedes into the background of a more general trend that we will now consider: the dispersal of influence.

The Dispersion of Influence

During the cold war era, networks of trade, arms, technology, and diplomacy tended to cluster. Countries in one network had a high probability of appearing in another. This meant that if you were in one cluster, your partners in that cluster would likely be your partners in all the other clusters of which you were a part. But now the trade, defense, and diplomacy networks are comprised of different clusters contributing to the breakdown of the West's hierarchical control within the global system.[8]

The larger trend in these global growth patterns, which also include social and information networks, is the increased autonomy of clusters and the diminishing role of linkages among clusters. This can be observed in overall UN voting, in patterns of global trade, in arms diffusion, and in the fragmentation of manufacturing. All form clusters of interaction, but these affiliations do not transfer to other networks. In the WTO, for example, China frequently votes with the same Western partners on matters of trade openness that it votes against in the UN Security Council on matters of sovereignty.

Arms transfers are exhibiting similar patterns of influence dispersion over time. In the early 1950s, sources of sophisticated weaponry were highly concentrated, allowing the primary producer, the United States, to exercise considerable influence over who gained access to them. By the late 1960s, when alternative suppliers, such as the Soviet Union, expanded their own arms manufacturing capabilities, countries that the United States considered its own satellites were able to buy weapons elsewhere. This impelled the United States to distribute weapons of high sophistication to countries of dubious loyalty and of uncertain stability. The Shah of Iran was able to demand and obtain a far greater range of weaponry during the Nixon administration than during Eisenhower's.

This change meant that the United States had far less leverage over the Shah's diplomatic forays or over those of other nations that received its arms shipments.

Around the world, the cohesiveness of the security networks that the United States was trying to establish suffered. By the early twenty-first century, the manufacturing of complex armaments had become so widespread that armies in Latin America, largely dependent on US supplies from 1950 until 1990, were purchasing weaponry from a variety of manufacturers, from China and Russia (Venezuela and Bolivia), from Germany (Argentina and Chile), and from France (Brazil), with only Peru and Columbia relying predominantly on the United States after 2000. Small-arms manufacturing and distribution obey the same pattern. Small-arms manufacturing is so diffuse that dissemination cannot be influenced by any single power or coalition of powers. The impending proliferation of nuclear weapons systems will further reinforce this trend of diffusion observed in other categories of weaponry. The increased trade in weaponry of all kinds is dependent on another trend in the global political economy: open markets have increased the amount of trade, and the accumulation of wealth has increased the demand for sophisticated weaponry.

Fragmentation of Manufacturing

Global trade data also reveal a pattern of consistent diffusion since the end of World War II, when few countries exported complex industrial products. This gave the few centers of manufacturing considerable leverage in diplomacy. But industrial capacity, like trade, has experienced diffusion that reduces the considerable leverage once enjoyed by the major manufacturing centers over their subsidiary trading partners. Emerging manufacturing centers have a choice of suppliers for inputs; and natural resource producers have a larger range of consumers with whom to trade and invest in domestic mineral exploitation. For example, a bottleneck to Chinese growth was the limited number of countries from which it could obtain natural resources. Rather than compete with the West in those countries, Chinese overseas investment has concentrated on developing new sources, often considered rogue nations by the West. These new partnerships diminish Western diplomatic leverage and weaken both the impact of sanctions and conditionality in the allocation of development assistance.

Value-Added Manufacturing

The fragmentation of global production chains receives considerable attention because of its impact on jobs, balance of payments, and prosperity. But it too has an effect on geopolitical alignment.

Value chains have become so intertwined that they defy efforts by governments to follow the movement of goods and services beyond the production phase and through the distribution process. It is easy to follow a widget from where it originated to its various stages in its production chain, but that product may then become a component in another product, manufactured in another country. When the finished good arrives at its point of final consumption, the investment and income flows embedded in it are difficult to untangle. In a product as complex as a commercial jetliner, the supply chain is intertwined in manufacturing processes dispersed around the globe.

The international fragmentation of manufacturing makes unraveling the valued-added component difficult. The production chains of many industrial manufacturers are so intertwined that governments are unable to determine the extent, or value, of foreign content. Investment flows, income flows, and even final ownership become more difficult to measure, ascertain, or monitor. Even such questions as the foreign content of domestic products elude measurement. This problem has bedeviled efforts by US government officials to assess national competiveness by measuring manufacturing output and overall productivity. Moreover the swift dynamics of these production and distribution processes obstruct the ability of a central command center to construct tax and controls, or to craft effective priorities for national industrial policy.

The fragmentation of industrial manufacturing reduces the influence that Western incumbents can exercise over global trade. A declining role in valued-added manufacturing is causing productivity growth of the West to decline as well. The process of decline is self-reinforcing because productivity growth in a high-cost supplier like the United States is likely to diminish when manufacturers at home switch to low cost-suppliers overseas.

The decline of US manufacturing output fell by 11 percent between 2000 and 2010, yet many analysts claim that this decline is benign and only represents the increasingly important role that knowledge and services play in the US economy (ITIF 2012). The problem is that high-value manufacturing also supports the growth of the service sector. As manufacturing moves to other centers, the service industries that support those manufacturing activities will also move or close. As US companies become more dependent on global suppliers and markets, they become less likely to support the diplomatic initiatives of domestic political leaders, again reducing US diplomatic leverage overseas. In short, international comparisons of export data in value-added production and distribution demonstrate the breakdown of hierarchical networks, reflecting the same pattern of a dispersal of influence that other global data sources reflect. The fragmentation of global value chains adds to the diffusion of global influence, as does the multiplication of trade treaties.

Until recently, building an industrial economy was about joining the right sociopolitical clusters—either the West or the bloc of socialist nations. This logic motivated the rising nations of East Asia to adopt the forms of sociopolitical legitimacy preferred by their primary trading partner, the Western democratic nations. But in the future, building value-chain complementarity will be less dependent on conforming to the sociopolitical preferences of a major partner, especially as the economic prospects of East Asia will depend increasingly on trade with China. This will render value creation in the global economy independent of ideological affinity and dilute the normative influence of liberal internationalist models of modernization.

In sum, the top of the global power hierarchy is not as high as it once was. Hegemony is on the wane; it is not liberal internationalism that is declining. Those nations that have been at the top have less structural power and therefore their norms are more difficult to transfer or to impose on others. Influence dispersal is an outcome of complexity, of a world in which many opportunities or niches for novelty and innovation exist. It is a micro level consequence of a system level change. Moreover there is less incentive for other leaders to join the liberal system. If they can partner with China for trade, why risk signing on to a program that might reduce their personal power and diminish their longevity in office?

Manufacturing Complexity and the Fragmentation of Influence
Relying on export data, economist Ricardo Hausmann and his colleagues at Harvard's Kennedy School of Government have built the first quantitative model that measures the complexity of productivity of a nation's

goods and services (Hausmann et al. 2011). Their index computes the value chain of competencies that national economies possess: [9]

Some goods, like medical imaging devices or jet engines, embed large networks of people and organizations. By contrast, wood logs or coffee embed much less knowledge, and the networks required to support these operations do not need to be as large. Complex economies are those that can weave vast quantities of relevant knowledge together across large networks of people (density) to generate a diverse mix of knowledge-intensive products. Simple economies, in contrast, have a narrow base of productive knowledge and produce fewer and simpler products, which require smaller webs of interaction. Because individuals are limited in what they know, the only way societies can expand their knowledge base is by facilitating the interaction of individuals in increasing complex webs of organizations and markets [structure]. (p. 18)

Hausmann's insight is that both the density and the structure of network connectivity drive value creation for firms, as well as nations. Global competition will depend increasingly on gaining key competencies required for participation in high-value knowledge networks. An economy's role in global value construction will depend on the degree of specific and unique competencies it possesses, not replicated by others. At the elementary level will be those economies that only produce raw materials; just above these will be economies that also process raw materials. The next level will be economies that are platforms for the assembly of complex manufactured goods. But the most important source of value will come from the role that national firms play in the design and marketing of complex products demanded in the global marketplace.

To be among the global elite of countries that produce the high-value products demanded on the world market, emerging countries must integrate into networks of science and technology. Leaders who provide insufficient connectivity to the nodes of growth and creativity in the global economy, who deny their populations the means to link, search, and navigate to high-value chains, will stifle their nations' chances of matching the capabilities of the global trendsetters and hinder their trajectories.

Value creation at the national level will also depend on increasing the number of interdependent linkages with other domestic manufacturing centers. This makes it imperative for leaders to harness the diversity of local knowledge to create a greater variety of better products globally. The role national economies will play in value creation in the unfolding international system will depend on the degree of complexity of their sociopolitical structures. Countries that aspire to operate at the world's technological frontier will need to host networks of high value that source, sell, hire, and design globally. Such networks will provide far more meaningful opportunities for knowledge acquisition than connections among producers of natural resources that offer only limited opportunities for domestic social networks to expand their skills and talents. The domestic policy challenge will be to construct public goods that enable networks of adaptive individuals, firms, and nations to interact on the basis of self-organizing complexity. How effectively networks create, pool, and disseminate productive knowledge is becoming the most important driver of future global prosperity. It will be one of the chief determinants of resilience of the international system itself.

The Global Complexity Transition and Networked Interdependence

While specialists in various policy communities readily concede that socioeconomic development is a complex undertaking, the programs and initiatives they design rarely follow logically from the true complexity of the problems they address. Grappling with global terrorism, our policy designates that we take efforts to seek and destroy hidden terrorist networks, but these networks can exist only because collective sociocultural processes that involve millions of people nurture them. Similarly the war on drug trafficking does not address the collective socioeconomic processes that sustain the trade. Nor do standardized tests that measure the performance of students and teachers solve the highly complex problem of matching pupils with programs that fit their specialized needs and abilities. Seeking a standardized product through centralized curriculum evaluation and testing is an Industrial Age anachronism. Problems that are large in scale but simple to implement, and those whose complexity requires specialization in distributing action and authority, require very different policy responses.

Conventional approaches to complex human environments, such as that of the interactions among nations, presume the necessity of a hierarchical command of either inserting a ruler, a ruling party, an area of influence, or a superpower at the top. Yet highly complex environments are not amenable to top-down control and—like ecology, evolution, the weather, the human nervous system—can form without planning. So why do conventional theories of international relations rely on the notion that solving social dilemmas of collective action requires a captain at the helm? It is because we are acting from an old script, one in which hierarchies were effective for many of the collective tasks and functions a society had to perform.

Throughout history people, organizations, and cultures have influenced one another through hierarchies that placed people into well-separated parts of an organization. These traditional hierarchies were designed to achieve scale in activities in which many individuals repeated identical tasks. The military represents hierarchy in its idealized form, with many individuals performing collectively under a single command structure. Typically the armed forces have been the measure of the effectiveness of a society's organization and the best-organized hierarchies have won in the competition among human societies.

Hierarchy has reflected the collective aspirations of almost every human collective. European society organized itself during the Middle Ages as a tripartite hierarchy, with those who fought at the top, followed by those who prayed, then by the rest who plowed. This simple structure may have protected Europe from the domination by other civilizations, also conceived as hierarchies. In traditional China, bureaucrats sat at the top, next to the emperor, and in the Hindu world priests were placed at the apex, followed by separate classes of warriors, merchants, and artisans. Regardless of which group possessed the greatest status, the tasks of traditional civilizations were sufficiently repetitive that they could best be managed hierarchically.

Networks accord opportunities for learning and problem-solving that change how individuals organize, transmit knowledge, and experience and interpret history, but these networks and the self-organizing processes that create them are not panaceas to the problems of living in a complex world. Networks are unstable; they constantly shift and are costly to maintain. Their members are called on to make considerable trade-offs and often must compromise individual rights and values. Some networks are lethal, and must be eliminated, while others are predatory and work against the collective interests of the greater number. The divergent properties of networks often depend on their structure, and understanding these properties will enable us to perform many highly complex tasks that cannot be managed via hierarchical mechanisms.

Conclusion: Rewriting the Narrative of Globalization

Globalization is dead—long live globalization! The combined effects of global technology diffusion and global resource dependency are producing "interacting dancing landscapes" in which the payoffs from activity in one sector of the global economy depend on the actions of interacting agents. The result is a human complexity revolution in which global development will require shared social learning algorithms that create and diffuse common knowledge. The most daunting challenge posed by global interdependence will be to create and disseminate common knowledge about the human condition.

Complexity has a global emergent property derived from the interactive effects of the interdependent parts. A complex a system is not reducible to its parts in isolation. Studying any one part of complex system in isolation will fail to reveal the dynamic and decentralized manner in which the components keep changing. Change in a complex system is not linear, and what goes in is not what comes out. Change cycles are not only incremental—they can reframe the overall system-level rules and transform outcomes. No formula, no matter how successful in the past, assures future success. A single action intended to improve efficiency on one dimension can precipitate volatility on another, pushing the system into a critical state and triggering extreme events that range from traffic jams to market crashes.

The evolutionary theory of complexity outlined in this book will enable global thinkers to rewrite the narrative of globalization and map the path to future sources of global prosperity. It provides the widest base for the creation of common knowledge about global change processes. Complexity is the analytical foundation that can integrate diverse cultures into a shared conception of the global future. It is the appropriate analytical vehicle to convey common knowledge about the human experience in the emerging global environment because it can include the endowments, beliefs, and technologies of agents of diverse origins. It reveals how globalization weaves together economies, cultures, and polities of all levels of development in shared networks of competition and symbiosis. And it offers a framework that validates both Western and non-Western experiences. It can lead developing and developed countries to find common cause in shaping and accelerating global development.

Glossary

Mapping the Concepts: Translating Complexity to Social Systems

This lexicon includes terms common in studies of evolutionary biology, complexity theory, and international relations. It attempts to develop complexity's deeply intuitive logic into new problem-solving strategies for contemporary political economy.

Adaptation: The ability to increase fitness through evolution; a contributing factor to survival and reproduction. A system is adaptive if it undergoes evolutionary change and selection.

Additive: The nature of a linear development of sequences in which quantitative characteristics are the sum of all the inputs. In conventional economic theory, progress or efficiency is said to be additive, comprising the accumulation of inputs toward a linear goal. Complex adaptive systems are inherently nonadditive. The behavior of the whole is not reducible to the sum of its parts.

Agent: An interactive element of a system. It can be a nerve cell in the central nervous system, a species in an ecosystem, or a household or firm in an economy. Even a landscape can be an agent.

Algorithm: A code that expresses the rules of interaction of the agents whose behaviors generate a complex adaptive system.

Bifurcation: An irreversible change that occurs in the evolution of living organisms and that differentiates the evolution of one organism from another. Bifurcation points are minor variations at the beginning that produce large variations at the end so that lineages diverge despite sharing a common ancestor. In complex systems bifurcations produce *emergent* outcomes.

Bounded rationality: Herbert Simon elaborates the concept of bounded rationality (1982a, b; 1972), referring to the process of problem-solving when information may be too limited or too vast, making it too costly for agents to seek the best possible solution. In bounded rationality, people seek solutions that are "good enough," rather than optimal. They "satisfice" rather than optimize. "Rule-of-thumb" solutions are examples of bounded rationality. Traditional models in economics assume that agents are optimizers who have full information and seek the best decisions. In complex systems, agents are not optimizers. Simon's insistence on the finite information-processing capacity of humans is the most pervasive critique of the rational choice models popular among economists. For more discussion on bounded rationality and politics, see Cook and Levi (1990).

Centralized network (i.e., hub-and-spoke network): A complex system in which the nodes, called hubs, have very few links with other nodes in the system. A centralized network may provide greater opportunities for information access, timing, monitoring and control. Fewer redundant contacts increase the efficiency of information flow to the center and require less effort to maintain clusters of influence (Burt 1992, 17–25). However, hub-and-spoke networks are deficient in resilience. Should the center break down, the system may fail. Because the nodes are built to connect to the center, but not to each other, the system will lose cohesion and disintegrate.

Coevolution: Unlike evolution, which is conventionally understood as a march toward a global optimization in which the fittest survive, coevolution involves ongoing self-organization, adaptive moves, and perhaps several optima toward which each agent in a system aspires. Responses to the adaptive moves of others can raise or lower the fitness levels of the coupled environments, and thus the overall system.

Complex adaptive system: A system in which there are levels of self-organization and where agents at one level are the building blocks of the next. A change at one level alters the options for change at another, making it difficult to predict the behavior of individuals in constantly shifting environments and organizational formations. The complex aggregate behavior in a complex system cannot be understood from the behavior of the parts. The whole emerges from the interaction of its components. Interdependency among connected but diverse parts is a primary characteristic that distinguishes a complex system from a merely complicated system, such as a pendulum or a sewing machine. In a complicated system, if one part is removed, the other parts will not respond. In a complex adaptive system, a change to one of the parts will change the behavior of the remaining components.

Connectivity (interconnectedness): The linkages of agents within a given landscape. Kinship, trade, treaties, social networks, or physical infrastructure may connect agents.

Convergence: Modernization theory and other conventional notions of globalization presume a general convergence toward an optimum standard of fitness defined by Western social, political, and geopolitical values. But convergence does not explain current social trajectories, and it does not represent the irreversible effects of bifurcation that produce the evolution of diverse human settlements and identities.

Convergent evolution (parallel evolution): In evolutionary biology, convergent, or parallel, evolution is the increasing similarity of unrelated species. For example, the bat, the bird, and the flying insect all developed wings, but there is no common point at which they all became capable of flight. In social evolution, environments with dissimilar antecedents may face similar challenges and thus develop similar but unrelated social capacities and institutions.

Dancing (complex) landscapes: An environment whose combinatorial complexity is intensified by the frequency and intensity of interdependent actions among agents to such a degree that the very ecology shifts, and this shifting alters the sets of available options even further, making the system itself unstable. In a dancing landscape, the movements of local peaks make finding an optimal path to the highest peak improbable.

Economic complexity: A society's ability to recombine and put knowledge to use to create a variety of better products. In the *Atlas of Economic Complexity*, Ricardo Hausmann et al. (2011) attempt to quantify the amount of productive knowledge by nationality to account for the enormous income differences between nations of the world. A complete map to belief diffusion in the global economy will have to consider not only the volume of trade but also the network effects (policy diffusion) of learning associated with high value-added production.

Emergence: Any behavior that occurs between agents that contributes to a more complex behavior of the whole. Emergence describes the process through which a system acquires new structures and behaviors that its individual components did not possess. Understanding of the behavior of the parts is insufficient to explain the emergent behavior of the system. An example of emergence is consciousness, a characteristic of a brain, even though no particular cell or synapse within the brain can be described as "conscious." Liquidity has no meaning for the individual molecules of which water is comprised. Development is a type of emergence, a condition of a social collective that the individual elements cannot possess.

Epistasis: Change that occurs when one or more agents modify the behavior of another agent. Epistasis makes a particular change contingent on other factors in the same environment, but it should not be mistaken for dominance. In a highly interconnected system, epistasis can interfere with efforts of individual agents to adapt. Unfortunately, to attain greater productivity in the global system, the choices most societies, firms, or organizations face involve considerable epistasis. As well, an epistatic system depends on the interdependence of its components; the choice of one element determines the choice of other elements. Epistatic change is difficult to reverse because it requires coordinated alteration of integrated components.

Equilibrium system: If left in isolation, an equilibrium system achieves an unvarying macroscopic state. It has no internal spatial structure that can stimulate change over time. A complex system does have an internal structure comprised of many interacting parts that change over time.

Feedback loop: Information that allows agents to learn and to adjust their behaviors to others' actions, thereby constantly re-creating the environment in which they all operate.

Fitness: A measure of the probability that a group or agent will reproduce. Fitness can also be understood as the adaptiveness of a population to new conditions. Finding an analog to biological fitness in a human economy or society is problematic.

Fitness landscape: A conceptual basis for visualizing problems of optimization or adaptation (problem-solving) within a given environment, using height and distance as figurative exertions. Problem-solving is conceived of as an uphill climb, and the peaks are solutions. The highest peak represents fitness and is the optimal solution. Local peaks are points on the landscape from which all paths head downward. High connectivity, when the peaks are connected to other peaks, may cause the system to settle at a level of fitness that is lower than if the landscape had only one peak. A fitness landscape can explain deviations from global norms anticipated by modernization theory.

Gradualism: The accumulation of many small changes that lead to a qualitative impact. The growth of China during imperial rule is an example of gradualism and had the result of thwarting innovation.

Institutions: As defined by Douglass North, institutions are "'the rules of the game,' the patterns of interaction that govern and constrain the relationship of individuals. Institutions include formal rules, written laws, formal social conventions, informal rules of behavior, and shared beliefs about the world, laws as well as the means of enforcement" (North, Wallis, and Weingast 2009, 15).

Interdependence: The linkages among multiple agents from which it would be costly for any agent to withdraw and in which the action of one partner affects the payoffs or fitness of others. Interdependence refers to the direct influence one part of a system has on another. Interdependence, rather than interconnectedness, is the essential dynamic property of a complex system. Interdependence is also distinct from interactivity; even strong interactions need not imply interdependence.

Liberal internationalism: An evolving ideology that involves the relationships between open markets, international institutions, cooperative security, democratic community, collective problem-solving, and the rule of law (Ikenberry 2009). The normative objectives of liberal internationalism are constantly in flux. The ideology traces its roots to neoclassical liberalism of the nineteenth century, in which international cooperation meant trade in goods without political preconditions. The expression of modern liberal internationalism that emerged after World War I emphasized state sovereignty and nonintervention, and shared with classical liberalism the belief that trade has a modernizing effect on social norms and increasing the prospects for mutual cooperation. But the failure to avoid World War II led the victorious liberal West to seek more interventionist and complex forms of international cooperation that limit sovereignty and, within nations, prescribe standards of political authority, such as accountability, participation, and transparency. The derivation of these terms, nevertheless, is culturally and historically specific. To non-Western societies and minorities within Western societies, liberal internationalism represents a collection of interventionist strategies. Imperiled by a common security threat during the cold war, the West adhered to common notions of what a core liberal order should look like. Liberal internationalism has set the foreign policy agenda since then. Western solidarity, however, no longer suffices to push the liberal agenda forward as a basis for effective global cooperation. Emerging nations that lack a common history with the West are ineffective as receptors and inefficient transmitters of liberal internationalist values. Consequently both the nature of the rules and the location of authority within the international system remain unresolved, and contested issues often situate developed and newly emerging powers on opposing sides.

Liberal hegemony: An American-led liberal international order that dominated global politics after World War II. Liberal hegemony is predicated by the position of the United States as system "administrator." Should the United States cease to play the role of a central administrator, the sustainability of the liberal system will be problematic, not because its role may be replaced by another rising power but because such a role may no longer exist.

Lineage bifurcation: See **speciation.**

Lock-in: When more than one solution is viable but only one solution appears persistently. This occurs as an organism or system matures and increases its fitness to a point of assured survival. Then adaptation slows to an incremental pace and growth rates taper. In social evolution, lock-in occurs in countries with high fitness levels. When the vested interests of institutions and interest groups become entrenched, lock-in holds back change causing institutional stasis.

Macroevolution: Evolutionary change that occurs at the species (system) level and above, and that creates new adaptive niches by creating new system level rules. Macroevolutionary effect occurs at the species level, as in the emergence of ears for hearing or eyes for sight, or the transition from asexual to sexual reproduction. In social systems a macroevolutionary change can occur at the state level and above, for example, as when states that win wars are positioned to decide the legitimate order for other states (Bobbitt 2002). Macroevolutionary outcomes can also be generated by long-term social demographic trends (Goldstone 1991), or by microbes and plagues like those that razed the ancient empires of Central and South America. See **punctuated equilibrium.**

Modernization theory: A theory of social change that presumes a universal and linear sequence of developmental processes. The theory lends support to the idea that democracy and economic growth go hand in hand, and that authoritarian regimes that refuse to democratize do so at their own peril and at the risk of eventual economic stagnation. China's trajectory provides a critical test of this proposition. Beginning in the 1980s, many developing countries with undemocratic and corrupt regimes experienced rapid growth while many poor democracies have languished. The high degree of connectivity of global processes renders global development far too complex to be accurately described by modernization theory.

Microevolution: Evolutionary change taking place within a species. It occurs at a scale that can be observed. A microevolutionary change would be the differences in the placement, size, or the capacity of the eye or the ear in a specific species.

Mutation: In evolution, a change that disrupts functions and traits that have been accumulated by the gradual process of natural selection. A genetic mutation may increase fitness in one organism but will likely have deleterious consequences for the system as a whole. The effect of mutations on fitness is almost always harmful because they can produce utterly random outcomes.

Mutualism: Interaction between two species that confers benefits to both partners. An example of mutualism in biology is the evolution of internal parasites that become host-specific; after colonizing a host, they coevolve with that host, which also defines their fitness landscape. This interaction is not necessary for the continuous improvement of the environment; it serves the immediate survival needs of the parasite and illustrates the idea that success depends less on the attributes of an individual agent than on where that agent happens to be situated in the system.

Neopatrimonial regime: A regime whose formal institutions must compete with preexisting informal social norms. A full set of institutions may be constitutionally specified in neopatrimonial regimes, but in actuality, relations are still governed by informal roles so that more than one mechanism determines the behavior. Typically, when liberal institutions are imposed on patrimonial regimes, patronage networks do not disappear. Liberal institutions are simply layered on top of preexisting patronage networks. The competencies of clientelistic exchange are maintained and are simply transferred to the new institutions. These regimes usually fail to make credible commitments to implement announced policies. See **patrimonialism**.

Network: Within the larger system, a set of nodes and the links and connections between the nodes. Members of a network can find paths to solving problems that are not apparent to nonmembers. Markets, for example, arise from and rely on networks of exchange among buyers and sellers, producers and suppliers, who in turn coevolve in a network of interdependency with other components of the social system. How agents in a network are connected has implications for the behavior that results. Differences in a network structure, be they *centralized* or *scale-free*, give rise to different types of behavior. Networks can map resource flows, communication and even perspectives.

New institutional economics: An influential socioeconomic discourse arising in the 1980s after the fall of the Berlin Wall that presumed to be able decipher the structures of social institutions and norms, and identify the building blocks of long-term economic growth. The rise of the NIE in academic circles is related to the expansion of the "good governance agenda" in policy circles. Yet emerging trends transforming the global ecosystem during the first decade of the twenty-first century defy NIE's conception of the processing fundamentals of economic growth. Finding a common institutional framework to overcome the ideological and cultural boundaries between developed and developing societies seems much less likely than the institutionalists had anticipated.

Niche: The specific role and requirements of a particular population within a larger community.

Niche construction: Local resource distribution in an ecosystem that alters the subsequent evolution of resource dependency.

Nonlinearity: A function characteristic of complexity. In a complex adaptive system, the agents interact according to shared and evolving rules of behavior that constantly redefine the environment in which they operate. Thus evolution is not a linear march toward a single goal, but a shifting series of adaptations. A given action should not be expected to produce the same result every time. The whole is not a simple function of its parts. The independent variable does not have a constant effect on the dependent variable. By contrast, in a linear system, the whole is the sum of the parts; we analyze linear systems by looking at the parts individually and then adding them together.

Normal distribution: An environment in which the most likely events occur near the mean, typically represented by a bell curve.

Optimization: The most efficient and beneficial use of resources to achieve a particular end. In a complex system, where no single "administrator" exists, there is no march toward a global optimization. The agents effect their own optimizing; there are multiple adaptive moves and perhaps several optima toward which each agent aspires.

Parallel processing: An essential evolutionary process in which agents "process" information from different sources simultaneously. The need for such processing increases with the degree of interaction. Parallel processing implies that each agent acts both independently, in pursuit of its own advantage, and interdependently, as it reacts to and produces adaptive responses in its neighbors. When multiple agents engage in parallel processing and perform their particular optimizations at the same time, they fundamentally change the behavior of the whole system. Parallel processing and *interdependency* are at odds in the functioning of complex systems.

Path dependency: A developmental trajectory that is inescapably historical and irreversible. Path dependency is sometimes used to explain the irreversibility of institutional design. But the real cause of irreversibility is *epistasis*—a term that more accurately captures what economic historians imply in their discussions of path dependency is *sensitivity to initial conditions*. A key implication is that the behavior outcomes of a small part in isolation differ from its behavior outcomes on the larger system.

Patrimonialism: Political recruitment on the basis of kin selection and reciprocal altruism among individuals sharing a common blood-line (Fukuyama 2011). In this sense, patrimonialism can be considered the opposite of bureaucratic rule. Ancient and contemporary history offers many examples of bureaucratic offices filled by a ruler's kin. A powerful biological impulse compels such recruitment. In its more general use, the term refers to political authority modeled on that of a father within a family. Max Weber refers to patrimonial rule being projected beyond the family to an entire society or even nation. His main point is that patrimonial domination eventually gives way to bureaucratic rationalism in the governance of modern states. Many current and past dictatorships are described as possessing a patrimonial political economy. The domination of India's politics since independence by a single family exhibits the power that patrimonial identification can have over an entire culture. Patrimonialism also suggests why state- and nation-building can be at odds. A state requires depersonalized institutional capacity, but national identity can be embodied in a patrimonial leader. The Gandhi family, which has ruled over India for most of its post-independence history, enjoys an influence rivaling that of constitutionally established institutions and rules of law.

Patronage networks (patron–client networks, patron-clientelism): Networks of dependence and inequality in which power brokers create a following by exploiting control over scarce resources—not only material wealth, but resources that confer status or prestige. The patron gains power by delivering benefits selectively, according to the value of the loyalty that can be extracted from the recipient. Such networks are most durable when the debts of the weaker partner can never be paid off or when the clients have limited channels of communication with the outside and depend on the patron for access to other power brokers in the wider society.

The extent of patronage networks was traditionally limited by the need to maintain a face-to-face relationship, but modern political parties allow patronage webs to be woven across entire nations. Webs of patronage typically hold the political parties in many immature democracies together. India's Congress Party in its formative days before 1973 was such a network. The resilience of clientalistic social reciprocity is well established in studies of evolutionary psychology and is ubiquitous among recently formed states. There is a benevolent side in that patrons often depend on their clients for political support and need this support to win elections. The patron gains moral authority by being able to represent and protect a local clientele in national or subnational arenas.

Phase transition: A sudden change in a system's macro-properties, such as when water becomes ice. Large-scale phase transitions are very rare in biology, where evolution takes place primarily in genes and their lineages. Phase transition in societies can result from the purposeful actions of the agents, though that action may not always be rational or efficient. The Arab Spring can be understood as an unpredictable phase transition stemming from the influence of social networks and their information cascades, and causing an abrupt change in the social environment.

Private good: A commodity whose consumption by one agent limits usage of the same commodity by another.

Public administration: The state infrastructure essential for institutional, economic, or social development.

Public good: A commodity whose consumption by one agent does not reduce its availability in the same quantity to another user

Punctuated equilibrium: A contributor to macroevolution. In evolutionary biology it refers to changes to the global ecology characterized by the sudden disappearance of one set of dominant species and their replacement by another. Punctuation can produce macroevolutionary effects on the system as a whole. European history is replete with instances of punctuated equilibrium arising from innovations in military technology and resulting in novel social structures.

Reductionism: The assertion that the whole of reality is nothing but the sum of its parts. Modernization theory is reductionist in its presumption of a universal, linear sequence of social changes in which the trajectory of newcomers will converge to Western patterns.

Regime: A stable set of institutions within a given ecology.

Replicator: In modernization theory the vehicle (economy) through which social and political order develop. A replicator mediates the selection of traits to be replicated. Recent studies, in contrast, suggest that the economy itself is a complex system and cannot act as a replicator of social order.

Resilience: The capacity to survive shocks; the ability to reorganize during intense cycles of change and remain in a cohesive state. According to Fikret Berkes, Johan Colding and Carl Folke, it is also a measure of a system's capacity to promote learning and adaptation, thus ensuring *self-organization*, which is the adaptive or innovative face of resilience (2002). A system's resilience is augmented by the diversity of opportunities and options it provides to participants.

Rugged landscape: A fitness landscape defined by multiple peaks and valleys in which agents are trapped. Interdependency and interaction between the actions of multiple players make a landscape rugged. When the choices of numerous interdependent players interact, they cannot see beyond local peaks (solutions), and have great difficulty finding an optimal solution or in acting cooperatively.

Rules: The laws governing complex systems. If one is to analyze a complex system, one must first develop the tools to assess the rules that govern agent behavior. General laws of social complexity that apply to all levels are unlikely because at each level of complexity the identity of the agents shifts. New rules must be derived at each level and for each variety of complex system, and for this reason the laws governing ecosystems in nature can never be mapped directly to social systems. But treating both as complex adaptive systems, we can discover shared general principles:

1. A network is comprised of agents.
2. Complex adaptive systems show sensitivity to initial conditions.
3. Networks progress through a series of bifurcations, like the branching of an ancestral tree.
4. In complex systems, bifurcations produce emergence.
5. Complex adaptive systems comprise levels of organization; agents at one level are the building blocks of the next.
6. In complex systems, the "rules" constitute the transition function.

Scale-free network: A complex system in which the nodes, called hubs, have numerous links with other nodes in the system. The traditional European system of aristocratic domination by multiple houses spread across the continent represents a scale-free system of distributed authority. A failure of one lineage did not trigger a systemwide failure.

In nature, insect colonies, the immune system, the nervous system, the brain, ecosystems, the weather, oceans, deserts are all examples of scale-free networks that arise through self-organization. Yet they are robust because a significant number of components can be eliminated before the system itself will fail.

Selection: The process that ensures the survival of those traits whose superior fitness increases the frequency of their appearance in a given population. Selection deletes poorly performing entities from the population.

Selectorate: The portion of the population with a voice in selecting the leadership. See **winning coalition**.

Self-organization: The process through which order emerges without a designated leader, as in a flock of birds or a school of fish. A society's self-organizing capacity refers to its ability to learn and adapt. A measure of the capacity of self-organization is the ability of a social system to survive shocks or extreme events.

Sensitivity to initial conditions: See **path dependency**. Sensitivity to initial conditions can cause a small perturbation in a complex system to have a huge systemwide effect. For this reason small differences in complex systems cannot be ignored. In systems that tend toward equilibrium, small differences in system description do not matter, and these are the systems where analytical social science is taken as a model. The result is that in normal science, irregular behavior is typically ignored. Sensitivity to initial conditions differs from path dependency, which is irreversible change.

Small-world network: A network in which every element appears to be close to every other; even those that in reality are far away are perceived to be close. Small-world networks are surprisingly frequent, such as when two strangers find a common acquaintance, although the world contains many people. The small-world network structure of the Europe-wide aristocracy acted as the source of systemwide continuity; in such small-world networks, the components themselves are not linked, but a small number of connections links most nodes to any other. Europe's embedded and cross-linked structure could adapt to shock without a loss of systemwide functionality. The system's resilience derived from the density of connections among large numbers of interacting parts. A small-world network can have very few connections relative to the size of the population.

Social network: The system of interconnections or linkages among members of a social system, ranging from informal and interpersonal to formal and international.

Speciation: The process by which new species are formed and or stabilize. New species result from *bifurcation*. The key problem for science is to identify the cause of variation. Was it intrinsic to the organism, or did the environment induce it?

State-making (state-building, state formation): The process of creating institutions and other infrastructure necessary for efficient functioning of a state. Several of the essential properties of state-building make it suitable to the epistemology of complexity:

1. State-building is a process in which tensions exist between interactions that are self-ordered and spontaneous and those that are organized and purposeful.

2. As open systems, states and their constituents obtain information from many other environments, both internal and external, with which they interact.

3. State-building involves processes whose effects and causes are often interchangeable.

4. State capacity is a quintessential example of emergence. That capacity is a composite of its system-level properties, such as effective administration, legitimacy in the eyes of its people, resilience and adaptiveness to environmental change, along with prescience in recognizing national interest.

5. States are hosts to interactive processes among actors that produce emergent outcomes, such as industrialization or secularism.

6. States do not exist in isolation; they interact with other states and those interactions form a system. A nested hierarchy exists in which components of lower or inner levels of the organization are combined into higher levels. States are not only composed of networks, but they comprise parts of other networks.

System: An environment composed of agents, niches, networks, and fitness landscapes whose behaviors affect each other and the system itself.

Tipping point: A point at which a system deviates from its existing state to a new macro condition. A celebrated example is the Schelling segregation model, which at some point tips and heterogeneous neighborhoods become highly segregated.

Top-down: Functional differentiation that is imposed from a central location. In a bottom-up system, functionality self-organizes and coordination arises through decentralized feedback loops.

Winning coalition: The subset of the population on which a leader depends to stay in power. The leadership rewards this group to maintain its support. The group is not exclusively elite and can include influential members of various strata. Generally, only the winning coalition is rewarded with private goods. See **selectorate**.

Notes

Chapter 1

1. "The common, if completely hidden, foundation to development agents, agencies, and agendas is modernization, which, for lack of anything else, everyone still relies on as bedrock" (Pritchett, Woolcock, and Andrews 2010, 4).

2. Modernization theory contributes to the agenda of liberal internationalism in which the trajectory of newcomers will converge to Western patterns, facilitating the integration of late-comers into the liberal order. Yet one need only look at Turkey's and China's integration into the global economy to see that their economic success only heightens their efforts to achieve political and cultural authenticity.

3. Liberal internationalism and classical liberal theory are fundamentally different. The growing intensity of interconnection among states (or among national economies) is the core assumption of classical liberal theory. Classical liberalism as expressed in the writings of David Ricardo (1772–1823) idealizes a system of international political economy in which nations cooperate as equal partners. This assumes a web of economic connections free from any sort of political intervention, and that occurs on the basis of relative advantages in economic activities (Ricardo 1817). Its focus is only on the centrality of "interconnectedness"; thus the economic theory of classical liberalism presumes an "atomistic" character to the operation of the global (or national) marketplace, in which entities act only in their own self-interest.

Ironically today liberal internationalism is a system of values that espouses hierarchically structured interventions to promote open markets, open economies, and an international regime of shared governance. The strongest advocates of liberal internationalism are interventionists who reject classical liberalism. Political scientist John Ikenberry, a prominent advocate of liberal internationalism, lauds the essential role of the United States as a liberal leviathan. Liberal internationalism projects a global political economy landscape based on hegemonic stability that requires a central authority. This is a sharp contrast with classical liberalism's ideal of complex economic interdependence free from political intervention.

4. For example, the power to plan and execute large-scale coordination made the industrial oligopolies that once dominated the domestic markets of capitalist nations seem formidable. But networked systems of production have supplanted

the supremacy of the large corporation that designed, built, and distributed its products through a single chain of command.

5. When the adversary is a network, and not a state, the logic of defensive strategy must be altered so as not to expect a victory. Since there can be no decisive solutions, defensive efforts must be concentrated on disruption rather than defeat.

6. Stuart Kauffman writes, "Both biological and technical evolution consist in the invention of slightly or profoundly novel organisms, goods, or services which integrate into the ecological or economic mesh and thereby transform it. . . . In an ecosystem or economic system, the very interactions and couplings among the organisms, or among the goods or services, create the conditions and niches into which new organisms, goods or services can integrate" (1993, 370).

7. US post–cold war strategy assumes that as a country moves closer on the scale to US values, it is more likely to become an ally. Many political scientists have contributed to the view that countries are less likely to attack countries sharing similar preferences. Lemke and Werner (1996) argue that similarity in political institutions shapes alignment choices in international crisis. The case that democracies rarely go to war with one another is made by Köchler (1995); Maoz and Russet (1993); Ray (2003); Rummel (1997).

8. The nations that advocate liberal internationalism as an international norm generally do so after social institutions exist that offer individuals insurance options, such as a social safety net including unemployment compensation and socially provided disability insurance and retirement accounts. When social safeguards against personal calamity exist then citizens no longer have to invest all of their wealth to self-insure and can lift their sights toward distant horizons.

9. Ikenberry asserts that international liberalism is the bedrock of the international system (2011a, b). But this underestimates the newcomers' desire to change the rules. Emerging powers may enjoy the security of an international system if the alternative is chaos, but the rules they prefer are not necessarily those based on liberal principles.

10. Backlashes against globalized elites take the form of what game theorists call ultimatum games (Root 2008). Players in an ultimatum game will reject an unfair offer that makes both of them better off, in order to punish the purveyor of the offer, even if in the end both players get nothing. The implication is that when participation in a market economy creates new levels of inequality, it may precipitate rejection by masses, or if it amplifies the power of emergent groups, it may provoke rejection by elites.

11. Traditional systems theory works from system aggregates to the individual agent, whereas a complex adaptive system is built from interactions of the agents.

12. World systems analysis developed by Immanuel Wallerstein in the 1970s relates individual societies or nation-states to the world system in which they are embedded (1974, 1979, 1980, 1984).

13. The International Monetary Fund–US Treasury complex has successfully helped developing countries to expand the capacity of central banks to absorb enormous flows of international capital. During peacetime especially, the interac-

tive capacity of local economic institutions is far greater than that of social institutions. A central bank can more quickly replicate the global optimum than can a system of education or family relations.

14. Yi Feng (2003) measures the key transition processes associated with globalization.

Chapter 2

1. GDP per capita assesses the average productivity of individuals across and within nations.

2. The idea that the rules of social and economic interaction within a particular state mirror the macro-level properties of the system in which they are embedded will raise new questions: What degree of variation is needed to maintain system-level functionality? When does variation enable the system to respond to changing circumstances, and when does variation prevent a necessary, coordinated response? Can different parts of the same system change at different rates but still maintain their relationships with the whole? How does the amount of variation within the system reflect the pattern of interconnections and the extent of interdependencies? How does component variation contribute to systemwide innovation?

3. "It is because we cannot describe the whole without describing each part, and because each part must be described in relation to other parts, that complex systems are difficult to understand" (Bar-Yam 1997, 1).

4. Irreversibility brings order out of chaos (Prigogine and Stengers 1984, 292).

5. Evolutionary biologists also debate when change is the result of punctuation, and when it is the result of gradualism. The debate over the influence of gradual versus punctuated change in evolution has produced one of the twentieth century's sharpest intellectual polemics among biologists. On the one side, the followers of Richard Dawkins believe that life forms have changed very little over the course of the last 500 million years because evolution is capable of envisioning only a limited library of possible solutions to solve basic functional design necessities. They are adamant that change among living organisms accumulates over long periods of time and that the agents of evolution can only be genes and coalitions of gene lineages that persist over time and compete with other gene lineages. Yet along with John Maynard Smith and Eors Szathmary, Dawkins concedes that the rate of "evolvability" can be changed by innovation, and that innovations will engender new innovations. Nevertheless, prior adaptations constrain evolutionary pathways, and both Maynard Smith and Dawkins emphasize that natural selection over long periods of small steps is essential to the "adaptiveness" of more fit social agents over time making evolutionary change different from social change processes.

The followers of Stephen Jay Gould, on the other side, provide evidence that many changes are not the consequence of gradual reforms; macroevolutionary patterns of systemwide change, such as the transition from asexual to sexual reproduction or from cold- to warm-blooded organisms, have occurred that cannot be fully explained by slow, gradual selection at the individual level; nor can they be interpreted by events that can be measured in local populations. They emphasize punctuation—sudden, systemwide shifts that represent fundamental changes in the rules of the game (Eldredge and Gould 1993; Eldredge 1985; Gould 2002). What is the origin of such macro-change processes? According to Gould, the vehicle for change is not always the individual organism. Change can act at both the level of the system and the level of individual components. An external shock, such as the Cambrian Explosion, can trigger system-level pressures that can cause cascades of self-organizing transformations.

6. To avoid the high risk of extinction, evolution avoids long jumps across fitness landscapes. Rapid shocks or genetic mutations can increase fitness but are more likely to lead to extinction. The Cambrian Explosion that established most of the body forms that currently exist may have generated ten extinct taxonomic groups, or phyla, for every three extant today. But this percentage of surviving phyla is unprecedented in evolutionary history. In subsequent evolutionary bursts of invention, such as the Permian period about 200 million years ago, 96 percent of the species that formed went extinct. Scientists believe the Cambrian was unique because many empty niche spaces were already open. The survival rate of new species declines as the environment fills up. Stuart Kauffman suggests that finding fitter variants is greater in early development than in later development. Fitness increases adaptation via progressively minor variation as the environment fills (1993, 76–77).

7. One of the theories that have had imprints on the research program of both Daron Acemoğlu and Douglass North is *structural functionalism*, with its broad focus on functionally differentiating the structures that shape a society as a whole. A state is separated into its key components, such as the political system, which is again divided into key components, such as interest groups, political parties, or branches of government. Sociologist Talcott Parsons, for example, suggests that development is a product of the degree of *functional separation* between key societal components, such as culture, community, polity, and economy. The distinction between premodern and modern societies is therefore the degree of functional differentiation of the parts. Unlike Parsons's followers who are sociologists looking for stability and solidarity, North and Acemoğlu, as economists, seek efficiency, or effectiveness. In North's account, structures are linked to respective functions, such as the capacity of institutions to reduce transaction costs that impede fruitful exchanges. The underlying notion for all forms of functionalism is that society can be understood as the sum of all the parts working together, and that the parts are a microcosm that replicates the structure of the whole. The evolutionary theory of complexity does not emphasize either efficiency or solidarity, but rather seeks resilience that derives from adaptive changes in the rules of interaction among system components.

8. Extractive regimes set up the same vicious circles in cases that include Argentina, Guatemala, Sierra Leone, Zimbabwe, Venezuela, the Soviet Union, and Roman, Incan, Aztec, Spanish, and Ottoman empires. This framework makes it hard to explain the durability of stagnant regimes and the volatility of regimes

that exhibit faster than historical growth rates, as France did on the eve of the French Revolution.

9. The first Human Development Report was published fifteen years later in 1990 with direction from Pakistani Economist Mahbub ul Haq and collaboration from Indian economist Amartya Sen.

10. Perpetually long-lived institutions are essentially bureaucratic offices that delegate authority according to competence in carrying out the organization's mission. Administrative hierarchies ensure that private and official roles are separate. This contrasts with patrimonial authority, which is familial and personal, and is modeled on the mechanics of a household.

11. In natural states, "a predominance of social relationships is organized along personal lines, including privileges, social hierarchies, laws that are enforced unequally, insecure property rights, and a pervasive sense that not all individuals were created or are equal" (North, Wallis, and Weingast 2009, 12).

12. No state, no matter how powerful or centralized, can control all the activities within its boundaries. Nevertheless, only states can make binding rules concerning their populations. The state is the central player responsible for creating and maintaining order at the transnational level within the global system.

13. If a species changes, all members of that species must change or be removed from the gene pool. A state may change its formal constitution, but this does not generate a similar level of absolute downward causation on its members' social behavior or organization.

Chapter 3

1. A replicator passes its structure to successive replications. In modernization theory, the replicator of social and political order is the economy; it mediates the selection of traits to be replicated, such as the transfer of liberal values to the rest of the polity.

2. William H. McNeill (1963, 1992) publishes a narrative of world history in which markets overwhelm and transform prior systems of social order and disrupt existing social structures anywhere on the globe.

3. For example, in the United States the rights to incorporate, a pillar of capitalism, were originally assigned as charters of social responsibility (Lehne 2001).

4. After two decades of writing on governance reform for the World Bank, the Asian Development Bank, the IMF, the OECD, the UNDP, and the US Department of the Treasury, I returned to USAID to design the project's analytical content, having contributed to good governance initiatives in a variety of international development organizations. In the late 1980s, I helped pioneer the study of governance in development in a USAID-funded project on economic on economic regulation in Madagascar. Then the need for meritocratic bureaucracies, social capital, and an effective state-society interface was a taboo subject. It was still the cold war, and donors did not choose where to spend money on the basis of how well a

country used it. Management Systems International, a Washington, DC, consulting firm that specializes in international development, was the primary contractor.

5. The concept originated in work co-authored with Bruce Bueno de Mesquita while we were fellows at the Hoover Institution, and was published as *Governing for Prosperity* by Yale University Press (Bueno de Mesquita and Root 2000). Based on the selectorate model, we developed tools to examine the broader context of political economy in which sector-level policies are framed and in which sector-level operations occur, and which could be applied across a broad spectrum of USAID activities.

6. The winning coalition is that portion of the selectorate sufficient to select a leader. Generally, only the winning coalition is rewarded with private goods.

7. Replicating institutional innovations presents a problem similar to that of cloning extinct species. Once the DNA of an extinct species is decoded, and before it can be implanted in the womb of an existing creature, mundane details must be determined: how long will the gestation take, and in what sequence are the DNA activated? The internal dynamics of sequencing cannot be fathomed from a structural blueprint of the key ingredients.

8. In practice, it is common to make suggestions that may be beneficial for some parts of the system. For example, we offered suggestions for restructuring the incentives in the Indonesian Ministry of Marine Life and Fisheries (DPK) so that officials would have stronger rewards for catching violators of agency policy. The DPK secretary general who partnered with us was removed from his job as soon as he endorsed our proposal to create a separate coast guard to monitor the nation's depleting fisheries. Those above him believed the changes would not be beneficial for the overall system, and the cabinet minister of President Susilo Bambang Yudhoyono rejected the proposal. The ministry was an instrument for patronage and corruption from which the central administration gained great utility, and that was exactly how it remained.

9. Complexity shares with the Austrian school of economics a concern with the spontaneous origin of social norms, but the Austrians typically presume the ability of social actors to start their institution-building trajectory from scratch. If we started at zero, it would be relatively easy to find the institutional arrangement that is optimal. But the future benefits of transition must be discounted at some rate of interest, which reduces the economic benefits of switching from one set of rules to another. The only way to calculate the benefits of switching is to have complete knowledge of a system's history.

10. The Maghribis were Jewish traders who migrated to the Maghreb from Baghdad in the tenth century. During the next three centuries, they successfully conducted long-distance trade, substituting social sanctions for weak legal institutions.

11. Darwin saw evolution operating by passing genotypes from one generation to another, but in political economy and among social organizations, no analogy of a genotype exists; as a result Hayek and Marshall gave up working on the idea before they finished.

12. Three distinctive evolutionary research agendas exist in the social sciences: (1) to find analogies for biological properties in economic systems (Hayek 1988; Marshall 1890); (2) to view social systems as one class of living systems, an approach pioneered by Kent Flannery, James G. Miller, and Anatol Rapoport; each sought general knowledge about such systems (Flannery 1972; Miller 1965; Rapoport 1986); and (3) to find what general laws these "systems" share. Eric Beinhocker (2006) makes an important and highly readable effort to view the economic system, including firms and business models, as one manifestation of a complex adaptive system.

13. In conventional analysis, the economic system is presumed to be either in equilibrium, veering toward equilibrium, or moving among a sequence of equilibriums, this approach does not capture the dynamics of continually evolving self-organization. One, two, or an infinite number of agents are rational maximizers, or optimizers, of expected utility; they are homogenous and exhibit stable and rational expectations. With little diversity, limited interdependence or connectivity among agents, the environment will exhibit neither robustness nor complexity. With no internal dynamics of their own, the values change in response to external stimulators, such as new information or a change in the supply of a commodity. Analogies in economics are generally mechanical systems that are merely complicated rather than complex, such as oscillators, pendulums, a spinning wheel, or an orbiting planet. Understanding the laws that govern how cells interact with other cells to form organisms, ecologies, economies, and societies is the future challenge that will require unifying all of the sciences that study human life. Understanding biological complexity will be the springboard for understanding social complexity. To understand human life and human society as one complex whole will require reconfiguring how knowledge is created and disseminated in the academy.

14. In the West after the Concordant of Worms, the Catholic Church legitimized itself through its development of canon law, creating a separate sphere for the rule of law that was essential to protect private capital from revenue-hungry monarchs. Without the institutionalization of a separate sphere of spiritual authority, property rights protection might never have solidified in the West. Economist Timur Kuran (2010) links stunted economic performance to the weakness of key wealth-building concepts in Islamic law.

15. Simon Levin's highly influential contribution to the study of environment and ecology, laid the theoretical foundation for the study of spatial ecology showing that "the problem of pattern and scale is the central problem in ecology" (1992). The regularities of the biosphere derive from interacting self-organizing processes, rather than from being parts of a unified or centralized whole (Levin et al. 2009, 772). The structure and dynamics of one scale of a socioecological system will depend on the dynamics of the system at scales above and below. The scale that we care to affect, such as economic or political development, is connected to and affected by activities occurring at various scales of the system. A state is similar to an ecological system, being composed of a hierarchy of interconnected adaptive cycles that operate at multiple scales. Complexity exists because any one scale is linked to hierarchies that govern systemwide behavior. An economy also has a multiple-scale structure and is strongly influenced by cross-scale dynamics.

16. When a system is far from equilibrium, many solutions are possible. Systems in equilibrium offer only one solution.

Chapter 4

1. The BRICs (Brazil, Russia, India, and China) are turning out to be uncooperative multilateral partners for the United States.

2. Institutional change is a perennial topic of social science, and the masterpieces are still read with the urgency with which they were written. They are typically strongly grounded in the geopolitical economy of their day: Thomas Hobbes and the European wars of religion; John Locke and England's Glorious Revolution; Karl Marx and the barricades of Paris in 1848; Max Weber and the rise of Prussian militarism. These writers established universal truths in the context of specific and current debates. History is written in reference to current needs, Croce wrote in *History as the Story of Liberty* (1941).

3. Fukuyama never claimed that non-Western societies would follow a similar sequence of developmental steps toward modernization. He has always been careful to avoid being understood as saying that comparable institutions require similar conditions or that a country's unique history predisposes it to a single future path that cannot be altered.

4. For an alternative view representing dependency theory, see André Gunder Frank (1998).

5. The term *third world* has its philosophical roots in the term *third estate*, which described the nonprivileged in the Constituent Assembly on the eve of the French Revolution. Their goal was to change the civil organization of French society.

6. Robert Keohane is a central contributor to the literature on how international regimes foster cooperation, emphasizing the role of institutions to overcome barriers to cooperation (1977, 1984).

7. Francis Fukuyama makes the same point (1992, xxiii).

8. "All the more spectacular origins of new structures or habits in the history of organisms were due to a change of ecological role. Such shifts splendidly illustrate the opportunism of evolution" (Mayr 1981, 207).

9. Modern economics, like modern religion, seeks to be true in all times, in all places, and for all people, never specifying a connection between ideas and the contexts that engendered them. Hirschman's *The Passions and the Interests* (1997) takes strong exception to this pretension.

10. This view is particularly linked to the writings of Gabriel Almond and Sidney Verba (1963).

11. Sociologist Martin Lipset (1960) and economist Robert Barro (1997) documented the strong correlation between economic liberalization and democratization, and concluded that the relationship could not be accidental. They postulated that as people become wealthier through economic opportunities, their desire to consume more democracy will increase, and that as their interests proliferate, democracy will emerge to manage conflicts.

12. The coevolution of democracy and autocracy can cause *disaptation*, defined in ecology as a "character that decreases its possessor's average rate of survival and reproduction relative to contrasting conditions evident in a population's evolutionary history; a primary disaptation is disadvantageous within the population context when it first appears; a secondary disaptation acquires a selective liability not present at its origin as a consequence of environmental change or an altered genetic context" (Levin et al. 2009, 93).

13. Philip Cerny writes about a shift in the state's role from being the source of social risk management to being a promoter of global opportunity (1995, 1999, 2007). Ramesh Mishra highlights globalization's role in diminishing the capacity of the traditional welfare state to protect citizens from global competition (1999).

14. In 2007, for example, 40 percent of countries lacking competitive multiparty elections attracted more private investment than the median country with competitive elections (Gehlbach and Keefer 2011). Fukuyama recognizes this outright reversal of democratic gains (2011, 10–13).

15. A lack of competitive voting or a free press traps authoritarian regimes in two institutional dilemmas: they have limited means to monitor lower level governments and they are unable to identify which local groups pose a danger to the state. Central leadership requires mechanisms to monitor local officials and extend central control over local elites (Root and May 2008). These impediments will be discussed at length in chapter 9. The result is an inability to supervise lower level local officials to ensure their compliance with centrally determined governance standards and with revenue goals. Thus countries in which information is too tightly controlled lose a mechanism to supervise lower level officials and local jurisdictions, an often-cited cause of the fall of the Soviet Union.

16. J. H. Hexter (1961) criticized the almost universal acceptance, enjoyed by explanations of long-term historical change, of the myth of the rising middle classes; "every significant phenomenon in European, and especially English history for three centuries, the Renaissance, the Reformation, the colonial expansion of Europe, the New Monarchy, nationalism, the Rise of the House of Commons, the Puritan Revolution was attributed to its rise." François Furet (1981), Alfred Cobban (1964), and George Taylor (1964) each extended Hexter's skepticism concerning the revolutionary role of the rising middle classes to rethink the origins of the French Revolution.

17. Mancur Olson (1965, 1982) attributes economic growth to contract-intensive transactions. This places institutions in the context of classical liberal assumptions that markets reflect a natural order. An alternative view expressed by Geoffrey Hodgson is that markets are institutions that can either enable or restrict economic activity (1988, 1993, 1996).

18. Lowi offers the following critique of pluralism "The group process is dynamic and cumulative when groups have an institutional structure against which to compete. Without that formal structure, the group process is not truly pluralistic at all. It is merely co-operative. And it is ineffective. Worse, it converts mere ineffectiveness into illegitimacy" (Lowi 1969, 156).

19. By reducing distances, information technology plays a critical role: it enables global supply chains, allowing people to engage in business with partners from

all over the globe. Comparative advantage, rather than central planning, drives the process.

20. Frances Cairncross writes that the communication revolution would be democratic and liberating, and eliminate distances between small and large, and rich and poor, and end the separation of the world's population into isolated local nations (1997).

Chapter 5

1. The end of the cold war was fertile ground for the belief that opening a society to market forces will lead to individual property rights, democratization, and the rule of law.

2. The challenges facing NIE as a policy directive are discussed in chapter 3 as the "transplanter's dilemma."

3. The IMF and World Bank seek to address good governance in policy dialogues with borrowers to insert good governance as a condition in loan covenants (Kapur and Webb 2000).

4. The Quality of Government Institute at Sweden's University of Gothenburg publishes an extensive library of surveys, data, and readings on institutional quality. Available at http://www.qog.pol.gu.se.

5. See "Worldwide Governance Indicators," World Bank.

6. NIE has proved to be very adept at identifying institutional gaps that separate high performers from the rest. The missing institutions are then presumed to be the explanation of international differences in economic development. However, gap assessments are a key source of the failure of development economics. As economist William Easterly observes, every time one gap is identified, another gap appears. First, there was a gap of capital, then education, then good policies, and finally NIE comes along and identifies a gap of good governance itself. International financial institutions continue to make gap assessments to calculate the relationship between investment and growth. To justify its continued use, defenders of this methodology argue that although filling gaps is not sufficient, it is a necessary condition for growth (2002, 29).

7. Hall and Taylor (1996) identify three distinctive varieties of new institutionalism, with the NIE program being a subset of rational choice institutionalism. This variant, which concerns itself with the relationship between institutions and economic development, is the sole concern of this chapter.

An earlier variant, historical institutionalism, flourished in the 1960s and 1970s, and had a structural functionalist orientation in which institutions, rules, processes, and procedures arose to serve power relations in society, defined in either pluralist or neo-Marxist terms. Once formed the institutions structure social relations along a set of paths. James March and Johan Olsen critiqued historical approaches for under-analyzing the effect of institutions on behavior and for lacking a theoretical point of reference (1984). Acemoğlu and Robinson (2012) revive the neo-Marxist perspective.

A third variant, sociological institutionalism, emphasizes symbolic systems that give meaning to social action. This approach eliminates the barriers of institutions and culture by treating culture as an institution. Persistent inefficiencies of social institutions are related to prescriptive norms of behavior. Institutional templates define socially appropriate responses to stress. The sociological approach is weak on specifying change mechanisms or on assessing strategic interaction among actors; none of the variants adequately link the interaction of micro foundations with macro outcomes.

8. Game theory is often summoned to examine the relationship between the rules and behavior and to determine why a change in the institutional parameters does not lead to a change in behavior. A frequently reported result is that coordination may fail due to distributional uncertainties, asymmetric information, or free-rider problems. Since people may not believe that a given set of rules will be followed, they will continue to presume previous rules of behavior. The new rules fail to become self-enforcing.

9. "A single gene may have simultaneous effects on several types of the phenotype . . . interactions among genes are of decisive importance for the fitness of individuals and for the effects of selection" (Mayr 2001, 272). A gene is a genetic unit comprised of base pairs that seem to function within a decentralized network that does not break down easily because it is protected by redundancy (Barabasi 2002, 181–83).

10. Authority is personal and familial, modeled on the mechanics of a household, which contrasts with the concept of a rational bureaucracy governed by formal rules, where authority is delegated according to competence. Administrative hierarchies ensure that the private and official roles are clearly separated.

11. How different regimes enact rule enforcement is difficult to observe. A civil service system may exist in law, but sitting bureaucracies may be induced to do the governing parties' bidding. Typically, when liberal institutions are imposed on patrimonial regimes, norms of social reciprocity between unequal members do not disappear. The competencies of clientelistic exchange are simply transferred to the new institutions and leaders to tailor their skills to identify groups or powerful individuals whose support can be obtained by material inducements. Rather than dispersing moderate benefits across a broad audience, clientelistic politicians concentrate benefits on voter constituencies whose support can bring victory in the next election (Kitschelt and Wilkinson 2007, 12).

12. A useful analogue is the nervous system. "The nervous system operates as a closed network of interactions, in which every change of the interactive relations between certain components always results in a change of the interactive relations of the same or of other components" (Capra 1996, 96). In a network, "the function of each component is to help produce and transform the components while maintaining the overall circularity of the network" (p. 96). Humberto Maturana and Francisco Varela originally formulated these ideas in the early 1970s.

13. Dani Rodrik, (2008, 52) sums up the consensus among the institutionalists, "In the long run, the main thing that ensures convergence with the living standards of advanced countries is the acquisition of high-quality institutions." Re-

lentless advocacy of institutional factors encouraged a shift in economic research away from the social welfare consequences of policies and toward the institutions, the rules of the game, that both implicitly and explicitly determined the selection of policies in the first place.

14. For example, in North, Wallis, and Weingast (2009), elites learn that cooperation is a functionally efficient means to maximize collective wealth.

15. China's regime differs from ordinary personality-based autocracies because its leaders are members of an organization that discounts the future less than an individual leader does. This is why communist regimes can act programmatically to invest for the future, whereas neopatrimonial regimes generally fail.

16. If Canada tried to rival the United States, conflict might upset an otherwise peaceful coexistence.

17. Among the most frequently cited examples of the race to find the genetic formula of social growth is the seminal contribution of Rafael La Porta, Florencio López-de-Silanes, Andrei Shleifer, and Robert Vishny. "The Quality of Government" links divergent developmental paths to their legal origins (1999). Another granular study compiles lists of checks and balances. An especially ambitious quantitative study is Richard Roll's and John Talbott's effort to regress nine highly significant institutional variables to explain gross national income (2003). But Roll's definition of good governance often refers to policy outcomes that are not institutions, but are variables of another variable. The indexes of institutional quality typically hit this sort of bottleneck when trying to distinguish cause from effect. Reverse causality is obscured since the institutional variables are generally measured at the end of a period of growth or decline.

Chapter 6

1. If an organism seeks to attain the highest fitness peaks, it will find that mutation and selection are insufficient to search long distances over an entire space of possibilities, as each new creature creates a nutrient needed by another. Thus coevolution can also create small and large bursts of speciation; new forms arise, while others are driven to extinction. "Adaptive moves in biological evolution and technical evolution drive avalanches of speciation and extinction" (Kauffman 1993, 28). "Endogenous coevolutionary changes may trigger bursts of speciation and extinction, as well as the integration of new species into the ecosystem" (Kauffman 1993, 227). These periods during which an exploding rate of innovation occurred in natural history are replicated in human-made history in which technological change drives one set of goods to extinction, while creating niches for others to survive. Avalanches of change are generated by the coevolutionary dynamics of small best choices made by agents competing among themselves to survive.

2. Dancing landscapes are generally referred to in landscape theory as complex. A landscape is truly complex when structure exists at every scale so that many forms of evolutionary behavior can occur, making it impossible to infer a model of general behavior (Bar-Yam 1997, 553–54).

3. Page and Miller (2007, 228).

4. A global peak is the highest local peak in a given landscape. Usually only one global peak exists.

5. Many accounts of the roots of India democracy stress the training of the Congress elite in British schools and their emulation of British parliamentary models. But it was the usefulness of those models for their own self-interested objectives that explains their choice of institutions. Pakistani leaders were trained in the same models but did not apply them once independence was obtained.

6. Notable exceptions are Mohandas Gandhi and SubhasChandra Bose.

7. The Red Queen's Hypothesis derives its name from Lewis Carroll's *Through the Looking Glass*. After constantly running but getting nowhere, Alice says to the Red Queen, "Well, in our country, you'd generally get to somewhere else—if you run very fast for a long time, as we've been doing." "A slow sort of country!" said the Queen. "Now, here, you see, it takes all the running you can do, to keep in the same place. If you want to go somewhere else, you must run at least twice as fast as that!" The implication is that in a coevolutionary system, continual adaptation is needed to maintain relative fitness.

8. Indian Planning Commission members who were also academicians includes: Dr. K. Kasturirangan (Member [Science] in the Planning Commission [July 2009–present]; Chancellor of Jawaharlal Nehru University (JNU) [March 2012–present]; Honorary Professor of Physics at the Physical Research Laboratory, Ahmedabad; Jawarharlal Nehru Centre for Advanced Research, Bangalore; Professor Emeritus at National Institute of Advanced Studies, Bangalore); Dr. Abid Hussain (IPC member [1985–1990]; Chancellor of English and Foreign Languages University, Hyderabad; Chancellor of ICFAI Foundation for Higher Education; Professor Emeritus at Indian Institute of Foreign Trade; Professor Emeritus at the Foreign Service Institute of Ministry of External Affairs); Dr. Jagdish N. Bhagwati (Indian Planning Commission [1961–1963]; Professor of International Trade at the Delhi School of Economics; Professor at MIT [1968–1980]; Professor, Economics and Law at Columbia University [1980–present]; Dr. A. Vaidhyanathan (ten years in Perspective Planning Division of the Planning Commission; later Professor at the Centre for Development Studies, Trivandrum Professor Emeritus at MIDS (Madras Institute of Development Studies [1984-2005]); Dr. Anwarul Hoda (Member of the Planning Commission, Government of India in the rank of Minister of State in the Union Government [2004–2009]; Chair Professor, Trade Police and WTO Research Programme at Indian Council for Research on International Economic Relations (ICRIER [2009–present]; Dr. G. S. Bhalla (Member Planning Commission, Government of India [1990–1991]; Professor of Economics, CSRD, Jawaharlal Nehru University [1975–1993] during tenure as IPC member and beyond; Professor Emeritus, Jawaharlal Nehru University [1993–present]); Dr. Surya Sethi (Principal Adviser for Power and Energy, Planning Commission, Government of India [2001–2009]; Core Climate Negotiator, Planning Commission, Government of India [2001–2009]; currently Professor at Lee Kuan Yew School of Public Policy, Singapore [2009–present]; Dr. Abhijit Banerjee; Dr. Jean Drèze; Dr. Abhijit Sen; Dr. Swapan Garain (Member of the Government of India's Planning

Commission Steering Committee on Voluntary Sector for the 10th [2002–2007] and 11th [2007–2012] Five Year plans; Associate Professor of Tata Institute of Social Sciences [July 1985–present]; Visiting Professor of Welingkar Institute of Management [July 2008–May 2009] during tenure as IPC member); Dr. Ramesh Chandra (Planning Commission, Government of Uttar Pradesh [February 1985–2011]; Professor and Founder Director, Dr. B.R.Ambedkar Center for Biomedical Research [February 1985–present]; Professor, Former Vice-Chancellor and Founder Director, ACBR [March 1991–present]); Dr. V. K. R. V. Rao (Member, Planning Commission [1963–1966]; National Professor, Government of India [1985–1990]); Dr. Suresh D. Tendulkar (Member, Expert Group on Estimation of Proportion of the Number of Poor appointed by the Indian Planning Commission [July 1993]; latest employment in academe: Professor of Economics, Delhi School of Economics, University of Delhi [August 1978–February 2004]; Member of the Economic Advisory Council to the Prime Minister [2004–2008] and chairman of the Council [2008–2009]; Dr. R. P. Sinha (Former Principal Advisor, Planning Commission; started career as an academic in 1960, returned to this field after retirement in 2001 as Visiting Professor in the Institute of Applied Manpower Research); Dr. Arjun Sengupta (Member Secretary of IPC, under Deputy Chairman Pranab Mukherjee [circa 1993]; Professor of International Economic Organization, School of International Studies, Jawaharlal Nehru University [1998–2002]; served as the Adjunct Professor of Development and Human Rights, Faculty of Public Health, Harvard University); Dr. V. Krishnamurthy (Member, Planning Commission of India [1991–1992]; Member, Board of Governors, Administrative Staff College of India, Hyderabad [1975–1979] and [1990–present]; Dr. Arun Kumar Ghosh (Former member of IPC; Returned to full-time academe, as a Fellow of the Nehru Memorial Museum and Library); Dr. Bagicha Singh Minhas (Member of the Indian Planning Commission [1971–1973]; Head of the Planning Division at the Indian Statistical Institute [1971–1986]; Senior Fellow at the Institute of Development Studies (IDS) at the University of Sussex [1976–1978]; Visiting Professor at John Hopkins; Rufus Putnam Visiting Professor at Ohio). List compiled by Vashnavi Venkatesh, MPP student, George Mason University.

9. The inability to switch course after repeated examples of mediocre growth and persistent digressions from the goals of the plan was due to political economy. In a symbiotic relationship, politicians and bureaucrats found that both groups gained enhanced status. More red tape meant more power for the bureaucrats, and the need to intervene to get things done proved to be a valuable source of rents for the politicians (Root 2006, 124–30).

10. After learning by copying each other, Chinese firms expanded their product range by copying the processes and manufactures of global firms, causing friction with potential trading partners.

11. Kauffman submits that any biological form is possible, constrained by function, and that the total numbers and types of species are limited to the solution of a fundamental set of requirements in which the above-stated dynamics can be played out.

12. For a detailed explanation, see Kauffman (1993, 644).

Chapter 7

1. In a scale-free, decentralized system, the web of relationships retains functional coherence, despite the introduction of new organizations, goods, or services. The possibilities of transformation arise from self-organization. The web governs its own change processes (Kauffman 1993, 370).

2. Western hegemons ebb and flow on the international stage. Charlemagne was emperor of the West for only fourteen years, and after his death in 814, Europe became a battlefield that no one power was able to dominate for more than a few centuries. Ottonian Germany dominated the early Middle Ages, and France dominated the later Middle Ages, but the French territories were split by the English in the west, and by the Burgundians in the east and the north (Huizinga 1924). Portugal, after taking a lead during the Age of Discovery, was subdued by the Spanish Hapsburgs, who were eclipsed by the Dutch. The British cowed both Bourbon France and Dutch. Germany surpassed Britain, and both were overtaken by the United States. Russia enjoyed its first system-defining role during the cold war.

3. Tight feedbacks highlight future options, helping agents to identify how a system will respond to change. It enhances the capacity of agents to attain future desired outcomes. Weak feedback loops make it difficult for agents to apprehend the consequences of their behavior.

4. Dissertation of Yan Li, George Mason University.

5. The map of political and social power of the European state system resembles a modern-day airline routing map; the linkages are widely distributed and connect with hubs. Instead of the nodes being airports connected by direct flights, the nodes are aristocratic houses linked by intermarriages. Just as the airport routing map is dominated by a few hubs, such as Atlanta, Chicago, Los Angeles, and New York, the hubs of the European system comprised the great families, the dukes, princes, and monarchs.

6. Institutional scholars like Joseph Strayer (1970) trace the origins of the modern state to its medieval antecedents.

7. A microevolutionary change would be the differences in the placement size or the capacity of the eye or the ear in a specific species.

8. Initially, the view that species come into existence rapidly and then do not change significantly was characterized as "non-Darwinian," but it has fallen under the umbrella of Darwinian evolution and helps to distinguish micro- from macroevolution. On the differences between micro- or macroevolutionary perspectives, see Rose and Lauder (1996).

9. Geoffrey Hodgson challenges the gradual view of institutional selection, writing that "a period of disruption is both the impulse and opportunity for economic change. . . . Large-scale disruptive events can create the opportunity to recast structures and institutions and lay down more modern and progressive habits and routines" (1996, 401).

10. Military revolutions that dramatically transformed the conduct of war have been identified by Michael Roberts (1956), C. J. Rogers (1993, 1995), Geoffrey

Parker (1988, 1996), Jeremy Black (1999), Michael Howard (1976, 2000), John A. Lynn (2002, 1997), David Eltis (1998), Robert Bates (2001), and Charles Tilly (1992). These authors address the sociological and organizational consequences of military revolutions.

11. The Swiss lacked comparative advantage in mounting a cavalry attack but learned how to defeat the cavalry of their enemies by forming defensive units of infantry consisting of pikemen (1421) and eventually handgunners to face down the charge of mounted knights. Geoffrey Parker observes "short bursts of rapid change" punctuated European military history. "Thus, in the fourteenth century, after a long period in which infantry had slowly but steadily increased in importance, Swiss pikemen and English archers suddenly and dramatically enhanced their role; then, after about a century of experiment, gunpowder artillery began in the 1430s to revolutionize siege craft; and about a century after that, following constant (and extremely expensive) experiment, a new defensive technique known as the artillery fortress brought positional warfare back into balance. Each innovation broke the prevailing equilibrium and provoked a phase of raid transformation and adjustment" (Parker 1995, 6).

12. First deployed in the Hundred Years' War, in 1346 at the Battle of Crécy, English cannons proved indecisive, being too heavy were ineffective in the field. The English did not make subsequent investments in making cannons more mobile.

13. Intensive drilling allowed the Swedes to exploit the full potential of volley fire and linear formations.

14. Introduced at the Battle of Breitenfeld (1631) by the Swedish king Gustavus Adolphus.

15. In his quest to dominate continental Europe, the armies of Louis XIV reached five hundred thousand troops. Innovation in administrative structure was needed to manage and provision an army of such size. The Sun King began a series of bureaucratic reforms that enabled France to dominate European politics for almost two centuries, but his quest for additional economic resources to further expand political power led to growing dependence on the skills of non-elites. Louis, like most early-modern European rulers, did not conceive of continuous productivity and growth (wealth) through technological innovation. He believed that wealth was acquired by employing the state's coercive capacity for economic expansion. For France to be first in commerce, Louis considered it essential to crush Europe's leading commercial nation, Holland. Declaring war against bourgeois Holland, he initiated fifty-three years of virtually constant warfare. Ironically, the heirs of François I, the founder of the Bourbon monarchy, became increasingly dependent on matching the technological innovations of rival nations. Thus unrelenting intra-European rivalry intensified the French crown's dependence on merchants, financiers, and legal specialists. A constant quest for funds led the crown to alienate authority to non-elites from the Third Estate in the form of royal offices and royal privileges and exemption from taxation.

16. State legitimacy was punctuated quite frequently by strategic events, or rather upheavals, "not least . . . a strategic event so cataclysmic as losing a war" (Bobbitt 2002). Long periods of stasis occur after innovators attain legitimacy through a

successful military intervention; "although wars may create and mold states, it is the State that creates legitimacy both domestic and external, and it is legitimacy that maintains peace" (2002, xvi).

17. Essentially, two kinds of military revolutions occurred in pre-modern European history. The infantry revolution of the fourteenth century and the artillery revolution of the fifteenth were technological. The expansion of bureaucracy, procurement and revenue systems during the seventeenth century and the *levee en masse* of the late eighteenth were tactical and strategic. Both types of military revolution transformed social organization.

18. Napoleon correctly observed that Russia was always part of the European state system, and just like the other components of that system, from the sixteenth century onward, Russia was either in a European war or preparing for the next one. To respond to the need to fight the better-equipped forces of Sweden and Turkey, Peter the Great launched Westernization reforms (1709–1723). A century later, Catherine the Great (1762–1792) re-imposed serfdom on the peasantry while both recentralizing and remilitarizing the state. She subordinated the nobility to mandatory military service for the purpose of expanding Russia's capacity to play a role as a major European power.

World War I revealed another great gap between Russia and capitalist powers of the West. Again, competition with other Western powers forced a change on the structure of the Russian state. Concern about the decline of military power due to economic and technological backwardness justified Joseph Stalin's internal regime of persecution and brutality. But it also resulted in a massive catch-up effort that industrialized Russia in a matter of a few decades.

19. Napoleon had himself anointed by the Church as emperor, thus marrying his family with royalty and restoring the clergy. His goal was to protect the revolution's core values by coopting the symbolism of the old regime.

20. The political hierarchy of authority in Europe was trans-territorial. The territorial basis of sovereignty allegiance was established during the nineteenth century, but the trans-territorial characteristics of authority and aristocratic status were not entirely effaced until after World War II.

21. Emancipation of minorities like Jews played a part in Prussia's mobilization strategy. Equal rights were granted to Jewish inhabitants in 1812, and military service was opened in 1848. In 1862, Albrect von Roon ordered that all Prussian citizens were liable for military conscription, including Jews. Austria did not do the same for its more significant Jewish population until 1867.

22. The Austrians also practiced trade discrimination; the empire did not become a single market until long after the German Customs Union (*Zollverein*), established in 1818, rapidly expanded the Prussian economy. By 1866 most German states were members. Austria's highly protected industry made it ineligible for membership. The Austrian empire still had internal tariffs until 1851. By contrast, the German union limited trade and commercial barriers among members. Austria had only one bank, the *Creditanstalt*, while Prussia had a more developed banking system.

23. After the former Hapsburg lands became nation-states, the gap between German-speaking and Slavic lands started to diminish.

24. Acemoğlu and Robinson claim that elites cede franchise rights to non-elites to surmount a crisis; in Prussia the elites ceded non-elites a greater role in the nation's primary institution, the army (2006, 2000).

25. The Austrian political and military system was being destabilized by distrust among different national and social groups. The deepest problem came from the poor technical education of the Austrian recruits. The Austrians did not possess the technical skill or manufacturing capacity to update their battlefield weapons until well after their European rivals.

Superior technical education enabled the Prussians to equip their infantry with breech-loading rapid-fire Dreyse needle guns. In the Franco-Austrian War of 1859, Austria's slow muzzle-loading Lorenz rifles were no match for the better-equipped French.

26. The Chinese classic *The Art of War* is not about technological or tactical innovations that require changes in the structure of the state or in the system of command.

27. Just a generation earlier, during World War II, Great Britain's prime minister, Winston Churchill, and John Maynard Keynes, who represented Britain at Bretton Woods in 1944 and in 1946, both claimed descent from the Norman invaders of the eleventh century. Many leaders of French society who fell to the Nazi attack similarly could trace their ancestry back centuries to knights on horseback. The European elite continued to stay intact and endured far longer than rival networks of social power. A paradox of the European state system is that novelty, functionality, and order arose from the bottom up, but rulers did not.

28. To restore order, a new Chinese dynasty would typically repudiate all ties to previous dynasties by instituting new codes of dress, annihilating and rebuilding all official buildings in a new style. The new regime generally declared that it was rebuilding the entire society in order to root out the sources of disorder, extirpating architectural and even intellectual remnants of a previous regime. Even religions were cast aside to signal the new era, which aspired to a more perfect social order. Yet the network structure of authority of the previous regime was replicated in the new one. The only exception to this pattern of radical rejection of the old was the Qing dynasty, which replaced the Ming dynasty with Manchu rule in 1644. Coming from a minority tribe, the Manchus emphasized continuity. In this regard they were similar to the Hapsburg rulers of the Austrian empire.

29. A frequent conjecture among military historians is that artillery was not needed, since the great threat to China's security came from nomadic invaders of inner Asia who did not possess fortifications. Gunpowder, they argue, was used primarily as a means to attack fortifications, but China's adversaries did not have fortifications.

30. Chinese policy was vigilant to avoid the dangers of rebelliousness posed by the autonomy of armed men and merchants. "Like organized resort to armed force, private riches acquired by personal shrewdness in buying and selling violated the Confucian sense of propriety. Such persons could be tolerated, even

encouraged, when their activity served official ends. But to allow merchants or manufactures to acquire too much power, or accumulate too much capital, was as unwise as to allow a military commander or a barbarian chieftain to control too many armed men. Wise policy aimed at breaking up undue concentrations of wealth just as an intelligent diplomacy and a well-designed military adminis-tration aimed at preventing undue concentrations of military power under any one command. Divide-and-rule applied in economics as much as in war. Officials who acted on that principle could count on widespread popular sympathy, since plundering armies and ruthless capitalists seems almost equally detestable to the common people." (McNeill 1982, 36)

31. Reference to the Japanese invasion of China are found in Perrin (1979).

32. The entire land belonged to the shogun, who dispensed it among the lords, with the shogun's portion always being larger than any feasible combination. This weakened the horizontal dynamics that might have led to rivalry with the center. The domain lords owed unqualified loyalty to the shogun. The system owed its stability to the concentration of power in the hands of a superior at each step in the hierarchy. It was feudalism under strong vertical control. On his own lands, an individual vassal was the supreme power.

33. By the end of the Tokugawa era, samurai were aristocratic bureaucrats for the *daimyo*. Their *daisho*, their swords (cf. long *katana* and short *wakizashi*), became merely symbolic, except when used against a disrespectful commoner (*kiri sute gomen*).

34. The curtain closed on individual bravery and prowess in 1877, when a mas-sive army of peasant conscripts put down a samurai uprising in the southwest.

35. Scheve and Stasavage (2012) tested for the effects of political rights on the expansion of progressive taxation by linking their data with the long-run evolu-tion of income inequality, and found a weak linkage between regime type and progressive taxation; suffrage extension alone did not generate the large increases in tax progressivity. Sacrifices in war change societal views about fairness, they conclude. After examining the increase in top tax rates in a large number of coun-tries from 1850 to 1970, they eliminated electoral democracy or the existence of left political parties as a principal cause of progressive taxation.

36. The European state made war, and war made the state, so quipped Charles Tilly (1992).

37. Trying to understand the Tiananmen Square massacre of 1989, Stuart Kauff-man speculates, "The Chinese government knew that, with a few features of their system altered, the entire edifice stood in danger of dramatic transformation" (1993, 370).

Chapter 8

1. The East Asian wave began with "people power" in the Philippines that top-pled the Marcos regime, then inspired democratic transitions in South Korea, Taiwan, Thailand, and finally in Indonesia after the 2008 financial crisis forced

the resignation of Suharto. Democracy in this region remains unstable, setbacks are frequent, institution building has lagged, and patronage has been persistent.

2. The Gülen movement's roots lie in eastern Turkey's Nurcu Order. Its founder, Bedi Üzzaman Sait Nursi (1876–1960), was from eastern Turkey and influenced by Sufism.

3. Some believe that the Gülen movement is an Islamist extremist movement, an enemy of democracy and secularism, and that Gülen himself aims to take over the country and set up an Islamic state by infiltrating every layer of the society and government through the control of media and education (Sharon-Krespin 2009). His defenders claim he is an advocate of a peaceful and nonviolent way of life, democracy, and civil liberty, and that he is respectful to the secular Turkish state and a corrective to the dangers of reactionary Islamist extremism (Harrington 2011).

4. In game theory, when players have the prospect of future interactions, they are more likely to cooperate. This applies to the AKP; most Turks presume that only a major economic setback will push the party out of power in the near future. The memory of previous disastrous policies has discredited all rival political parties. The AKP has the only prospect for the political change, until a new party arises that can attract members away.

5. Affinity with the Arab Spring can drive Turkey further from the West. It can strengthen Erdoğan's campaign to isolate the secular higher brass of the military through mass arrests and resignations. Electoral populism may compel Turkey to seek leadership of an Islamic bloc and align its democracy with like-minded neighbors that advocate Islamic over individual rights.

6. A notable twelfth-century treatises that employs logic is *Four Books of Sentences, Decretum (Concord of Discordant Canons) Glossa Ordinaria, Historia Scholastica, Summa Theologica*, and *Summae*, or *Summulae logicales* of Gratiani.

7. A deep-seated suspicion of political and economic power is as old as the republic, according to Simon Johnson and James Kwak. Both Jefferson and Madison feared that concentrated wealth would lead to concentrated power that could threaten democracy (2010, 14–38).Vigilance against the formation of a "small elite with a dangerous amount of economic and political power" (p. 20) has distinguished the US experience from that of Mexico and Latin America more generally, where powerful and unfettered financial interests can distort the economy for their own purposes.

8. In East Asia, authoritarian governments in South Korea, Taiwan, and Thailand successfully implemented land reform by providing formal land titling, public goods, extension services, small-scale producer credit, and help with exporting, processing, and packaging; this made owning land a market opportunity for the poor. By contrast, the elected governments in the Philippines failed successfully carry out their version of the US Homestead Act because rural poor property rights were granted without providing the rural poor with the means to take advantage of market opportunities, expropriation and re-concentration of holdings resulted.

9. The more people feel that their future can be improved through social alliances with outsiders, the more standard was their speech (Nettle 1999, 29). Nettle explores this logic in case studies drawn from several African examples (1999). Arab-speaking populations in the Middle East failed to create strong states. Do the hardships of maintaining regular communication across a continent-wide desert cause sociological decomposition? Another hypothesis is that "elite institutions have been the determinants of language spread in only a minority of cases until very recently" (p. 94). Mandarin Chinese and French are important exceptions in that strong administrative systems in China and France imposed a national language.

10. "Melanesian society is organized tribally into what anthropologists call segmentary lineages, groups of people who trace their descent to a common ancestor. Numbering anywhere from a few dozen to a few thousand kinsmen, these tribes are known as *wantoks*, a pidgin corruption of the English words 'one talk,' or people who speak the same language" (Fukuyama 2011, 2–3). Nettle points out that if China had the same ratio of languages to people that Papua New Guinea has, it would have over 200,000 languages (1999, 65).

11. Japan's precocious integration as a national culture has been commented upon by scholars. Mary Berry writes about "the unprecedented formation in early modernity of common 'customs, attitudes, and practices' within national or proto-national units" (1999, 103). According to Edwin Reischauer and Alfred Craig (1989), during the Tokugawa shogunate of the Edo period (1600–1868), Japan "achieved a greater degree of cultural, intellectual, and ideological conformity . . . than any other country in the world . . . before the nineteenth century" (cited in Lieberman 1999, 103). Berry concurs that integrating structures permeate the Islands: "a centralized polity has generated a capacious, hierarchical officialdom; regional and even national markets have generated both a specialized, commercial agriculture and a specialized, vertically organized workforce. Additional integral forces are reliable transport, urbanization, and schooling" (1997, 548).

12. Samuel Huntington's *Clash of Civilizations* and Francis Fukuyama's *Origins of Political Order* elaborate this point (Fukuyama 2011; Huntington 1996).

Chapter 9

1. Notable efforts to define state capacity are Almond and Powell (1966); Katzenstein (1978); Zysman (1983); Migdal (1988); Ikenberry (1988); Organski and Kugler (1980); Skocpol (1985); Kugler and Tammen, eds. (2012).

2. *Extractive capacity* generally refers to the absolute value of the revenue captured by the state or the percentage of the gross domestic product that is captured. Although this measurement is relatively easy to measure, it is a poor proxy for overall state capacity.

3. In China, by contrast, more distance from pre-modern norms has occurred than in India because intermediary groups of ancient pedigree were dissolved during the cultural purges of the Mao Zedong period.

4. Patron clientelism is studied in Brazil (Ames 2000; Abers 1998), in Argentina (Auyero 2000), in the Philippines (Coronel 1998; Coronel and Severino 1996), in Thailand (Dixit and Londregan 1996; Doner and Ramsey 1997; Glaeser and Shleifer 2005; Medina and Stokes 2007; Diaz-Cayeros, Estevez, and Magaloni 2004; Robinson and Verdier 2002; Robinson, Torvik, and Verdier 2006), and in Benin (Wantchekon 2003). Redistributive networks in Africa are limited, and few members of the population benefit, compared to South Asia (Van de Walle 2001). Sharp ethno-cultural divisions facilitate clientelistic exchanges, as evidenced from Madhya Pradesh, reported in Singh et al. (2003). Other patron–client networks like drug cartels or the yakuza in Japan can also be nationwide.

5. The impact of clientelism on political regimes is examined by Kitschelt (2000); Scott (1972a, b); Tarrow (1977)." Kitschelt and Wilkinson (2007, 12). Brinker-hoff and Goldsmith (2002) review the literature on patronage and democratic governance for USAID.

6. Although the role of the local big man is best known for its prevalence in Africa, the practice to extend the appeal of the Congress Party is noted in Kothari (1970); Weiner (1957, 1967).

7. A grievance presented to the king by a Burgundian lord in 1756 asserted that the essence of lordship was the ownership of land combined with the exercise of public authority. That grievance concerned the right of the lord to select the new village schoolmaster. The seigneur forwarded his grievance to the King's Council, but in vain. The council refused to consider the complaint and referred it to the *intendant*, who supported the peasantry's initiative and warned the seigneur in question, Loppin de Gemeau, that he would lose the case even if it went through all the levels of provincial justice. The King's Council, the *intendant* said, would reverse any decision that might prohibit the village assembly from meeting without the lord's consent. Thus, in Burgundy and elsewhere, the *seigneurie* was losing the judicial and administrative justifications of its economic rights and privileges.

8. The Chinese Communist Party, similarly, has provided a formal venue for local communities to address grievances against local party officials. The plaintiffs lose most of the cases, which only makes their assertion of rights more vehement (Pei 1997, 837).

9. The crown made claims to exercise personally the rights that belonged to the state itself. Roman concepts of a unified public authority eventually undermined the concept of *l'etat c'est moi*.

10. Traditionally war training was acquired by practice under a supervisor. The heroic virtues required for leadership were presumed to be an inherited characteristic derived from one's social origin. In 1751 the crown created the École Militaire Royale to instruct younger members of noble houses. As scientific branches of military activity, such as artillery and engineering, became more important, non-noble recruits were admitted. The war colleges established the importance of the need for instruction by inventors, who generally came from socially inferior backgrounds. This created a demand for greater access to officer status by non-noble recruits on the basis of merit rather than birth.

11. The Bank of England was permitted to borrow money on security of Parliament, to deal in bullion and bills of exchange, and to act as pawnbroker. By the end of 1694, by leveraging liabilities to the public, the bank had advanced sums greater than its total capital to the state in the form of bills, which the exchequer accepted in lieu of tallies used to pay government creditors. The bank thus became indispensable to the government as a source of credit and a channel for making remittances to soldiers overseas. As the issue of bank notes grew and became standardized over the course of the eighteenth century, the bank's ties with the government became more intimate.

12. In the Philippines, social stratification in the domestic arena is shaped by the country's position in the international arena, which enables the elite to exchange geopolitical policy concessions for the resources to stay in power, but dependence on external resources weakens the stimulus for developing institutions to create government accountability. In contrast, the elites of communist China, cut off from outside sources of influence, derive status, position, and authority entirely from local sources.

13. This difference between the two leaders is not readily explained by two of the most popular incentive theories of political leadership, that of Bruce Bueno de Mesquita and of Daron Acemoğlu, which address why leaders increase the franchise or choose to create public goods. Bueno de Mesquita et al. emphasize coalition size, also known as the selectorate (Bueno de Mesquita and Root 2000; Bueno de Mesquita et al. 2003). This literature emphasizes that the relationship between the regime's budgetary resources and the size of the winning coalition determine the leader's strategy for allocating the budgetary surplus at his or her disposal. When the winning coalition is small, the ruler maintains support by integrating it into the patronage network, provisioning private goods to essential supporters. Should the expenditure on private goods provision needed to keep the winning coalition loyal exceed the revenue supply, the ruler must acquire the capacity to provide public goods to pay off a much larger winning coalition. But how does one identify the winning coalition in East Asian autocracies in which there is no selectorate and where the selection of the leadership is opaque? Deng had to establish power as the leader of an oligarchy, while Mao was a leader of the masses, and this makes it difficult to make a comparison about differences in the size of their winning coalitions. Moreover they faced similar constraints on financial resources. To identify the boundary of the winning coalition in China is far more difficult than in personalized autocracies that operate as neopatrimonial regimes.

14. Deng decentralized enterprise management by exposing private enterprise managers to decentralized market opportunities. To do this, market reforms were introduced piecemeal, and many were based on "particularistic contracting" with local officials in exchange for their loyalty (Shirk 1993). State-owned enterprises and small- and medium-size private enterprises obtained greater autonomy; however, a system of exemptions, special cases, and local experiments creates many channels for abuse.

15. A principal–agent problem is a conflict of interest that arises when a principal delegates to an agent a specific task that is either costly or not in the interests of the agent to perform.

16. China has been less successful than Europe in fostering independent business organizations that entail cooperation and management beyond kinship ties. As a result it remains out of alignment with the scale-free structures of a networked world economy because its legal system is not suited to activities of private firms that compete through access to third-party adjudication. Its centralized network system, the one-party system, impedes the development of strong private-sector firms in favor of state-managed and state-funded firms, which also tend to be China's largest. Private firms are mostly family-run, their growth limited to the extent of family networks. The weakness of private networks for trade and investment stems from the weakness of an independent rule of law framework in China.

17. This policy of strengthening less productive, state-owned enterprises represents the misallocation of capital by standards of optimal capital allocation efficiency (Song, Storesletten, and Zilibotti 2011).

18. China's experiments in providing greater voice and accountability have been the subject of an extensive literature (Florini, Lai, and Tan 2012). See Lowenthal (1970, 1976) on authoritarian mobilization under Mao.

Chapter 10

1. Mahinda Rajapaksa represents a Sri Lanka Freedom Party-led coalition called the People's Alliance.

2. *Japan Times* article from March 4, 2009.

3. In 2004 Angola abandoned its loan negotiations with the IMF and accepted China's offer of a loan of $2 billion without conditions, at a lower interest rate and longer repayment terms. China's support of Sudan and Zimbabwe similarly nullifies international efforts to stimulate domestic reforms. These interventions fall under the policy of helping countries develop toward independence and self-reliance while recognizing equality and mutual benefit. The benefits China receives in Sudan, Zimbabwe, Myanmar, and elsewhere include access to natural resources and support for Chinese initiatives in international organizations. With little fanfare, 750,000 Chinese have settled in Africa over the past decade, according to Xinhua News Agency, as cited by an August 8, 2007, story, "Entrepreneurs from China Flourish in Africa," in *New York Times*.

4. R. Premadasa (appointed in 1988) was the first president from a low-caste background, Rajapaksa, in contrast, belongs to the traditionally high caste—the Goyigama (farmer) caste—but hails from a rural background, unlike his predecessors, and is the first to marginalize the English-speaking elites, so his rise had far-reaching social implications.

5. "Report of the Secretary-General's Panel of Experts on Accountability in Sri Lanka," March 31, 2011 (UNSG 2011). The report alluded to a culture of im-

punity in which violations of human rights include the use of excessive force in densely populated areas.

6. Resolution A/HRC/S-11/L./Rev.2 passed on May 27, 2009. Twenty-nine countries were in favor (Angola, Azerbaijan, Bahrain, Bangladesh, Bolivia, Brazil, Burkina Faso, Cameroon, China, Cuba, Djibouti, Egypt, Ghana, India, Indonesia, Jordan, Madagascar, Malaysia, Nicaragua, Nigeria, Pakistan, Philippines, Qatar, Russian Federation, Saudi Arabia, Senegal, South Africa, Uruguay, and Zambia); twelve countries were against (Bosnia and Herzegovina, Canada, Chile, France, Germany, Italy, Mexico, Netherlands, Slovakia, Slovenia, Switzerland, and United Kingdom); and six abstained (Argentina, Gabon, Japan, Mauritius, Republic of Korea, and Ukraine).

7. Sri Lankan External Affairs Minister Gamini Lakshman Pieris reported that the UN panel will not be permitted to enter the country to investigate allegations of human rights abuses during the last months of the Sri Lankan civil war. The government rejected the appointment of the panel. Peiris indicated that the panel was unnecessary and noted that Sri Lanka would not issue visas to its members (DPA, IANS 2010).

8. US sources see the $1 billion investment as a potential refueling and docking station for the Chinese navy on patrol in the Indian Ocean. Sri Lankan sources see it as merely commercial opportunity for Chinese construction firms.

9. These would allow the population to migrate to the coastal regions and eventually relieve the congestion in the heart of the country around Colombo and Kandy, with dramatic ramifications for the traditional commercial elites in Colombo and the traditional elites that descend from Kandy, to dominate national politics. One of these roads in the south (the Galle-to-Hambantota segment) was considered by the Asian Development Bank, but the Chinese vice president of the bank, a former official of the Chinese Export-Import Bank, instructed ADB staff not to pursue an initiative to guarantee its underwriting. The Exim Bank then took up the project in collaboration with a Chinese contractor.

10. A senior member of the Sri Lankan government verbally confirmed this information, 2011.

11. Interview conducted in Sri Lanka, 2011.

12. Reported by a number of MPs in personal interviews with the author who agreed not to disclose their identity, 2011.

13. Wijedasa (2010) discloses that the terms and conditions under which Chinese ventures are secret: "China does not expect us to make sweeping macroeconomic changes. It expects nothing of us but the import of their material, technology, and labor and their repayment conditions. China gets a stronghold in this part of the world, and Sri Lanka gets her projects."

14. Fonseka has also been charged with treason for divulging state secrets in another case still in civilian court as of 2012.

15. Since Rajapaksa has come to power, both Polity and Freedom House have downgraded Sri Lanka's status as a democracy. Since 2006, Sri Lanka's scored on par with Burkina Faso, Georgia, Guatemala, Guinea-Bissau, Honduras, Kenya, Kuwait, Lebanon, Malaysia, Nepal, Nicaragua, and Tonga.

16. Although Sri Lanka has a long legacy of populist and intellectual resentment concerning the control and linkage of native industries to the industrial West, Rajapaksa must avoid trapping the educated middle class, for as they find less room to maneuver and their ideological leadership spurned, they may turn against the regime.

17. A reverse dynamic has been at play in North America, where pressures from the United States put Mexico on the road toward democratic stability long before its Latin American neighbors, who are pulled in other directions by local attractors, such as Brazil. As a democracy, Mexico still struggles with a weak environment for law enforcement and its politics are ridden by patronage and corruption. The expectation of the largest external player alters the options for domestic actors.

18. John Ikenberry believes "openness and rule-based relations enshrined in institutions such as the United Nations and norms such as multilateralism" will persist because rising powers will seek more authority within the system (2011b, 56).

Chapter 11

1. Walter Wriston's views in *The Twilight of Sovereignty* are replicated in a number of popular books written during the 1990s, such as Kevin Kelly's *New Rules for the New Economy* (1998), Frances Cairncross's *The Death of Distance: How the Communications Revolution Will Change Our Lives* (1997), Carl Shapiro and Hal Varian's *Information Rules: A Strategic Guide to the Network Economy* (1998), Manuel Castells's *The Rise of Network Society* (1996), and Jessica Lipnack and Jeffrey Stamps's *The Age of the Network: Organizing Principles for the 21st Century* (1994).

2. Among the many pessimistic scenarios is fear of the formation of mercantilist alliances and global fragmentation into parochial blocs and regional monopolies. In this scenario global trade may splinter the globe into a world of regional substructures, security complexes, and economic zones. Local hegemons, like Brazil, Iran, Turkey, Russia, Germany, and China, will come to dominate their smaller regional partners.

3. Huntington's civilizational cleavages are between Islam and the West, but he speculates that Islamic and Eastern societies might coalesce in their opposition to Western values.

4. Signatories of the accord on human rights in 1975 are Federal Republic of Germany, German Democratic Republic, United States of America, Austria, Belgium, Bulgaria, Canada, Cyprus, Denmark, Spain, Finland, France, United Kingdom, Greece, Hungary, Republic of Ireland, Iceland, Italy, Liechtenstein, Luxembourg, Malta, Monaco, Norway, Netherlands, Poland, Portugal, Romania, San Marino, Holy Sea, Sweden, Switzerland, Czechoslovakia, Turkey, Union of Soviet Socialist Republics, and Yugoslavia.

5. Turkey's globalized managerial class thrived because of its privileged ties to international economy and because of the regime's tight security alignment with the

antisocialist West. But the diminished threat of global communism has weakened the stature and influence of Western-looking elites.

6. According to the ECRF, in 2010 the list of the axis of sovereignty members, includes Algeria, Azerbaijan, Bangladesh, Belarus, Bolivia, China, Comoros, Cuba, Democratic Republic of Congo, Egypt, Equatorial Guinea, Guinea, India, Indonesia, Iran, Kyrgyzstan, Laos, Libya, Malaysia, Myanmar, Nicaragua, North Korea, Oman, Russia, Senegal, Sri Lanka, Sudan, Syria, Tajikistan, Tunisia, Venezuela, Vietnam, and Zimbabwe. But trending toward the axis of sovereignty (voting with the European Union less than 35 percent of the time) are Afghanistan, Angola, Bahamas, Bahrain, Barbados, Benin, Bhutan, Burkina Faso, Cambodia, Cameroon, CapeVerde, Central African Republic, Chad, Colombia, Congo, Côte d'Ivoire, Democratic Republic of Congo, Djibouti, Dominica, Dominican Republic, Ecuador, Eritrea, Ethiopia, Gabon, Grenada, Guinea-Bissau, Guyana, Iraq, Jordan, Kazakhstan, Kenya, Kuwait, Lesotho, Mali, Mauritania, Mozambique, Namibia, Nepal, Niger, Nigeria, Pakistan, Philippines, Qatar, Saint Kitts and Nevis, Saint Vincent and the Grenadines, Singapore, Somalia, South Africa, Suriname, Swaziland, Thailand, Trinidad and Tobago, Turkmenistan, Uganda, United Arab Emirates, Uzbekistan, Yemen, and Zambia (see http://ecfr.eu/page/-/the-eu-and-human-rights-at-the-UN-2010-review.pdf).

7. Brazil, China, Germany, India, and the Russian Federation abstained against adopting Resolution 1973 to protect civilians in Libya, and Russia and China vetoed the resolution to protect civilians in Syria.

8. These observations on network structure and global political economy are based on joint work with David Masad.

9. Early assessments of value-chain competencies was undertaken by Bill McKelvey (1999, 296).

References

Abers, Rebecca. 1998. From clientelism to cooperation: Participatory policy and civic organizing in Porto Alegre, Brazil. *Politics and Society* 26 (4): 511–37.

Acemoğlu, Daron, and James A. Robinson. 2000. Why did the West extend the franchise? Growth, inequality, and democracy in historical perspective. *Quarterly Journal of Economics* 115 (4): 1167–99.

Acemoğlu, Daron, and James A. Robinson. 2006. *Economic Origins of Dictatorship and Democracy.* Cambridge: Cambridge University Press.

Acemoğlu, Daron, and James A. Robinson. 2012. *Why Nations Fail: The Origins of Power, Prosperity, and Poverty.* New York: Crown.

Ader, Robert, and Nicholas Cohen. 1975. Behaviorally conditioned immunosuppression. *Psychosomatic Medicine* 37 (4): 333–40.

Alexandroff, Alan S., and Andrew F. Cooper, eds. 2010. *Rising States, Rising Institutions: Challenges for Global Governance.* Washington, DC: Brookings Institution Press.

Almond, Gabriel A., and G. Bingham Powell Jr. 1966. *Comparative Politics: A Developmental Approach.* Boston: Little, Brown.

Almond, Gabriel Abraham, and Sidney Verba. 1963. *The Civic Culture: Political Attitudes and Democracy in Five Nations.* Princeton: Princeton University Press.

Ames, Barry. 2000. *The Deadlock of Democracy in Brazil.* Ann Arbor: University of Michigan Press.

Amsden, Alice H. 1989. *Asia's Next Giant: South Korea and Late Industrialization.* Oxford: Oxford University Press.

Amsden, Alice H. 2001. *The Rise of "The Rest": Challenges to the West from Late-Industrializing Countries.* Oxford: Oxford University Press.

Amsden, Alice H. 2007. *Escape from Empire: The Developing World's Journey through Heaven and Hell.* Cambridge: MIT Press.

Amsden, Alice H. 2012. Elites and property rights. In Alice H. Amsden, Alice DiCaprio, and James A. Robinson, eds., *The Role of Elites in Economic Development.* New York: Oxford University Press, 19–28.

Amsden, Alice H., and Alisa DiCaprio. 2012. Understanding the dynamics of elite behaviour in a development context. In Alice H. Amsden, Alice DiCaprio, and

James A. Robinson, eds., *The Role of Elites in Economic Development*. New York City: Oxford University Press, 351–62.

Andersson, Krister P., and Elinor Ostrom. 2008. Analyzing decentralized resource regimes from a polycentric perspective. *Policy Sciences* 41 (1): 71–93.

Anonymous. 2011. When fundraising is a crime: A death sentence for a young businesswoman chills entrepreneurs. *The Economist* (April): 14.

Apter, David. 1959. *Ghana in Transition*, 2nd ed. New York: Antheneum.

Archer, Christon I., John R. Ferris, Holger H. Herwig, and Timothy H. E. Travers. 2002. *World History of Warfare*. Lincoln: University of Nebraska Press.

Arnoldy, Ben. 2010. Sri Lanka elections buoy ruling party: Tamils sidelined. *Christian Science Monitor*, April 19.

Arthur, Brian W. 1994. *Increasing Returns and Path Dependence in the Economy*. Ann Arbor: University of Michigan Press.

Arthur, Brian W. 2009. *The Nature of Technology: What It Is and How It Evolves*. New York: Free Press.

Arthur, Brian W., Steven Durlauf, and David Lane, eds. 1997. *The Economy as an Evolving Complex System II. Series in the Sciences of Complexity*. Reading, MA: Addison-Wesley.

Atkinson, Robert D., Luke A. Stewart, Scott M. Andes, and Stephen J. Ezell. 2012. *Worse Than the Great Depression: What Experts Are Missing about American Manufacturing Decline*. Washington, DC: Information Technology and Innovation Foundation (ITIF).

Auerswald, Philip. 2012. *The Coming Prosperity: How Entrepreneurs Are Transforming the Global Economy*. New York: Oxford University Press.

Auyero, Javier. 2000. The logic of clientelism in Argentina: An ethnographic account. *Latin American Research Review* 35 (3): 55–81.

Axelrod, Robert. 1984. *The Evolution of Cooperation*. New York: Basic Books.

Axelrod, Robert. 1997. *The Complexity of Cooperation: Agent-Based Models of Competition and Collaboration*. Princeton: Princeton University Press.

Axelrod, Robert, and Scott D. Bennett. 1993. Choosing sides: A landscape theory of aggregation. *British Journal of Political Science* 23 (April): 211–33.

Axelrod, Robert, and Michael D. Cohen. 2001. *Harnessing Complexity: Organizational Implications of a Scientific Frontier*. New York: Basic Books.

Axtell, Robert, and Joshua M. Epstein. 1996. *Growing Artificial Societies: Social Science from the Bottom Up*. Washington, DC: Brooking Institute Press.

Bak, Per, and Kim Sneppen. 1993. Punctuated equilibrium and criticality in a simple model of evolution. *Physical Review Letters* 71 (24): 4083–4086.

Bar-Yam, Yaneer. 1997. *Dynamics of Complex Systems: Studies in Nonlinearity*. Boston: Addison-Wesley.

Barabasi, Albert-Laszlo, and Eric Bonabeau. 2003. Scale-free networks. *Scientific American* (May): 50–59.

Barabasi, Albert-Laszlo. 2002. *Linked: The New Science of Networks, How Everything Is Connected to Everything Else and What It Means for Business, Science, and Everyday Life*. New York: Perseus.

Baran, Zeyno. 2008. Turkey divided. *Journal of Democracy* 19 (1): 55–69.

Barro, Robert. 1997. *Determinants of Economic Growth: A Cross-Country Empirical Study*. Cambridge: MIT Press.

Bates, Robert H. 2001. *Prosperity and Violence: The Political Economy of Development*. New York: Norton.

Becker, Marvin B. 1982. *Medieval Italy: Constraints and Creativity*. Bloomington: Indiana University Press.

Becker, Marvin B. 1988. *Civility and Society in Western Europe, 1300–1600*. Bloomington: Indiana University Press.

Becker, Marvin B. 1994. *The Emergence of Civil Society in the Eighteenth Century: A Privileged Moment in the History of England, Scotland, and France*. Bloomington: Indiana University Press.

Beinhocker, Eric D. 2006. *Origin of Wealth: Evolution, Complexity, and the Radical Remaking of Economics*. Boston: Harvard University Press.

Berkes, Fikret, Johan Colding, and Carl Folke. 2002. Synthesis: Building resilience for adaptive capacity in social-ecological systems. In Fikret Berkes, Johan Colding, and Carl Folke, eds., *Navigating Social-Ecological Systems: Building Resilience for Complexity and Change*. Cambridge: Cambridge University Press, 352–87.

Berman, Harold J. 1983. *Law and Revolution: The Formation of the Western Legal Tradition*. Cambridge: Harvard University Press.

Berry, Mary Elizabeth. 1997. Was early modern Japan culturally integrated? Special issue: *The Eurasian Context of the Early Modern History of Mainland South East Asia, 1400–1800*. *Modern Asian Studies* 31 (3): 547–81.

Berry, Mary Elizabeth. 1999. Was early modern Japan culturally integrated? In *Beyond Binary Histories: Re Imaging Eurasia to c. 1830*, ed. Victor Lieberman, 103–138. Ann Arbor: University of Michigan Press.

Besancon, Marie. 2003. *Good Governance Rankings: The Art of Measurement*. Cambridge: World Peace Foundation.

Black, Jeremy, ed. 1999. *War in the Early Modern World 1450–1815*. London: UCL Press.

Bobbitt, Philip. 2002. *The Shield of Achilles: War, Peace, and the Course of History*. New York: Knopf.

Bodin, Jean. 1606. *The Six Books of the Commonwealth*. Trans. from the Latin by Richard Knolles. London.

Bonner, John T. 1988. *The Evolution of Complexity by Means of Natural Selection*. Princeton: Princeton University Press.

Boserup, Ester. 1981. *Population and Technological Change: A Study of Long-term Trends*. Chicago: Chicago University Press.

Boserup, Ester. 1990. *Economic and Demographic Relationships in Development: Essays Selected and Introduced by T. Paul Schultz.* Baltimore: Johns Hopkins University Press.

Bowels, Samuel. 2004. *Microeconomics: Behavior, Institutions, and Evolution.* Princeton: Princeton University Press.

Bowels, Samuel. 2012. *The New Economics of Inequality and Redistribution.* Cambridge: Cambridge University Press.

Bowels, Samuel, and Herbert Gintis. 2011. *A Cooperative Species: Human Reciprocity and Its Evolution.* Princeton: Princeton University Press.

Bowen, J. Ray, and David C. Rose. 1998. On the absence of privately qwned, publicly trades corporations in China: The Kirby puzzle. *Journal of Asian Studies* 57 (2): 442–52.

Bremmer, Ian. 2010. *The End of the Free Market: Who Wins the War between States and Corporations?* London: Portfolio.

Brinkerhoff, Derick W., and Arthur A. Goldsmith. 2002. Clientelism, patrimonialism and democratic governance: An overview and framework for assessment and programming. Working paper. USAID, Washington, DC.

Bueno de Mesquita, Bruce, and George W. Downs. 2005. Development and Democracy. *Foreign Affairs* 84 (5): 77–86.

Bueno de Mesquita, Bruce, and Hilton L. Root, eds.. 2000. *Governing for Prosperity.* New Haven: Yale University Press.

Bueno de Mesquita, Alastair Smith Bruce, Randolph M. Siverson, and James D. Marrow. 2003. *The Logic of Political Survival.* Cambridge: MIT Press.

Burt, Ronald S. 1992. *Structural Holes: The Social Structure of Competition.* Cambridge: Harvard University Press.

Buzan, Barry, and Richard Little. 2000. *International Systems in World History: Remaking the Study of International Relations.* Oxford: Oxford University Press.

Campos, Jose Edgardo, and Hilton L. Root. 1996. *The Key to the Asian Miracle: Making Shared Growth Credible.* Washington, DC: Brookings University Press.

Capra, Fritjof. 1996. *The Web of Life: A New Scientific Understanding of Living Systems.* New York: Anchor Books.

Cairncross, Frances. 1997. *The Death of Distance: How Communications Revolution Will Change Our Lives.* Boston: Harvard Business Review Press.

Carothers, Thomas. 2002. The end of the transition paradigm. *Journal of Democracy* 13 (1): 5–21.

Casson, Mark, ed. 2011. *Markets and Market Institutions: Their Origin and Evolution.* Cheltenham, UK: Elgar.

Castells, Manuel. 1996. *The Rise of Network Society. The Information Age: Economy, Society and Culture.* London: Blackwell.

Cederman, Lars-Erik. 1997. *Emergent Actors in World Politics: How States and Nations Develop and Dissolve.* Princeton: Princeton University Press.

Cerny, Philip. 1995. Globalization and the changing logic of collective action. *International Organization* 49 (4): 595–625.

Cerny, Philip. 1999. Globalization and the erosion of democracy. *European Journal of Political Research* 36 (1): 1–26.

Cerny, Philip. 2007. Multi-nodal politics: Towards a political process theory of globalization. Http://www.mendeley.com/library/.

Chang, Ha-Joon. 2011. Institutions and economic development: Theory, policy and history. *Journal of Institutional Economics* 7 (4): 473–98.

Chaussinaud-Nogaret, Guy. 1970. *Les Financiers de Languedoc au XVIIIe siècle.* Paris: SEVPEN.

Coase, Ronald. 1937. The nature of the firm. *Economica* 4 (16): 386–405.

Coase, Ronald. 1960. The problem of social cost. *Journal of Law and Economics* 3 (October): 1–44.

Coase, Ronald. 1998. The new institutional economics. *American Economic Review* 88 (2): 72–74.

Cobban, Alfred. 1964. *The Social Interpretation of the French Revolution.* Cambridge: Cambridge University Press.

Cook, Karen S., and Margaret Levi, eds. 1990. *The Limits of Rationality.* Chicago: University of Chicago Press.

Coronel, Sheila S., ed. 1998. *Pork and Other Perks: Corruption and Governance in the Philippines.* Manila: Institute for Popular Democracy.

Coronel, Sheila S., and Howie G. Severino, eds. 1996. *Patrimony: 6 Case Studies on Local Politics and the Environment in the Philippines.* Quezon City: Philippine Center for Investigative Journalism.

Croce, Benedetto. 1941. *History as the Story of Liberty.* Edward Kiev Judaica Collection. London: Allen and Unwin.

Dadush, Uri, and William Shaw. 2011. *Juggernaut: How Emerging Markets Are Reshaping Globalization.* Washington, DC: Carnegie Endowment for International Peace.

Darley, Vincent, and Alexander V. Outkin. 2007. *Nasdaq Market Simulation: Insights on a Major Market from the Science of Complex Adaptive Systems.* Singapore: World Scientific.

Darwin, Charles. 1876. *On the Origin of Species by Means of Natural Selection.* New York: Appleton.

David, Paul. 1985. Clio and the economics of Qwerty. *American Economic Review* 75 (2): 332–37.

Dawkins, Richard. 1997. Review: Human chauvinism. *Evolution; International Journal of Organic Evolution* 51 (3): 1015–20.

Dawkins, Richard. 2006. *The God Delusion.* Boston: Houghton Mifflin Harcourt.

Diamond, Jared. 1997. *Guns, Germs, and Steel: The Fates of Human Societies.* New York: Norton.

Diamond, Larry J. 2002. Thinking about hybrid regimes. *Journal of Democracy* 13 (2): 21–35.

Diaz-Cayeros, Alberto, Federico Estevez, and Beatriz Magaloni. 2004. The erosion of party hegemony, clientelism and portfolio diversification. The Programa Nacional De Solidaridad (PRONASOL) in Mexico, Working paper. Department of Political Science, Stanford University.

Dickson, Bruce J. 2010. China's cooperative capitalist: The business end of the middle class. In Li Cheng, ed., *China's Emerging Middle Class: Beyond Economic Transformation*. Washington, DC: Brookings Institution Press, 291–309.

Dixit, Avinash, and John Londregan. 1996. The determinants of success of special interests in redistributive politics. *Journal of Politics* 58 (4): 1132–55.

Doner, Richard, and Ansil Ramsey. 1997. Competitive clientelism and economic governance: The case of Thailand. In Sylvia Maxfield and Ben Ross Schneider, eds., *Business and the State in Developing Countries*. Cornell: Cornell University Press, 237–76.

Dorogovtsev, Sergey N., and José F. F. Mendes. 2003. *Evolution of Networks: From Biological Networks to the Internet and WWW*. Oxford: Oxford University Press.

Doyle, Michael. 1986. Liberalism and world politics. *American Political Science Review* 80 (4): 1151–69.

DPA, IANS. 2010. Sri Lanka to refuse entry to UN human rights panel. *The Gaea Times*, June 24, 1.

Dunning, Thad. 2008. *Crude Democracy: Natural Resource Wealth and Political Regimes*. Cambridge: Cambridge University Press.

Easley, David, and John Kleinberg. 2010. *Networks, Crowds, and Markets: Reasoning about a Highly Connected World*. Cambridge: Cambridge University Press.

Easterly, William R. 2002. *The Elusive Quest for Growth: Economists' Adventures and Misadventures in the Tropics*. Cambridge: MIT Press.

Eggertsson, Thrainn. 1990. *Economic Behavior and Institutions: Principles of Neoinstitutional Economics*. Cambridge: Cambridge University Press.

Eldredge, Niles, and Stephen J. Gould. 1972. Punctuated equilibria: An alternative to phyletic gradualism. In Thomas J. M. Schopf, ed., *Models in Paleobiology*. San Francisco: Freeman, Cooper, 82–115.

Eldredge, Niles, and Samuel J. Gould. 1993. Punctuated equilibrium comes of age. *Nature* 366 (November): 223–37.

Eldredge, Niles. 1985. *Time Frames: The Re-Thinking of Darwinian Evolution and the Theory of Punctuated Equilibria*. New York: Simon, Shuster.

Eldredge, Niles. 1989. *Macroevolutionary Dynamics: Species, Niches and Adaptive Peaks*. New York: McGraw Hill.

Elias, Norbert. 1983. *The Court Society (Die höfische Gesellschaft. Untersuchungen zur Soziologie des Königtums und der höfischen Aristokratie)*, Edmund Jephcott, trans. Oxford: Oxford University Press.

Eltis, David. 1998. *The Military Revolution in Sixteenth-Century Europe*. New York: Tauris.

Elton, Geoffery R. 1953. *The Tudor Revolution in Government: Administrative Changes in the Reign of Henry VIII*. Cambridge: Cambridge University Press.

England, Robert Stow. 2005. *Aging China: The Demographic Challenge to China's Economic Prospects*. Westport, CT: Greenwood.

Epstein, David L., Robert Bates, Jack Goldstone, Ida Kristensen, and Sharyn O' Halloran. 2006. Democratic transitions. *American Journal of Political Science* 50 (3):551–569.

Erman, Tahire. 2001. The politics of squatter (*Gecekondu*) studies in Turkey: The changing representations of rural migrants in the academic discourse. *Urban Studies (Edinburgh, Scotland)* 38 (7): 983–1002.

EuropeAid. 2008. *Addressing and Analyzing Governance in Sector Operations*. Brussels: European Commission InfoPoint–External Cooperation.

Evans, Peter. 1997. State structures, government–business relations and economic transformation. In Ben Ross Schneider and Sylvia Maxfield, eds., *Business and the State in Developing Countries*. Ithaca: Cornell University Press, 63–87.

Fairbank, John King. 1986. *The Great Chinese Revolution: 1800–1985*. New York: Harper, Row.

Fatton, Robert Jr. 1986. Clientelism and patronage in Senegal. *African Studies Review* 29 (4): 61–78.

Feng, Yi. 2003. *Democracy, Governance, Economic Performance: Theory and Evidence*. Cambridge: MIT Press.

Ferguson, William. 2013. *Collective-Action and Exchange: A Game Theoretic Approach to Contemporary Political Economy*. Palo Alto: Stanford University Press.

Finer, Samuel E. 1997. *The History of Government from the Earliest Times*. Vol. 2: *The Intermediate Ages*. New York: Oxford University Press.

Fingleton, Eamonn. 2008. *In the Jaws of the Dragon: America's Fate in the Coming Era of Chinese Hegemony*. New York: Dunne/St. Martin's Press.

Fisman, Raymond. 2001. Estimating the value of political connections. *American Economic Review* 91 (4): 1095–1102.

Flannery, Kent V. 1972. The culture evolution of civilizations. *Annual Review of Ecology and Systematics* 3 (November): 399–426.

Florini, Ann, Hairong Lai, and Yeling Tan. 2012. *China Experiments: From Local Innovations to National Reform*. Washington, DC: Brookings Institution Press.

Frank, Andre Gunder. 1998. *ReORIENT: Global Economy in the Asian Age*. Berkeley: University of California Press.

French, Patrick. 2011. *India: A Portrait*. New York: Knopf.

Frenken, Koen. 2006. *Innovation, Evolution and Complexity Theory*. Cheltenham, UK: Elgar.

Friedman, Thomas. 2005. *The World Is Flat: A Brief History of the Twenty-First Century*, 1st ed. New York: Farrar, Straus, Giroux.

Fukuyama, Francis. 1989. The end of history? *National Interest* 16 (Summer): 3–18.

Fukuyama, Francis. 1992. *The End of History and the Last Man*. Westminster: Penguin.

Fukuyama, Francis. 2011. *The Origins of Political Order: From Prehuman Times to the French Revolution*. New York: Farrar, Straus, Giroux.

Furet, François. 1981. *Interpreting the French Revolution*. Elborg Forester, trans. Cambridge: Cambridge University Press.

Gehlbach, Scott, and Philip Keefer. 2011. Private investment and the institutionalization of collective action in autocracies: Ruling parties and legislatures. Working paper. World Bank, Washington, DC.

Gellner, Earnst. 1983. *Nations and Nationalism*. Oxford: Blackwell.

Gellner, Ernst, and John Waterbury, eds. 1977. *Patrons and Clients in Mediterranean Societies*. London: Duckworth Center for Mediterranean Studies.

Gerschenkron, Alexander. 1962. *Economic Backwardness in Historical Perspective: A Book of Essays*. Cambridge, MA: Belknap/Harvard University Press.

Gibbons, Robert. 2005. Four formal(izable) theories of the firm? *Journal of Economic Behavior and Organization* 58 (2): 200–45.

Gilman, Nils. 2007. *Mandarines of the Future: Modernization Theory in Cold War America*. Baltimore: John Hopkins University Press.

Ginsburg, Tom, and Tamir Moustafa, eds. 2008. *By Law: The Politics of Courts in Authoritarian Regimes*. New York: Cambridge University Press.

Gintis, Herbert. 2000a. *Game Theory Evolving: A Problem-Centered Introduction to Modeling Strategic Interaction*. Princeton: Princeton University Press.

Gintis, Herbert. 2000b. Beyond *Homo Economicus. Ecological Economics* 35 (3): 311–22.

Glaeser, Edward, and Andrei Shleifer. 2005. The Curley effect: The economics of shaping the electorate. *Journal of Law Economics and Organization* 21 (April): 1–19.

Godement, Francois. 2010. A global China policy. Policy brief. European Council on Foreign Relations, Berlin.

Goldman, Emily O., and Leslie C. Eliason. 2003. *The Diffusion of Military Technology and Ideas*. Palo Alto: Stanford University Press.

Goldstone, Jack. 1991. *Revolution and Rebellion in the Early Modern World*. Berkeley: University of California Press.

Goldstone, Jack. 2010. The new population bomb: The four population megatrends that will change the world. *Foreign Affairs* 89 (1): 31–43.

Gould, Samuel J. 1982. The meaning of punctuated equilibrium and its role in validating a hierarchical approach to macroevolution. In Roger Milkman, ed., *Perspectives on Evolution*. Sunderland: Sinauer Associates, 83–104.

Gould, Stephen J. 1989. *Wonderful Life: The Burgess Shale and the Nature of History*. New York: Norton.

Gould, Samuel J. 2002. *The Structure of Evolutionary Theory*. Cambridge: Belknap Press/Harvard University Press.

Gould, Samuel J. 2007. *Punctuated Equilibrium*. Cambridge: Harvard University Press.

Gowan, Richard, and Franziska Branter. 2009. The EU and human rights at the UN: 2009 review. Policy brief. European Council on Foreign Relations, Berlin.

Granovetter, Mark. 1973. The strength of weak ties. *American Journal of Sociology* 78 (6): 1360–80.

Granovetter, Mark. 1978. Threshold models of collective behavior. *American Journal of Sociology* 83 (6): 1420–43.

Greif, Avner. 1993. Contract enforceability and economic institutions in early trade: The Maghribi traders' collection. *American Economic Review* 83 (3): 525–48.

Grossman, Sanford J. 1976. On the efficiency of competitive stock markets where trades have diverse information. *Journal of Finance* 31 (2): 573–85.

Grossman, Sanford J. 1981. An introduction to the theory of rational expectations under asymmetric information. *Review of Economic Studies* 48 (4): 541–59.

Grossman, Sanford J., and Joseph E. Stiglitz. 1980. On the impossibility of informationally efficient markets. *American Economic Review* 70 (3): 393–408.

Guillermo, O'Donnell, Philippe C. Schmitter, and Laurence Whitehead, eds. 1986. *Transitions from Authoritarian Rule*. Vol. 4: *Tentative Conclusions about Uncertain Democracies*. Baltimore: John Hopkins University Press.

Hage, Jerald, and Marius Meeus, eds. 2006. *Innovation, Science, and Institutional Change: A Research Handbook*. Oxford: Oxford University Press.

Hall, Peter A., and Rosemary C.R. Taylor. 1996. Political science and the three new institutionalisms. *Political Studies* 44: 936–57.

Harrington, James C. 2011. *Wrestling with Free Speech, Religious Freedom, and Democracy in Turkey: The Political Trials and Times of Fethullah Gulen*. Lanham: University Press of America.

Hart, Oliver, and John Moore. 1990. Property rights and the nature of the firm. *Journal of Political Economy* 98 (6): 1119–58.

Hartwell, Robert M. 1966. Markets, technology and the structure of enterprise in the development of the eleventh-century Chinese iron and steel industry. *Journal of Economic History* 26 (1): 29–58.

Hartwell, Robert M. 1967. A cycle of economic change in imperial China: Coal and iron in northeast China, 750–1350. *Journal of Economic and Social History of the Orient* 10: 102–59.

Hartwell, Robert M. 1971. Financial expertise, examinations and the formulation of economic policy in northern Sung China. *Journal of Asian Studies* 30 (2): 281–314.

Hausmann, Ricardo, César A. Hidalgo, Sebastián Bustos, Michele Coscia, Sarah Chung, Juan Jimenez, Alexander Simoes, and Muhammed A. Yıldırım. 2011. *The Atlas of Economic Complexity: Mapping Paths to Prosperity*. Harvard, Kennedy

School of Government. Cambridge: HKS Center for International Development/ MIT Media Lab.

Hayek, Friedrich A. 1973. *Law, Legislation and Liberty.* Vol. 1: *Rules and Order.* Chicago: University of Chicago Press.

Hayek, Friedrich A. 1988. The Fatal Conceit: The Errors of Socialism. In William Warren Bartley, ed., *The Collected Works of F. A. Hayek.* Chicago: University of Chicago Press, 66–88.

Hecht, Gabrielle, ed. 2011. *Entangled Geographies: Empire and Technopolitics in the Global Cold War.* Cambridge: MIT Press.

Heper, Metin. 1992. The strong state as a problem for the consolidation of democracy: Turkey and Germany compared. *Comparative Political Studies* 25 (2): 169–94.

Herbst, Jeffrey I. 2000. *States and Power in Africa: Comparative Lessons in Authority and Control.* Princeton: Princeton University Press.

Hexter, Jack H. 1961. *Reappraisals in History: New Views on History and Society in Early Modern Europe.* New York: Harper Torchbooks.

Hintz, Otto. 1906. *State Constitution and Military Organization. Proceedings from the Go Foundation in Dresden.* Dresden: Germany.

Hintz, Otto. 1975. *The Historical Essays of Otto Hintze.* Translation of *Staatsverfassung und Heeresverfassung,* Felix Gilbert and Robert M. Berdahl, trans. Oxford: Oxford University Press.

Hirschman, Albert O. 1970. *Exit, Voice, and Loyalty: Responses to Decline in Firms, Organizations, and States.* Cambridge: Harvard University Press.

Hirschman, Albert. 1997. *The Passions and the Interests: Political Arguments for Capitalism Before Its Triumph.* Princeton: Princeton University Press.

Hobbes, Thomas. 1651. *Leviathan Or The Matter, Form, and Power of a Common-wealth, Ecclesiastical and Civil.* London: Printed for Andrew Crooke at the Green Dragon in St. Paul's Churchyard.

Hodgson, Geoffrey M. 1988. *Economics and Institutions: A Manifesto for a Modern Institutional Economics.* Cambridge, Philadelphia: Polity Press/University of Pennsylvania Press.

Hodgson, Geoffrey M. 1993. *Economics and Evolution: Bringing Life Back into Economics.* Cambridge, Ann Arbor: Polity Press/University of Michigan Press.

Hodgson, Geoffrey M. 1996. An evolutionary theory of long-term economic growth. *International Studies Quarterly* 40 (3): 391–410.

Hodgson, Geoffrey M. 2006. *Economics in the Shadows of Darwin and Marx: Essays on Institutional and Evolutionary Themes.* Cheltenham, UK: Elgar.

Holland, John H. 1975. *Adaptation in Natural and Artificial Systems.* Ann Arbor: University of Michigan.

Holland, John H. 1992. *Adaptation in Natural and Artificial Systems: An Introductory Analysis with Applications to Biology, Control, and Artificial Intelligence.* Cambridge: MIT Press.

Holland, John H. 1995. *Hidden Order: How Adaptation Builds Complexity*. New York: Basic Books.

Holland, John H. 1998. *Emergence: From Chaos to Order*. Reading, MA: Addison-Wesley.

Howard, Michael. 1976. *War in European History: Reflections on War and International Order*. New York: Oxford University Press.

Howard, Michael. 2000. *The Invention of Peace*. New Haven: Yale University Press.

Huizinga, Johan. 1924. *The Waning of the Middle Ages: A Study of the Forms of Life, Thought and Art in France and the Netherlands in the Dawn of the Renaissance*, Fritz Hopman, trans. New York: Doubleday/Anchor Books.

Huntington, Samuel. 1993. The clash of civilizations? *Foreign Affairs* 72 (3): 22–49.

Huntington, Samuel. 1996. *The Clash of Civilizations and the Remaking of World Order*. New York: Simon, Schuster.

Ikenberry, John G. 1988. *Reasons of State: Oil Politics and the Capacities of American Government*. Ithaca: Cornell University Press.

Ikenberry, John G. 2009. Liberal Internationalism 3.0: America and the dilemmas of liberal world order. *Perspectives on Politics* 7 (1): 71–87.

Ikenberry, John G. 2011a. *Liberal Leviathan: The Origins, Crisis, and Transformations of the American World Order*. Princeton: Princeton University Press.

Ikenberry, John G. 2011b. The future of the liberal world order: Internationalism after America. *Foreign Affairs* 90 (3): 56–68.

Ikenberry, John G., and Daniel Duedney. 2009. The myth of autocratic revival: Why liberal democracy will prevail. *Foreign Affairs* 88 (1): 77–93.

Inglehart, Ronald, and Christian Welzel. 2005. *Modernization, Cultural Change, and Democracy: The Human Development Sequence*. New York: Cambridge University Press.

Jackson, Matthew O. 2008. *Social and Economic Networks*. Princeton: Princeton University Press.

Jervis, Robert. 1998. *System Effects: Complexity in Political and Social Life*. Princeton: Princeton University Press.

Johnson, Simon, and James Kwak. 2010. 13 *Bankers: The Wall Street Takeover and the Next Financial Meltdown*. New York: Pantheon.

Kagan, Robert. 2009. *The Return of History and the End of Dreams*. New York: Vintage.

Kalaycıoğlu, Ersin Mahmut. 2007. Religiosity and protest behaviour: The case of Turkey in comparative perspective. *Journal of Southern Europe and the Balkans* 9 (3): 275–91.

Kapur, Devesh, and Richard Webb. 2000. Governance-related conditionalities of the international financial institutions. *Proceedings of the United Nations Confer-*

ence on Trade and Development. Cambridge: Center for International Development Harvard University, 1–28.

Karpat, Kemal H. 2001. *The Politicization of Islam: Reconstructing Identity, State, Faith, and Community in the Late Ottoman State*. New York: Oxford University Press.

Katzenstein, Peter J., ed. 1978. *Between Power and Plenty: Foreign Economic Policies of Advanced Industrial States*. Madison: University of Wisconsin Press.

Kauffman, Stuart A., and Steven J. Johnson. 1991. Coevolution to the edge of chaos: Coupled fitness landscapes, poised states, and coevolutionary avalanches. *Journal of Theoretical Biology* 149 (4): 467–505.

Kauffman, Stuart A. 1993. *The Origins of Order: Self-Organization and Selection Evolution*. New York: Oxford University Press.

Kauffman, Stuart A. 1995. *At Home in the Universe: The Search for Laws of Self-Organization and Complexity*. Oxford: Oxford University Press.

Kaufmann, Robert R. 1974. The patron–client concept and macro-politics: Prospects and problems. *Comparative Studies in Society and History* 16 (3): 284–308.

Keefer, Philip, and Razvan Vlaicu. 2008. Democracy, credibility, and clientelism. *Journal of Law Economics and Organization* 24 (2): 371–406.

Kelly, Kevin. 1998. *New Rules for the New Economy: 10 Radical Strategies for a Connected World*. New York: Viking.

Keohane, Robert O., and Joseph S. Nye. 1977. *Power and Interdependence: World Politics in Transition*. Boston: Little, Brown.

Keohane, Robert O. 1984. *After Hegemony: Cooperation and Discord in the World Political Economy*. Princeton: Princeton University Press.

Keyman, Fuat E., and Berrin Koyuncu. 2005. Globalization, alternative modernities and the political economy of Turkey. *Review of International Political Economy* 12 (1): 105–28.

Kirişci, Kemal. 2009. The transformation of Turkish foreign policy: The rise of the trading state. *New Perspectives on Turkey* 40 (1): 29–57.

Kitschelt, Herbert. 2000. Linkages between citizens and politicians in democratic polities. *Comparative Political Studies* 33 (6–7): 849–79.

Kitschelt, Herbert, and Steven Wilkinson. 2007. Citizen–politician linkages: An introduction. In Herbert Kitschelt and Steven Wilkinson, eds., *Patrons, Clients, and Policies: Patterns of Democratic Accountability and Political Competition*. Cambridge: Cambridge University Press, 1–49.

Klein, Benjamin, Robert G. Crawford, and Armen A. Alchian. 1978. Vertical integration, appropriable rents, and the competitive contracting process. *Journal of Law and Economics* 21 (2): 297–326.

Knack, Stephen, and Philip Keefer. 1997. Does social capital have an economic payoff? A cross-country investigation. *Quarterly Journal of Economics* 112 (4): 1251–88.

Knox, Macgregor. 2000. October 1942: Adolf Hitler, Wehrmacht officer policy, and social revolution. *Historical Journal (Cambridge, England)* 43 (3): 801–25.

Knox, Macgregor, and Williamson Murray. 2001. *The Dynamics of Military Revolution, 1300–2050*. Cambridge: Cambridge University Press.

Köchler, Hans. 1995. *Democracy and the International Rule of Law: Propositions for an Alternative World Order*. New York: Springer.

Kohli, Atul. 2007. State and redistributive development in India. Working paper. United Nations Research Institute for Social Development (UNRISD), Geneva.

Kothari, Rajni. 1970. *Caste in Indian Politics*. London: Routledge.

Krasner, Stephen D. 1984. Approaches to the state: Alternative conceptions and historical dynamics. *Comparative Politics* 16 (2): 223–46.

Kugler, Jacek, and Ronald L. Tammen, eds. 2012. *The Performance of Nations*. Lanham: Rowman and Littlefield.

Kupchan, Charles A. 2012. *No One's World: The West, the Rising Rest, and the Coming Global Turn*. New York: Oxford University Press.

Kuran, Timur. 2010. *The Long Divergence: How Islamic Law Held Back the Middle East*. Princeton: Princeton University Press.

Kydland, F., and E. C. Prescott. 1977. Rules Rather Than Discretion: The Inconsistency of Optimal Plans. *Journal of Political Economy* 85 (3): 473–92.

Lampton, David. M. 2001. *Same Bed, Different Dreams: Managing U.S.–China Relations, 1989–2000*. Berkeley: University of California Press.

Landes, David S. 1998. *The Wealth and Poverty of Nations: Why Some Are So Rich and Some So Poor*. New York: Norton.

Lau, Lawrence J., Yingyi Qian, and Gérard Roland. 2001. Reform without Losers: An Interpretation of China's Dual-Track Approach to Transition. *Journal of Political Economy* 108 (1): 120–43.

Lee, J. S. 1931. The periodic recurrence of internecine wars in China. *China Journal* (March–April):111–163.

Lehne, Richard. 2001. *Government and Business: American Political Economy in Comparative Perspective*. New York: Chatham House.

Lemke, Douglas, and Suzanne Werner. 1996. Power parity, commitment to change, and war. *International Studies Quarterly* 40 (2): 235–60.

Levi, Margaret. 1997. *Consent, Dissent, and Patriotism*. New York: Cambridge University Press.

Levin, Simon A. 1992. The problem of pattern and scale. *Ecology* 73 (6): 1943–67.

Levin, Simon A. 2002. Complex and adaptive system: Exploring the known, the unknown and the unknowable. *Bulletin of the Mathematical Society* 40 (1): 3–19.

Levin, Simon A., Stephen Carpenter, Charles Godfray, Anne Kinzig, Michel Loreau, Jonathan B. Losos, Brian Walker, and David S. Wilcove, eds. 2009. *The Princeton Guide to Ecology*. Princeton: Princeton University Press.

Levinthal, Daniel A. 1997. Adaptation on rugged landscapes. *Management Science* 43 (7): 934–50.

Lewin, Roger. 1992. *Complexity: Life at the Edge of Chaos*. New York: Macmillan.

Li, David D. 1998. Changing incentives of the Chinese bureaucracy. Papers and Proceedings from the Hundred and Tenth Annual Meeting of the American Economic Association. *American Economic Review* 88 (2): 393–97.

Lieberman. Victor, B. ed. 1999. *Beyond Binary Histories: Re-Imagining Eurasia to C. 1830*. Ann Arbor: University of Michigan Press.

Lin, Justin Yifu. 1995. The Needham puzzle: Why the Industrial Revolution did not originate in China. *Economic Development and Cultural Change* 43 (2): 269–92.

Linz, Juan J., and Alfred C. Stepan. 1996. *Problems of Democratic Transition and Consolidation: Southern Europe, South America, and Post-Communist Europe*. Baltimore: John Hopkins University Press.

Lipnack, Jessica, and Jeffrey Stamps. 1994. *The Age of the Network: Organizing Principles for the 21st Century*. London: Wight.

Lipset, Seymour Martin. 1960. *Political Man: Where, How and Why Democracy Works in the Modern World*. New York: Doubleday.

Liu, Wanshun. 2012. Political institutions and riot management. Working paper. Peking University, Beijing.

Lohmann, Susanne. 1993. A signaling model of informative and manipulative political action. *American Political Science Review* 87 (2): 319–33.

Lohmann, Susanne. 1994. The dynamics of informational cascades: The Monday demonstrations in Leipzig, East Germany, 1989–91. *World Politics* 47 (1): 42–101.

Lowenthal, Richard. 1970. Development vs. utopia in Communist policy. In Chalmers Johnson, ed., *Change in Communist Systems*. Stanford: Stanford University Press, 33–117, 135–53.

Lowenthal, Richard. 1976. The ruling party in a mature society. In Mark G. Field, ed., *The Social Consequences of Modernization in Communist Societies*. Baltimore: Johns Hopkins Press, 81–118.

Lowi, Theodore. 1969. *The End of Liberalism: Ideology, Policy, and the Crisis of Public Authority*. New York: Norton.

Lustick, Ian. 2011. Secession of the center: A virtual probe of the prospects for Punjabi secessionism in Pakistan and the secession of Punjabistan. *Journal of Artificial Societies and Social Simulation* 14 (1): 7.

Lynn, John. 1993. How war fed war: The tax of violence and contributions during the grand siècle. *Journal of Modern History* 65 (2): 286–310.

Lynn, John. 1997. *Giant of the Grand Siècle: The French Army, 1610–1715*. Cambridge: Cambridge University Press.

Lynn, John. 1999. *Wars of Louis XIV: 1667–1714*. London: Longman.

Lynn, John. 2001. Reflections on the history and theory of military innovation and diffusion. In Colin Elman and Miriam Fendius Elman, eds., *Bridges and Boundaries: Historians, Political Scientists, and the Study of International Relations*. Cambridge: MIT Press, 359–82.

Lynn, John. 2002. *The French Wars 1667–1714: The Sun King at War*. Oxford: Osprey.

Macfarlane, Alan. 1978. *The Origins of English Individualism: The Family, Property and Social Transition*. Oxford: Blackwell.

Mahbubani, Kishore. 2011. The calls for global leadership will be unanswered. *Financial Times*, December 22.

Mahbubani, Kishore. 2013. *The Great Convergence: Asia, the West, and the Logic of One World*. New York: PublicAffairs.

Mandelbaum, Michael. 2007a. *Democracy's Good Name: The Rise and Risks of the World's Most Popular Form of Government*. New York: Public Affairs.

Mandelbaum, Michael. 2007b. Democracy without America: The spontaneous spread of freedom. *Foreign Affairs* 86 (5): 119–30.

Maoz, Zeev, and Bruce Russet. 1993. Normative and structural causes of democratic peace, 1946–1986. *American Political Science Review* 87 (3): 624–38.

March, James G., and Johan P. Olsen. 1984. The new institutionalism: Organizational factors in political life. *American Political Science Review* 78 (3): 734–49.

Marshall, Alfred. 1890. *Principles of Economics*. London: Macmillan.

Marshall, Alfred. 1923. *Money, Credit, and Commerce*. London: Macmillan.

Maturana, Humberto R., and Francisco J. Varela. 1980. *Autopoiesis and Cognition: The Realization of the Living*. Boston: Reidel/Springer.

Maxfield, Sylvia, and Ben Ross Schneider, eds. 1997. *Business and the State in Developing Countries. Cornell Studies in Political Economy*. Ithaca: Cornell University Press.

Mayer, Arno J. 1981. *The Persistence of the Old Regime*. New York: Pantheon.

Mayr, Ernst. 1992. The idea of teleology. *Journal of the History of Ideas* 53 (1): 117–35.

Mayr, Ernst. 2001. *What Evolution Is*. New York: Basic Books.

McKelvey, Bill. 1999. Avoiding complexity catastrophe in coevolutionary pockets: Strategies for rugged landscapes. *Organization Science* 10 (3): 294–321.

McNeill, William H. 1963. *The Rise of the West: A History of the Human Community*. Chicago: University of Chicago Press.

McNeill, William H. 1982. *The Pursuit of Power: Technology, Armed Force, and Society since A.D. 1000*. Chicago: University of Chicago Press.

McNeill, William H. 1992. *The Global Condition: Conquerors, Catastrophes, and Community*. Princeton: Princeton University Press.

Medina, Luis F., and Susan Stokes. 2007. Monopoly and monitoring: An approach to political clientelism. In Herbert Kitschelt and Steven Wilkinson, eds., *Patrons, Clients, and Policies*. Cambridge: Cambridge University Press, 68–83.

Menard, Claude, and Mary M. Shirley, eds. 2008. *Handbook of New Institutional Economics*. New York: Springer.

Metcalfe, Stan. 1995. The economic foundations of technology policy: Equilibrium and evolutionary perspectives. In Paul Stoneman, ed., *Handbook of the Eco-*

nomics of Innovation and Technological Change. New Jersey: Wiley-Blackwell, 409–512.

Migdal, Joel S. 1988. *Strong Societies and Weak States: State-Society Relations and State Capabilities in the Third World.* Princeton: Princeton University Press.

Milanovic, Branko. 2005. *World's Apart: Measuring International and Global Inequality.* Princeton: Princeton University Press.

Miller, James G. 1965. Living systems: Basic concepts. *Behavioral Science* 10 (3): 193–237.

Miller, John, and Scott Page. 2007. *Complex Adaptive Systems: An Introduction to Computational Models of Social Life.* Princeton: Princeton University Press.

Mishra, Ramesh. 1999. *Globalization and the Welfare State.* Cheltenham, UK: Elgar.

Mokyr, Joel. 1990a. Punctuated equilibria and technological progress. *American Economic Review* 80 (2): 350–54.

Mokyr, Joel. 1990b. *The Lever of Riches: Technological Creativity and Economic Progress.* Oxford: Oxford University Press.

Mokyr, Joel. 1991. Evolutionary biology, technical change and economic history. *Bulletin of Economic Research* 43 (2): 127–49.

Moore, Barrington Jr. 1966. *Social Origins of Dictatorship and Democracy: Lord and Peasant in the Making of the Modern World.* Boston: Beacon Press.

Mousnier, Roland. 1974. *Les Institutions de la France sous la monarchie absolute: 1598–1789.* Paris: Presses Universitaires de France.

Mousnier, Roland. 1980. *Les Institutions de la France sous la monarchie absolute.*Vol. 2: *Les Organes de l'etat et la société.* Paris: Presses Universitaires de France.

Nathan, Christopher. 1997. *China's Transition.* New York: Columbia University Press.

Needham, Joseph. 1954. *Science and Civilization in China.* Vol. 1: *Introductory Orientations.* Cambridge: Cambridge University Press.

Needham, Joseph. 1969. *The Grand Titration: Science and Society in East and West.* London: Allen, Unwin.

Nelson, Richard R., and Sidney G. Winter. 1982. *An Evolutionary Theory of Economic Change.* Cambridge: Harvard University Press.

Nettle, Daniel. 1999. *Linguistic Diversity.* Oxford: Oxford University Press.

Newman, Mark. Albert -Laszol Barabasi, and Duncan Watts. 2006. *The Structure and Dynamics of Networks.* Princeton: Princeton University Press.

Newman, Mark E. J. 2010. *Networks: An Introduction.* Oxford: Oxford University Press.

Nicolis, Gregoire, and Ilya Prigogine. 1989. *Exploring Complexity: An Introduction.* New York: Freeman.

North, Douglass C. 1981. *Structure and Change in Economic History.* New York: Norton.

North, Douglass C. 1990. *Institutions, Institutional Change and Economic Performance: Political Economy of Institutions and Decisions.* Cambridge: Cambridge University Press.

North, Douglass C. 1991. Institutions. *Journal of Economic Perspectives* 5 (1): 97–112.

North, Douglass C. 1992. Institutions and economic theory. *American Economist* 36 (1): 3–6.

North, Douglass C. 2005. *Understanding the Process of Economic Change.* Princeton: Princeton University Press.

North, Douglass C., John Joseph Wallis, Steven B. Webb, and Barry R. Weingast. 2007. Limited access orders and the developing world: A new approach to the problems of development. Policy research working paper 4359. World Bank, Washington, DC.

North, Douglass C., John Joseph Wallis, and Barry R. Weingast. 2009. *Violence and Social Order: A Conceptual Framework for Interpreting Recorded Human History.* Cambridge: Cambridge University Press.

Oatley, Thomas, W. Kindred Winecoff, Andrew Pennock, and Sarah Bauerle Danzman. 2013. The political economy of global finance: A network Model. *Perspectives on Politics* 11 (1):133–153.

O'Brien, Robert, and Marc Williams. 2004. *Global Political Economy: Evolution and Dynamics*, 2nd ed. Hampshire, UK: Palgrave Macmillan.

Olson, Mancur. 1965. *The Logic of Collective Action: Public Goods and the Theory of Groups.* Cambridge: Harvard University Press.

Olson, Mancur. 1982. *The Rise and Decline of Nations: Economic Growth, Stagflation, and Social Rigidities.* New Haven: Yale University Press.

Organski, Abramo. F. K., and Jacek Kugler. 1980. *The War Ledger.* Chicago: University of Chicago Press.

Ormerod, Paul. 1994. *The Death of Economics.* New York: St. Martin's.

Ormerod, Paul. 1998. *Butterfly Economics: A New General Theory of Social and Economic Behavior.* New York: Pantheon.

Ormerod, Paul. 2006. *Why Most Things Fail: Evolution, Extinction and Economics.* New York: Pantheon.

Ormerod, Paul. 2012. *Positive Linking: How Networks and Incentives Can Revolutionise the World.* London: Faber and Faber.

Ostrom, Elinor, Roy Gardner, and James Walker, eds. 1994. *Rules, Games, and Common-Pool Resources.* Ann Arbor: University of Michigan Press.

Ostrom, Elinor. 1990. *Governing the Commons: The Evolution of Institutions for Collective Action.* New York: Cambridge University Press.

Ostrom, Elinor. 2009. The governance challenge: Matching institutions to the structure of social-ecological systems. In Simon Levin, ed., *The Princeton Guide to Ecology.* Princeton: Princeton University Press, 748–53.

Ostrom, Elinor. 2005. *Understanding Institutional Diversity.* Princeton: Princeton University Press.

Ostrom, Elinor, Roy Gardner, and James Walker. 1990. Rent dissipation in a limited-access common-pool resource: Experimental evidence. *Journal of Environmental Economics and Management* 19 (3): 203–11.

Page, Jeremy. 2009. China helping Sri Lanka in battle against Tamil Tigers. *Times (London)* (May): 10.

Page, Scott E. 2007. *The Difference: How the Power of Diversity Creates Better Groups, Firms, Schools, and Societies.* Princeton: Princeton University Press.

Page, Scott E. 2010. *Diversity and Complexity.* Princeton: Princeton University Press.

Parag, Khanna. 2008. *The Second World: Empires and Influence in the New Global Order.* New York: Random House.

Parker, Geoffrey. 1988. *The Military Revolution.* Cambridge: Cambridge University Press.

Parker, Geoffrey, ed. 1995. *The Cambridge Illustrated History of Warfare: The Triumph of the West.* New York: Cambridge University Press.

Parker, Geoffrey. 1996. *The Military Revolution: Military Innovation and the Rise of the West 1500–1800,* 2nd ed. New York: Cambridge University Press.

Parker, Geoffrey, ed. 2005. *The Cambridge History of Warfare.* New York: Cambridge University Press.

Pei, Minxin. 1997. Citizens v. mandarins: Administrative litigation in China. *China Quarterly* 152: 832–62.

Perera, Amantha. 2010. How China and India displaced the West in Sri Lanka. *Time World,* October 3.

Perrin, Noel. 1979. *Giving up the Gun: Japan's Reversion to the Sword, 1543–1879.* Boston: Godine.

Perrow, Charles. 1972. *Complex Organizations: A Critical Essay,* 3rd ed. New York: McGraw-Hill.

Persaud, Avinash. 2000. Sending the herd off the cliff edge: The disturbing interaction between herding and market-sensitive risk management practices. *World Economy* 1 (4): 15–26.

Piattoni, Simona, ed. 2001. *Clientelism, Interests, and Democratic Representation: The European Experience in Historical and Comparative Perspective.* Cambridge: Cambridge University Press.

Pomeranz, Kenneth. 2000. *The Great Divergence: China, Europe, and the Making of the Modern World Economy.* Princeton: Princeton University Press.

La Porta, Rafael, Florencio Lopez-de-Silanes, Andrei Shleifer, and Robert Vishny. 1999. The quality of government. *Journal of Law Economics and Organization* 15 (1): 222–79.

La Porta, Rafael, Florencio Lopez-de Silanes, and Andrei Shleifer. 2008. The economic consequences of legal origins. *Journal of Economic Literature* 46 (2): 285–332.

Prigogine, Ilya I., and Isabella Stengers. 1984. *Order Out of Chaos: Man's New Dialogue with Nature.* London: Flamingo/Random House.

Pritchett, Lant, and Michael Woolcock. 2004. Solutions when the solution is the problem: Arraying the disarray in development. *World Development* 32 (2): 191–212.

Pritchett, Lant, Michael Woolcock, and Matt Andrews. 2010. Capability traps? The mechanisms of persistent implementation failure. Working paper 234. Center for Global Development, Washington, DC.

Qian, Yingyi. 2003. How reform worked in China. In Dani Rodrik, ed., *Search of Prosperity: Analytic Narratives on Economic Growth*. Princeton: Princeton University Press, 297–335.

Qing, Jiang. 2012. *A Confucian Constitutional Order: How China's Ancient Pat Can Shape Its Political Future*. Daniel A. Bell and Ruiping Fan, eds., Edmund Ryde, trans. Princeton: Princeton University Press.

Raghuram Rajan, G. 2010. *Fault Lines: How Hidden Fractures Still Threaten the World Economy*. Princeton: Princeton University Press.

Rapoport, Anatol. 1986. *General System Theory: Essential Concepts and Application*. Cambridge, UK: ABACUS Press.

Ray, James Lee. 2003. A Lakatosian view of the democratic peace research program. In Colin Elman and Miriam Fendius Elman, eds., *Progress in International Relations Theory: Appraising the Field*. Cambridge: The MIT Press, 205–44.

Reich, Robert. 2007. *Supercapitalism: The Transformation of Business, Democracy, and Everyday Life*. New York: Knopf.

Reischauer, Edwin O., and Albert M. Craig. 1979. *Japan, Tradition and Transformation*. Sydney: Allen, Unwin.

Ricardo, David. 1817. *Principles of Political Economy and Taxation*. London: Murray.

Richard, Guy. 1974. *Noblesse d'affaires au XVIII siécle*. Paris: Armand Colin.

Robert, I. Rotberg, and Rachel M Gisselquist. 2009. Strengthening African governance—Index of African governance: Results and rankings 2009. Kennedy School of Government and World Peace Foundation, Cambridge, MA. Available at http://data.nber.org/iag/iag2009.pdf.

Roberts, Michael. 1956. The military revolution, 1560–1660: An inaugural lecture delivered before the Queen's University of Belfast. In M. Boyd, ed., *Proceedings from an Inaugural Lecture Delivered before the Queen's University of Belfast*. Belfast: Queen's University of Belfast, 1–32.

Robinson, James A., Ragnar Torvik, and Thierry Verdier. 2006. Political foundations of the resource curse. *Journal of Development Economics* 79 (2): 447–68.

Robinson, James A., and Thierry Verdier. 2002. The political economy of clientelism. Discussion paper 3205. Center for Economic and Policy Research (CEPR), Washington, DC.

Rodrik, Dani. 2008. *One Economics, Many Recipes: Globalization, Institutions, and Economic Growth*. Princeton: Princeton University Press.

Rogers, Clifford J. 1993. The military revolutions of the Hundred Years' War. *Journal of Military History* 57 (2): 241–78.

Rogers, Clifford J., ed. 1995. *The Military Revolution Debate: Readings on the Military Transformation of Early Modern Europe*. Boulder: Westview Press.

Roll, Richards, and John Talbott. 2003. Political freedom, economic liberty, and prosperity. *Journal of Democracy* 14 (3): 75–89.

Root, Hilton L. 1985. Challenging the seigneurie: Community and contention on the eve of the French Revolution. *Journal of Modern History* 57 (4): 652–81.

Root, Hilton L. 1987. *Peasants and King in Burgundy: Agrarian Foundations of French Absolutism*. Berkeley: University of California Press.

Root, Hilton L. 1994. *La Construction de l'etat moderne en Europe: Le Cas de la France et de l'Angleterre*. Paris: Presses Universitaires de France.

Root, Hilton L. 1996. *Small Countries Big Lessons: Governance and the Rise of East Asia*. New York: Oxford University Press.

Root, Hilton L. 2006. *Capital and Collusion: The Political Logic of Global Economic Development*. Princeton: Princeton University Press.

Root, Hilton. L. 2008. *Alliance Curse: How America Lost the Third World*. Washington, DC: Brookings Institution Press.

Root, Hilton L. 2012. The policy conundrum of financial market complexity. In James R. Barth, Clas Wihlborg, and Chen Lin, eds., *Research Handbook on Banking and Governance*. Northamption, UK: Elgar, 360–77.

Root, Hilton L., and Karen May. 2008. Judicial Systems and Economic Development. In Tom Ginsburg and Tamir Moustafa, eds., *Rule By Law: The Politics of Courts in Authoritarian Regimes*. Cambridge: Cambridge University Press, 304–25.

Rose, Michael R., and George V. Lauder. 1996. *Adaptation*. Maryland Heights: Academic Press.

Rostow, W. W. 1960. *The Stages of Economic Growth: A Non-Communist Manifesto*. Cambridge: Cambridge University Press.

Rudolph, Lloyd I., and Susanne Hoeber Rudolph. 1967. *The Modernity of Tradition: Political Development in India*. Chicago: University of Chicago Press.

Rummel, Rudolph J. 1997. *Power Kills: Democracy as a Method of Nonviolence*. New Brunswick: Transaction Publishers.

Sachs, Jeffrey. 2005. *The End of Poverty: Economic Possibilities for Our Time*. New York: Penguin.

Schedler, Andreas. 2002. Elections without democracy: The menu of manipulation. *Journal of Democracy* 13 (2): 36–50.

Schelling, Thomas C. 1978. *Micromotives and Macrobehavior*. New York: Norton.

Scheve, Kenneth, and David Stasavage. 2012. Democracy, war and wealth: Lessons from two centuries of inheritance taxation. *American Political Science Review* 106 (01): 81–102.

Schrödinger, Erwin. 1944. *What Is Life?: The Physical Aspect of the Living Cell*. Lanham: University Press.

Scott, James C. 1972a. Patron–client politics and political change in Southeast Asia. *American Political Science Review* 66 (1): 91–113.

Scott, James C. 1972b. *Comparative Political Corruption*. Englewood Cliffs, NJ: Prentice-Hall.

Sengupta, Somini. 2008. Take aid From China and take a pass on human rights. *New York Times*, March 9.

Shapiro, Carl, and Hal R. Varian. 1998. *Information Rules: A Strategic Guide to the Network Economy*. Boston: Harvard Business School Press.

Sharon-Krespin, Rachel. 2009. Fethullah Gülen's grand ambition Turkey's Islamist danger. *Middle East Quarterly* 16 (1): 55–66.

Shirk, Susan L. 1993. *The Political Logic of Economic Reform in China*. California Series on Social Choice and Political Economy. Berkeley: University of California Press.

Simon, Herbert A. 1969. *The Sciences of the Artificial*. Cambridge: MIT Press.

Simon, Herbert A. 1972. Theories of bounded rationality. In C. B. McGuire and R. Radner, eds., *Decision and Organization*. Amsterdam: North-Holland, 161–76.

Simon, Herbert A. 1982a. *Models of Bounded Rationality*. Vol. 1: *Economic Analysis and Public Policy*. Cambridge: MIT Press.

Simon, Herbert A. 1982b. *Models of Bounded Rationality*. Vol. 2: *Behavioral Economics and Business Organization*. Cambridge: MIT Press.

Singh, Vikas, Bhupendra Gehlot, Daniel Start, and Craig Johnson. 2003. Out of reach: Local politics and the distribution of development funds in Madhya Pradesh. Working paper 200. Overseas Development Institute, London.

Skocpol, Theda. 1985. Strategies of analysis in current research. In Peter B. Evans, Dietrich Rueschemeyer, and Theda Skocpol, eds., *Bringing the State Back*. Cambridge: Cambridge University Press, 3–37.

Smick, David M. 2008. *The World Is Curved: Hidden Dangers to the Global Economy*. London: Penguin.

Smil, Vaclav. 2008. *Global Catastrophes and Trends: The Next Fifty Years*. Cambridge: MIT Press.

Smith, John Maynard, and Eörs Szathmáry. 1995. *The Major Transitions in Evolution*. Oxford: Oxford University Press.

Smith, Vernon L., Gerry L. Suchanek, and Arlington W. Williams. 1988. Bubbles, crashes, and endogenous expectations in experimental spot asset markets. *Econometrica* 56 (5): 1119–51.

Song, Zheng, Kjetil Storesletten, and Fabrizio Zilibotti. 2011. Growing like China. *American Economic Review* 101 (1): 196–233.

Southern, Sir Richard W. 1953. *The Making of the Middle Ages*. New Haven: Yale University Press.

Steinmo, Sven. 2010. *The Evolution of Modern States: Sweden, Japan and the United States. Cambridge Studies in Comparative Politics*. Cambridge: Cambridge University Press.

Strange, Susan. 1996. *The Retreat of the State: The Diffusion of Power in the World Economy*. Cambridge: Cambridge University Press.

Strayer, Joseph R. 1970. *On the Medieval Origins of the Modern State*. Princeton: Princeton University Press.

Strogatz, Steven H. 2003. *Sync: The Emerging Science of Spontaneous Order*. New York: Hyperion.

Talbott, Strobe. 2008. *The Great Experiment: The Story of Ancient Empires, Modern States, and the Quest for a Global Nation*. New York: Simon, Schuster.

Tarrow, Sidney. 1977. *Between Center and Periphery: Grassroots Politicians in Italy and France*. New Haven: Yale University Press.

Taylor, George V. 1964. Types of capitalism in eighteenth-century France. *English Historical Review* 79 (312): 478–97.

Thompson, Edward P. 1971. The moral economy of English crowd in the eighteenth century. *Past and Present* 50 (1): 76–136.

Tilly, Charles. 1985. War making and state making as organized crime. In Peter B. Evans, Dietrich Rueschemeyer, and Theda Skocpol, eds., *Bringing the State Back*. Cambridge: Cambridge University Press, 169–91.

Tilly, Charles. 1992. *Coercion, Capital and European States: AD 990–1992*. Hoboken, NJ: Wiley-Blackwell.

Tilly, Charles. 2007. *Democracy*. Cambridge: Cambridge University Press.

de Tocqueville, Alexis. [1856] 1955. *The Old Regime and the French Revolution*. Gilbert, Stuart, trans. New York: Anchor.

Trager, Robert. 2011. Multidimensional diplomacy. *International Organization* 65 (3): 469–506.

Treverton, Gregory F., and Agrell Wilhelm, eds. 2009. *National Intelligence Systems: Current Research and Future Prospects*. Cambridge: Cambridge University Press.

United Nations UN Secretary-General (UNSG). 2011. Report of the Secretary General`s panel of experts on accountability in Sri Lanka, March 31. Available at: http://www.unhcr.org/refworld/docid/4db7b23e2.html.

United States Department of State. 2010. *Advancing Freedom and Democracy Report 2010*. Washington, DC: US Department of State. Available at: http://www.state.gov/j/drl/rls/afdr/2011/index.htm.

United States Senate Committee on Foreign Relations. 2009. *Sri Lanka: Recharting U.S. Strategy after the War*. Report prepared for the 111th Cong., 1st sess., December 7, United States Senate. Washington, DC: Government Printing Office.

Veblen, Theodore. 1915. *Imperial Germany and the Industrial Revolution*. London: Macmillian.

Wade, Robert. 2003. *Governing the Market: Economic Theory and the Role of Government in East Asian Industrialization*. Princeton: Princeton University Press.

Van de Walle, Nicolas. 2001. *African Economies and the Politics of Permanent Crisis, 1979–1999*. Cambridge: Cambridge University Press.

Voeten, Erik. 2004. Resisting the lonely superpower: responses of states in the United Nations to the U.S. dominance. *Journal of Politics* 66 (August):729–754.

Wallerstein, Immanuel. 1974. *The Modern World-System*. Vol. 1: *Capitalist Agriculture and the Origins of the European World-Economy in the Sixteenth Century.* New York: Academic Press.

Wallerstein, Immanuel. 1979. *The Capitalist World Economy.* Cambridge: Cambridge University Press.

Wallerstein, Immanuel. 1980. *The Modern World-System.* Vol. 2: *Mercantilism and the Consolidation of the European World-Economy, 1600–1750.* New York: Academic Press.

Wallerstein, Immanuel. 1984. *The Politics of the World-Economy: The States, the Movements and the Civilizations.* Cambridge: Cambridge University Press.

Wantchekon, Leonard. 2003. Clientelism and voting behavior: Evidence from a field experiment in Benin. *World Politics* 55 (3): 399–422.

Watts, Duncan J. 1999. Networks, dynamics, and the small-world phenomenon. *American Journal of Sociology* 105 (2): 493–527.

Watts, Duncan J. 2003. *Small Worlds: The Dynamics of Networks between Order and Randomness.* Princeton: Princeton University Press.

Weber, Max. 1946. *From Max Weber: Essays in Sociology*, Hans H. Gerth and C. Wright Mills, eds. New York City: Oxford University Press.

Weber, Max. 1978. *Economy and Society.* Vol. 2: *An Outline of Interpretative Sociology,* ed. Guenther Roth and Claus Wittich, eds. Berkeley: University of California Press.

Weiner, Myron. 1957. *Party Politics in India: The Development of a Multi-party System.* Princeton: Princeton University Press.

Weiner, Myron. 1967. *Party Building in a New Nation: The Indian National Congress.* Chicago: University of Chicago Press.

Weingast, Barry. 1991. Institutional foundations of the "Sinews of Power": British financial and military success following the Glorious Revolution. Working paper. Hoover Institution, Stanford.

Wijedasa, Namini. 2010. Chinese projects in Sri Lanka and the Karadiyanaru explosion. Accessed April 10, 2013. http://transcurrents.com/tc/2010/10/chinese_projects_in_sri_lanka.html.

Williamson, John. 1990. What Washington means by policy reform. In John Williamson, ed., *Latin American Adjustment: How Much Has Happened?* Washington, DC: Institute for International Economics, 7–38.

Williamson, Oliver E. 1975. *Markets and Hierarchies, Analysis and Antitrust Implications: A Study in the Economics of Internal Organization.* New York: Free Press.

Williamson, Oliver. E. 1985. *The Economic Institutions of Capitalism: Firms, Markets, Rational Contracting.* New York: Free Press.

Wong, Bin R. 1998. *China Transformed: Historical Change and the Limits of European Experience.* Ithaca: Cornell University Press.

Wright, Robert. 2000. *Nonzero: The Logic of Human Destiny*. New York: Pantheon.

Wright, Sewall. 1932. The roles of mutation, inbreeding, crossbreeding and selection in evolution. In *Proceedings of the VI International Congress of Genetrics*, vol. 1. Chicago: University of Chicago, 356–66.

Wriston, Walter B. 1992. *The Twilight of Sovereignty: How the Information Revolution Is Transforming Our World*. New York: Scribner's.

Zeleza, Paul Tiyambe. 2008. The causes and costs of war in Africa: From liberation struggles to the "war on terror." In Alfred Nhema and Paul Tiyambe Zeleza, eds., *The Roots of African Conflicts: The Causes and Costs*. Athens: Ohio University Press, 1–35.

Zysman, John. 1983. *Governments, Markets, and Growth*. Ithaca: Cornell University Press.

Index

fitness landscapes and, 10 (*see also* Fitness landscapes)
globalization and, 71–73
governance and, 218, 233–34
gradualism and, 21
innovation and, 251n5
institutional selection fallacy and, 43–46
interdependence and, 95–96, 99–101, 104–108, 111–12, 114, 260n1, 261n7
international systems and, 117–18, 124, 126, 137–38, 263n8, 267n35
late starter advantage and, 111–13
liberal internationalism and, 57–58, 69–72, 213, 256n8, 257n12
lock-in and, 241
macroevolution and, 10, 20, 33, 121, 125, 137–38, 165, 241, 244, 251n5, 263n8
microevolution and, 12, 131, 137, 241, 263n7
natural selection and, 21–22, 36, 86, 241, 251n5
networks and, 1–2, 7–14, 238, 250n6
new institutional economics (NIE) and, 79–82, 85–87, 91, 260n18
niche construction and, 242
phase transition and, 244
punctuated equilibrium and, 241, 251n5
self-organization and, 10 (*see also* Self-organization)
speciation and, 55, 84, 246, 260n1
survival of simple and, 85–87
Extractive capacity, 167–68, 192, 269n2
Extractive regimes, 24–25, 252n8

Fairbank, John K., 133–34, 137, 187
Fascism, 23, 66
Feedback loops
state capacity and, 168
defined, 239
governance and, 218
international systems and, 119, 263n3

Feudalism, 163
international systems and, 119, 122, 124–25, 139, 141, 267n32
shoguns and, 138–39, 267n32, 269n11
state capacity and, 173–79
Financial bubbles, 50–51
Finer, Samuel E., 132, 135, 158
France
bureaucracy and, 174–79, 191
cannons, artillery, and, 122–23
China and, 191
civil law and, 87
Constituent Assembly 1789 and, 178, 256n5
democracy and, 156, 269n9
feudal privileges and, 124–25
François I and, 174
French Revolution and, 23, 85, 124, 126–27, 133, 177, 179, 190, 252n8, 256n5, 257n16
global interdependence and, 112
governance and, 229, 274n4
intendants and, 176, 179, 191
international systems and, 122–28, 130, 133, 263n2, 264n15
l'etat c'est moi concept and, 175
levée en masse and, 125
liberal internationalism and, 68, 202, 273n6
Louis XI and, 174
Louis XIII and, 176
Louis XIV and, 124–25, 127, 175–77, 264n15
Louis XV and, 176–77
Mitterrand, François and, 133
monarchy and, 122–23, 174–79
Napoleon and, 125–28, 140, 179, 183, 265nn18, 19
New World policy of, 127–28Prussia and, 130, 183–84
Richelieu and, 176
social revolution and, 174–79
state capacity and, 165, 168, 174–80, 183–84, 190–91, 194
War of the Grand Alliance and, 180–81

Islam
All-India Muslim League and,
102–103
democracy and, 37–38, 145–55, 162,
268nn3,5
fundamentalists and, 3, 37–38
governance and, 221, 274n3
identity politics and, 147
liberal internationalism and, 66
middle class and, 147
philosophy and, 154–55
social networks and, 3, 9
Turkey and, 147–55, 162

Japan, 211
as between East and West, 138–40
bureaucracy and, 173–74
China and, 28
Commander Perry and, 123, 139
Edo period and, 138, 269n11
European threat and, 138–40
feudalism compared with Europe,
139
firearms and, 139
innovation and, 11, 138, 139, 161
international systems and, 138–40
language diffusion and social risk,
160–62
lock-in and institutional stages, 112–13
Meiji Restoration and, 138–39, 161
sensitivity to initial conditions and,
158–59
shoguns and, 138–39, 267n32,
269n11
Tokugawa Ieyasu era and, 138–39,
267n33, 269n11
warfare and, 138–40
Jews, 44, 130, 254n10, 265n21

Kant, Immanuel, 60, 66
Kauffman, Stuart A., 8
avalanches of change and, 114
complexity explosion and economic
takeoff, 137–38, 250
fitness peaks and China's institutional maturity, 110
fitness values and, 100, 252n6

global fitness optimum and, 57, 72,
interacting dancing landscapes and,
99
optimization of function and, 111,
252n6
social planner's job and, 100
Tiananmen Square massacre and,
267n37
Kinship
bureaucracy and, 169
China and, 272n17
nepotism and, 135, 174, 210–12,
224
patrimonialism and, 168–71, 185,
194, 242–43
social structures and, 44–45, 62,
168–71, 185, 238, 272n17
Korea, 44, 158–59, 186, 193, 209–11,
223, 268nn1, 8, 273n6, 275n6
Kydland, F., 167

Landes, David S., 59
Language
Asia and, 160–62, 269n10
China and, 269nn9, 10
diffusion and, 160–62
international systems and, 117
self-organization and, 34
social networks and, 2
Law
civil law, 87, 260n16
common law, 53, 87, 181, 260n16
contract enforcement, 27, 28, 29,
51, 53–55, 43–47, 67–70, 80, 83,
92, 235
Late starter's advantage, 111–13
Legitimacy
China and, 193–94, 197–215
cultural authenticity and, 222–23,
249n2
democracy and, 153, 157–58
global interdependence and, 96
governance and, 226–27, 231
international systems and, 124–25,
131, 140, 265n16
liberal internationalism and, 58, 65,
69, 72, 197–215, 257n18

evolution and, 241, 251n5
innovation and, 244
macroevolution and, 121
military and, 244
social networks and, 14
technology and, 121–26, 244

Rational actor models, 39–41
Rationalism, 163–64, 178, 243
Reciprocity, 161, 259n11
  patron-clientelism and, 169, 171,
    243–44, 270n4
  state capacity and, 169–71, 185
Red Queen's Hypothesis, 104–108,
  261n7
Religion
  Brahmins and, 27, 103
  Buddhism and, 134
  caste, 27, 61, 103, 157, 202, 272n4
  Christianity and, 120, 123, 129,
    155–56, 158, 255n14
  Confucianism and, 104, 134, 137,
    158–59, 188, 192, 195, 267n30
  fundamentalists and, 3, 37–38
  global interdependence and, 103
  Hinduism and, 102, 157, 234
  international systems and, 135, 145–
    48, 151–55, 158, 163, 266n28
  Islam and, 3 (*see also* Islam)
  Napoleon and, 265n19
  philosophy and, 154–56
  Protestant Reformation, 123, 127,
    257n16
  state capacity and, 192
  Sufism and, 268n2
Replicators
  defined, 244
  international systems and, 118
  modernization theory and, 9, 37, 54,
    118, 244, 253n1
Resilience
  defined, 244
  European system and, 121–26
  global interdependence and, 101, 114
  governance and, 220, 233
  international systems and, 115, 117–
    18, 120–26

new institutional economics (NIE)
  and, 80–83
  redundancy and, 80
  second-best path to, 82–83
  social networks and, 11, 117–18,
    120, 238, 244, 246
  state capacity and, 167, 246
Ricardo, David, 226, 249n3
Robinson, James A., 24, 28–29, 39,
  55, 131, 182–83, 266n24
  democratization, 131, 182, 266n24,
    271n13
  and global development, 23–31, 33,
    252n7
  Why Nations Fail (with Daron
    Acemoğlu), 24
Rodrik, Dani, 81, 83, 259n13
Root, Hilton L., 159, 211, 223
  Capital and Collusion (2006), 93
  Governing for Prosperity (2001,
    with Bruce Bueno de Mesquita),
    93, 254n5
  Peasants and the King in Burgundy
    (1987), 175–78
Rostow, Walter, 42, 187, 201, 256n2,
  258n7
Rugged fitness landscapes
  cost of searching on, 162
  defined, 98, 245
  global interdependence and, 98–100,
    107–108
  governance and, 218
  liberal internationalism and, 71–72
  optimization on, 10–11
Russia. *See also* Cold war era
  China and, 186
  Gorbachev and, 185
  governance and, 219, 221, 223, 225,
    229, 274n2, 275nn6,7
  human rights and, 203
  international systems and, 120, 125–
    27, 131, 265n18
  liberal internationalism and, 58–59,
    63, 66, 69, 203, 256n1, 273n6
  Peter the Great and, 265n18
  power transition and, 58–59
  social networks and, 5